AF478469

Minimum Wages and Employment

Static and Dynamic Non-Market-Clearing Equilibrium Models

Christian Ragacs
Vienna University of Economics and Business Administration
Austria

First published 2004 by
PALGRAVE MACMILLAN
Houndmills, Basingstoke, Hampshire RG21 6XS and
175 Fifth Avenue, New York, N. Y. 10010
Companies and representatives throughout the world

PALGRAVE MACMILLAN is the global academic imprint of the Palgrave Macmillan division of St. Martin's Press, LLC and of Palgrave Macmillan Ltd. Macmillan® is a registered trademark in the United States, United Kingdom and other countries. Palgrave is a registered trademark in the European Union and other countries.

ISBN 1–4039–3498–3

This book is printed on paper suitable for recycling and made from fully managed and sustained forest sources.

A catalogue record for this book is available from the British Library.

Library of Congress Cataloging-in-Publication Data

Ragacs, Christian, 1962-
  Minimum wages and employment : static and dynamic non-market clearing equilibrium models / Christian Ragacs.
p. cm.
    Includes bibliographical references and index.
    ISBN 1–4039–3498–3 (cloth)
      1. Minimum wage--Mathematical models. 2. Labor market--Mathematical models. I. Title.

HD4917.R34 2004
331.2'3'0151--dc22

                                                    2004044366

10   9   8   7   6   5   4   3   2   1
13   12   11   10   09   08   07   06   05   04

Printed and bound in Great Britain by
Antony Rowe Ltd, Chippenham and Eastbourne

For Magdalena and Rudolf,

My Parents

Contents

PART II: MINIMUM WAGES AND COMPARATIVE STATICS

PART III: MINIMUM WAGES AND ECONOMIC GROWTH

8 Conclusions

List of Tables

List of Abbreviations

CES:	Constant Elasticity of Substitution
COV:	Coverage
FOC:	First Order Condition
GDP:	Gross Domestic Product
Inters.:	Intersectoral
Kaitz:	Kaitz-Index
MW:	Minimum Wage
n.a.:	Not Available
OECD:	Organization for Economic Co-Operation and Development
R&D:	Research and Development
s.t.	Subject To
UK:	United Kingdom
US:	United States of America
WB:	Wage Bargaining
WIFO:	Österreichisches Institut für Wirtschaftsforschung (Austrian Institute of Economic Research)
WWW:	World Wide Web

Acknowledgments

In writing this book I have profited from many fruitful discussions. I appreciate the helpful comments and suggestions I have received from Werner Hölzl, Hansjörg Klausinger, Engelbert Stockhammer, and Martin Zagler, at the Vienna University of Economics and Business Administration. I have also benefited from discussions with colleagues from the Research Group "Growth and Employment in Europe: Sustainability and Competitiveness" and the Faculty Staff Research Seminar of the Department of Economics, both located at the Vienna University of Economics and Business Administration. I wish to thank the supervisors of my dissertation, Peter Rosner from the University of Vienna, and Herbert Walther from the University of Economics and Business Administration. I am grateful to the Viennese Federal Chamber of Labour ("Kammer für Arbeiter und Angestellte Wien") for providing support for this research. Finally, I would like to thank my wife Ursula Ragacs for her endless patience during the writing of this book.

CHRISTIAN RAGACS

1
Introduction

1.1 MINIMUM WAGES?

The notion of "minimum wage" is used quite differently in political and theoretical discussions. Theoretical literature dominantly describes the minimum wage as a wage floor based on laws and regulations. However, wages resulting from bargaining between unions and firms are also defined as minimum wages. In both cases the minimum wage applies only to employed persons.[1] A third interpretation of "minimum wage" is based on a completely different economic focus, as it describes the right to a specific level of income transfers, independently of the form of working effort, for every person in an economy. In this book we are interested in the economic effects of the first two cases.

Additionally, from our point of view it is not legitimate to merely interpret all bargaining outcomes as an equivalent to a minimum wage, as a short digression on bargaining behavior shows.[2] For the sake of simplicity, we assume that there exists only one firm and one union. The firm exhibits a concave utility function, U^f, which is given in the general form of $U^f = U^f(\pi(w, L))$, where π equals profit, w is the real wage and L employment. The concave utility function of the union, U^u, is given by $U^u = U^u(w, L)$.

We assume that the bargaining situation may be described by a (not necessarily asymmetric) Nash solution. The threat point of the firm is a profit of zero, $\pi_0 = 0$, the threat point of the union is a reservation wage R, $(R > 0)$, and ϕ, with $0 \leq \phi \leq 1$, is an indicator of the bargaining power of the firm.

We distinguish between three different kinds of bargaining situations.[3] In *"right to manage"* models, the union and the firm only negotiate the wage. Once the wage is fixed, firms unilaterally determine employment (Nickell and Andrews 1983). Let L^* be the optimal employment of the firm for a given wage level, so that the maximization problem is described by

$$\max_{w} \left\{ U^{f}\left(\pi(w, L^{*})\right) - U^{f}(0) \right\}^{\phi} \left\{ U^{u}\left(w, L^{*}(w)\right) - U^{u}(R) \right\}^{1-\phi}.$$

Possible bargaining results are therefore restricted to combinations of wage and employment levels that are conform to the standard labor demand function of the firm (i.e. points on its labor demand curve). Consequently, compared to the case of perfect competition, we obtain higher wages and lower employment in every case where the bargaining power of the union is not zero.

"*Monopoly models*" simply describe a specific form of "right to manage" models, where the bargaining power ϕ of the firm is zero (Oswald 1985).

In models of "*efficient bargaining*" the union and the firm negotiate wage and employment (McDonald and Solow 1981). Hence the underlying maximization problem changes to

$$\max_{w, L} \left\{ U^{f}(\pi(w, L)) - U^{f}(0) \right\}^{\phi} \left\{ U^{u}(w, L) - U^{u}(R) \right\}^{1-\phi}.$$

Knowing that isoprofit contours describe wage and labor combinations yielding identical profits for the firm, bargaining solutions will not lie on the traditional labor demand curve. In contrast to the "right to manage" model, we obtain efficient contracts which are given by tangential points ("contract curve") of the firm's isoprofit contours and the union's indifference curves.[4] The contract curve lies "to the right" of the labor demand curve of the firm.[5] Accordingly, for any agreed wage, we yield higher employment than in the undisturbed market economy.

However, when we examine the actual bargaining situations, where largely binding contracts are negotiated solely for the wage, the "right to manage model" seems to find convincing empirical support. Additionally, from the theoretical point of view it is easy to see that the economic outcome of this model is identical to that of legally set minimum wages. Hence in this book we focus on legal minimum wages and minimum wages as the outcome of bargaining situations which can be described with a "right to manage" model.

The next section presents a short overview of minimum wage systems. The overview is followed by a brief reference to new developments in the theory of minimum wages and a few examples of existing theoretical drawbacks. We state the necessity of extending the theoretical analysis by analyzing the effects of minimum wages not only on the labor market, but also on other markets. Based on this, we then provide arguments for the emphasis on the importance of human capital and economic dynamics in this book. In conclusion, specific research questions and an outline of the further work will be presented.

1.2   MINIMUM WAGE SYSTEMS: SELECTED STYLIZED FACTS

In the OECD, national or statutory minimum wages exist in 17 countries, but they differ in the relative level of the minimum wages and the extent of differentiation for region or age, the indexation systems and the wage setting mechanism (OECD 1998, 31). Machin and Manning (1997) distinguish between four different forms of existing minimum wage systems, namely:

- Statutory minimum wages which are set by the government. Such examples can be found in the Netherlands, the US, Portugal, Spain and France;
- National minimum wages as a result of collective bargaining as found in Belgium, Greece and Denmark;
- Different minimum wages for specific industries that are the result of wage bargains and also apply to non-union workers. Examples of this can be found in Austria, Germany and Italy.
- And finally, systems where industry-varying minimum wages are only set for certain low-payment industries, as found in Ireland.

Moreover, the existence of national minimum wages, the number of people paid at minimum wage level, the coverage of the minimum wage systems, and the union density strongly differ among OECD countries. Due to the completely different wage setting systems it is impossible to describe the different systems in detail. Therefore in the following we present a selection of indicators which should give a first impression of the wage setting systems and possible employment effects of the minimum wage. We are especially interested in indicators that help to answer the question whether minimum wages are binding in the neoclassical sense, or not.

Tables 1.1 and 1.2 provide further details for selected OECD countries. Table 1.1 focuses on the different minimum wage systems and the institutional settings. It presents the basic minimum wage system

Table 1.1   Minimum Wage Systems: Stylized Facts for Selected Countries I

Country	MW System[a]	Union[b] Density	Bargaining Level[c] Inters.	Sectoral	Firms
Austria	WB in all industries, results binding for all workers	39.8		•••	•
Belgium	National WB, legal MW	69.2	•••	•	•
Denmark	National WB	87.5	••	••	•
Finland	National WB	79.0	•••	•	•
France	Set by government, legal MW	9.10		•	•••
Germany	WB, expanded	29.7		•••	•
Greece	National WB, legal MW	32.5	•	•••	•
Ireland	"Labour Committees" in 16 low income industries legal MW	44.5	•••	•	•
Italy	WB	35.4		•••	•
Luxemburg	Legal MW	50.0		••	••
Netherlands	Legal MW	27.0		•••	•
Norway	WB	n.a.	n.a.	n.a.	n.a.
Portugal	Legal MW	30.0		•••	•
Spain	Legal MW	15.0		•••	•
Sweden	WB	79.0		•••	•
Switzerland	Industry specific WB	n.a.	n.a.	n.a.	n.a.
UK	Since 1999 national MW[d]	29.0		•	•••
US	Legal MW	13.5		•	•••

Notes:

MW: Minimum wage; *WB*: Wage bargaining; *Inters.*: Intersectoral.
Bargaining levels: • Existing at this level, •• Important, but not dominant level, ••• Dominant level.

Source:

a) Table 1 in Dolado et al. (1996) and table 5 in Charley (2003); *b)* Table 2 in Charley (2002). Data changing for 1998–2000; *c)* Table 2 in Charley (2003); *d)* Gregory and Swaffield (2002).

For all sources: Own simplifications and compilations.

(legal minimum wage, different forms based on bargaining), union density rates and different levels of wage bargaining. We distinguish between three levels of bargaining, namely on the intersectoral, the sectoral and the firm's level.

We see that the existence of national minimum wages and wage bargaining is not contradictory, but we find that legal minimum wages are more often implemented in countries with a lower union density rate. The density rate itself differs extremely, as it ranges from about 9 percent (France) to 88 percent (Denmark). However, the union density rate could become a problematic indicator for the effects of minimum wages if we recognize that in some countries, especially in Austria, the wage bargaining results are not just binding for union members, but also for non-union members.

The differences are also quite marked when one examines bargaining levels (Charley 2003): In three countries (Belgium, Finland and Ireland) intersectoral negotiations dominate, whereas eight countries show dominance on the sectoral level (Austria, Germany, Greece, Italy, the Netherlands, Portugal, Spain and Sweden). Finally, in two countries (Denmark and Luxemburg) we do not find a dominant bargaining level.

Ultimately, we see that France, the UK and the USA as a group seem to exhibit a different wage setting system compared to all other countries. In these three countries wage bargaining predominantly takes place at the firm's level and is accompanied by legal minimum wages. This gives rise to the possibility that the wage bargains are in relative terms less influenced by macroeconomic performance and yield stronger effects on employment.[6]

Table 1.2 presents data which should provide a more detailed impression of the economic impact of minimum wages. It describes the number of workers paid at the minimum wage level as the percentage of aggregate employment, and the Kaitz-Index, which defines the minimum wage as a percentage of the average wage. The coverage rate describes the percentage of workers whose wages or working conditions are regulated either by legal minimum wages or bargaining results.

As seen in table 1.2, in many countries the number of people covered, especially in industry, is extremely high. However, due to overpayments, many of these employees actually earn more than the minimum wage. Hence the coverage rate does not provide clear information on the number of people actually paid at the minimum wage level. Therefore, the data for minimum wage payments are more relevant in

Table 1.2   Minimum Wage Systems: Stylized Facts for Selected Countries II

Country	Workers[a]	Kaitz[b]	COV[c]	Variation by[d]
Austria	4	0.62 (1993)	98	Industry, region, age, job tenure; Youth: industry agreements
Belgium	4	0.60 (1992)	90+	Age, job tenure; Youth: small reduction
Denmark	6	0.54 (1992)	83	Industry, age; Youth: 40% (<18)
Finland	n.a.	0.52 (1993)	90	Age, occupation, industry, region
France	11	0.50 (1993)	90–95	Age, training; Youth: 80% (16), 90% (17), 30–75% (trainees)
Germany	n.a.	0.55 (1991)	67	Age, qualification, trainee status, region; Youth: industry agreements
Greece	20	0.62 (1995)	n.a.	Manual/non manual, job tenure, marital status, qualifications; Youth: lower rates for short job tenure
Ireland	n.a.	0.55 (1993)	n.a.	Age, industry, region, occupation, job tenure; Youth: varies, 63% (<18)
Italy	n.a.	0.71 (1991)	90	Age, industry, job tenure; Youth: industry agreements
Luxemburg	11	0,56	58	Age, skill, family characteristics; Youth: 70% (<21)
Netherlands	3.2	0.55 (1993)	88	Age; Youth: 34,5 % (16) rising to 84% (22)
Norway	n.a.	0.64 (1993)	n.a.	Industry, age, job tenure, job
Portugal	8	0.45 (1993)	87	Age, trainee status, industry; Youth: 75% (<18)
Spain	6.5	0.32 (1994)	81	Age, home workers, casual workers; Youth: 66% (<18)
Sweden	0	0.52 (1992)	90+	Age, industry, job tenure, occupation; Youth: 85% (<24)

Table 1.2 Continued

Country	Workers[a]	Kaitz[b]	COV[c]	Specific Arrangements[d]
Switzerland	n.a.	0.52 (1993)	n.a.	Age, industry; Youth: 0% (<21) (1986–93)
UK	n.a.	0.40 (1993)	36	Age, industry
US	4	0.39 (1993)	15	States, limited youth sub-minimum

Notes:

Workers: Workers paid at MW level in % of aggregate employment; *Kaitz.:* Kaitz-Index: MW as % of average wage, *COV:* Coverage, % of workers with regulated wages or working conditions.

Source:

a), b), d): Table 1 in Dolado et al. (1996); *c):* Table 3 in Carley (2003).

For all sources: Own simplifications and compilations.

describing the economic impact of minimum wages. At first glance these numbers, presented in percentages of total employment, do not seem (with the exception of France) to be very high. However, this would yield a completely wrong impression, because even if the coverage in many industries is small in terms of percentage, the number of people actually covered is likely to be greater than total employment. We must further consider that, due to wage drifts, minimum wages often have indirect effects on other, non-covered wages, thereby intensifying their economic impact.

The coverage rate differs significantly, ranging from 15 percent (US) to 98 percent (Austria). Differences in the Kaitz-Index are also remarkable, with values ranging from 32 percent (Spain) to 71 percent (Italy). Similar to table 1.1, the specific position of the UK and the USA is repeated with relatively small values for the Kaitz-Index and coverage rates. However, both indicators are problematic from a statistical point of view. This has already been discussed above for the coverage rate. The Kaitz-Index is strongly influenced by the level of the average wage. In many countries we find great differences among wage setting systems for different industries and occupations. Hence the minimum wage in one economic sector might be higher than the market wage in another, increasing the Kaitz-Index (Dolado et al. 1996, 322 ff.).

In spite of the fact that the UK, the US and to an extent France seem to exhibit a fundamentally different wage setting system in comparison to other countries, we must warn against drawing direct conclusions about minimum wage effects. We have only compared different wage setting mechanisms and simple economic indicators, but have not implemented them into general economic surroundings. We have not, for example, compared the labor productivity, growth performance and unemployment rates of the different countries.

1.3   THEORETICAL CONSIDERATIONS AND DRAWBACKS

The theory of minimum wages is firmly based on the traditional textbook theory. Hence, binding minimum wages clearly should reduce employment. In markets characterized by monopsony power employment is only reduced if the minimum wage "is high enough," as will be shown in chapter two. However, in the monopsony case, there also exists the possibility that minimum wages may increase employment. Furthermore, in particular in the recent literature we find several other theoretical approaches, where minimum wages could increase employment.[7] Moreover, more recent empirical studies yield contradictory results, as some authors find negative employment effects, while others may even refer to the positive employment effects of the minimum wage. An overview of this discussion, the theory of minimum wages, and the empirical results will be presented in chapter two.

However, this discussion represents only one element of the examination of minimum wages. From the author's point of view, important shortcomings exist in the "mainstream" analytical treatment of the topic. These lie mainly in the partial equilibrium setting, the reduction of the analysis to aspects of the labor market, and the static framework. Given these restrictions, a broadening of the analytical framework could aid in describing a wider range of economic effects of minimum wages. First, it seems appropriate to discuss changes in the behavior of economic agents when subjected to the introduction of a minimum wage in a general equilibrium framework. This leads to an analysis of possible effects on markets other than the labor market. However, as will be discussed later, the analytical treatment of minimum wages in a general equilibrium model seems to be complicated from an analytical point of view. Second, some crucial effects of minimum wages may be dynamic, such as their impact on the accumulation of human and physical capital, so that they cannot be captured in a static framework. Given these criticisms, it appears problematic that it is still common practice in political discussions to draw conclusions about the entire economy based on only static partial equilibrium results.

There are a lot of ways to broaden the focus of an analysis of minimum wages. The next section will state why the author is specifically interested in the integration of human capital and economic growth into the theory of minimum wages.

1.4   THE IMPORTANCE OF ECONOMIC GROWTH AND HUMAN CAPITAL

It is interesting that, although the theory of endogenous growth and the theory of labor economics are at the forefront of economic research, for quite some time very little was published on the integration of the two fields. However, when analyzing the economic effects of minimum wages, the impact of economic growth should not be ignored, as illustrated by simple examples.[8] Assume that a certain policy measure would shift a three percent growth rate by only 0.8 percentage points a year. This is by no means much, yet after only 16 years this would add up to an over two percent increase of the compounded growth rate. Only few discretionary policy reforms are able to induce such a large level shift. For instance, Ball and Mankiw (1995) note that abolishing 60 percent of US debt altogether would have a maximum effect of only three per cent on the GDP, providing that all savings go directly into private investment. Moreover, as a typical business cycle exhibits an amplitude of somewhat below two percent, after executing such a growth policy the bottom of the business cycle would lie above the current average level. Hence, the possible effects of minimum wages on economic growth and consequently on the levels of variables could indeed be much stronger (negative or positive) than predicted by a static theoretical approach.

This focus on dynamic processes facilitates the selection of additional economic variables to be implemented into the theory of the minimum wage. As will be pointed out in more detail in chapter two, one may distinguish between two central economic lines of reasoning in the theory of economic growth. While the first wave of perfect competition models (e.g. Romer 1986 and Lucas 1988) stressed the importance of external effects in human capital accumulation, leading to non-decreasing returns in accumulative factors of production, the second wave of papers stressed the importance of innovative activity in imperfectly competitive markets (Romer 1990 or Grossman and Helpman 1994). Both types of models lead to a permanent positive growth rate of output.

This book focuses on the first line of argumentation and maintains that human capital is an important element in the dynamics of an economy. This argumentation is based on the recent discussion of the effects of human capital on economic growth. However, let it be known that this discussion is still ongoing. While in some studies the empirical evidence for the positive effects of human capital on economic growth is very weak or zero (e.g. Benhabib and Spiegel 1994, Barro and Sala-I-Martin 1995), these results are contradicted by the argument that the insignificance is only caused by statistical misspecifications. The results are also contradicted by empirical studies which point out clearly positive effects of human capital on economic growth (e.g. Mankiw, Romer and Weil 1992, Lindahl and Krueger 1998, Temple 1999). Moreover, Topel (1998) found that a change in the initial level of education correlates positively with economic growth.

1.5   SPECIFIC RESEARCH QUESTIONS AND OUTLINE

Based on the previous discussion, this book first examines the methodological possibility of implementing minimum wages into a general equilibrium model, in order to analyze the effects on markets other than the labor market. Second, the specific effects of introducing human capital to the analysis in a simple static context are examined. Third, the effects of minimum wages in models of endogenous growth based on human capital accumulation are examined. Based on these considerations the structure of this book is as follows:

In chapter two we present a short overview of the relevant literature and we point out several specific drawbacks of the theoretical analysis of the effects of minimum wages. We focus in particular on the partial equilibrium bias and point out possible connections to the theory of endogenous growth.

In chapter three we present the methodological foundation that is necessary for the theoretical analysis conducted later. It is shown that it is problematic to analyze the effects of minimum wages in a simple Walrasian economy. It is also shown that the work of Malinvaud (1985) can help to generate an appropriate micro-based framework for the solution of this problem. Hence, the analysis will be based on so-called general "non-market-clearing" equilibrium models. However, the main interest lies in the adaptation of the formal basic structure of these models – apart from this, the entire analysis continues to move in a Walrasian-oriented economy without real money effects.

Based on these methodological considerations, we derive new contributions to the theory of minimum wages in the following four sections. In all of them the implementation of minimum wages in the theoretical framework of micro-based "non-market-clearing" equilibrium systems is discussed. Four different models are presented; two of them are static in nature and two are models of endogenous growth. However, the analysis is generalized in such a way that notation and basic assumptions are as similar as possible. Unemployment, if it exists, is involuntary in all four models.

Chapter four presents a simple and general Walrasian model involving only three markets. The model is modified to a static "non-market-clearing" equilibrium model through the introduction of a minimum wage in order to capture output, employment and welfare effects. The specific functional forms assumed here will also serve as a foundation for the static model presented in chapter five and dynamic enlargement throughout this examination.

Drawing on Lucas (1988) in section five, the basic model will be adapted by including educational decisions and the possible reactions of agents to the existence of unemployment. The additions reflect the importance of human capital for the economic outcome of an economy. It is assumed that the average level of human capital in an economy influences the production of the individual firm. Furthermore, it is assumed that the household's acquisition of skills is positively influenced by the level of unemployment. The economic intuition for this is that the fear of becoming unemployed influences the educational decisions of households, because they assume that a higher level of education decreases the probability of losing their job. It will be shown that these simple additions yield important changes to the model's results.

The next two chapters also focus on the importance of human capital, but in a dynamic sense. Chapter six exhibits a Lucas (1988) type model of endogenous growth with micro-based decisions on the optimal use of labor, leisure and educational time, and with external effects in production. The model from chapter four is made dynamic, the primary interest being the analysis of the effect of the minimum wage on steady state economic growth and employment.

In chapter seven the assumption of external effects in production has been omitted and we implement the basic idea of the static model presented in chapter five. Hence we develop a Lucas type model of endogenous growth, where households think that a higher level of education decreases the probability of unemployment. The effects of minimum wages on steady state growth and employment are also examined here.

A short summary of the main results will conclude the book. More complex mathematical derivations can be found in the mathematical appendix.

Part I:
On Theory and Methodology

2
An Inquiry into the Theory of Minimum Wages

2.1 INTRODUCTION

In recent years the discussion of the economic effects of minimum wages has experienced a revival, strongly based on empirical estimations that yield missing negative or even positive employment effects of minimum wages. This discussion is often focused on the controversy over perfect-competition versus monopsony power in the labor market, but we also find alternative theoretical foundations for the analysis of the employment effects of the minimum wage.

In this chapter we will present a short overview of the theoretical discussion on the employment effects of minimum wages in addition to a summary of the newest empirical results. As mentioned in chapter one, this book focuses on legal minimum wages and on bargaining results that are to be interpreted as the outcome of a "right to manage model." Hence, for this survey we only provide contributions within that framework and omit theoretical and empirical considerations based on other possible forms of the union's behavior. Furthermore, following the alignment of this book we restrict this overview to theoretical and empirical work that analyzes the employment and growth effects of minimum wages. We present older theoretical results as well as recent approaches and build up the ongoing presentation on the different methodological settings found in the literature.

The analysis of minimum wages is largely carried out in a comparative static framework. In chapter 2.2 we present an overview of the respective theoretical discussion. In spite of its simplicity, the "textbook version" of the analysis of minimum wages still has a strong influence on the theoretical and political discussion. Thus, we point out its central argumentation and drawbacks and use it as a benchmark for the following description of existing alternative theoretical models.

The standard alternative model for the analysis of minimum wages is based on the monopsony type of labor markets. We also present the textbook model and point out the possibility of positive employment effects of minimum wages. Another important direction of research can then be found in "two-sector models." These models are characterized by the assumption of the existence of a labor market with coverage by a binding minimum wage, and a second labor market that may be modeled in different ways, as will be shown later. Finally, we find partial equilibrium models used for the analysis of minimum wages that are also based on monopsony power, but this monopsony power is not founded on the existence of only one firm. Instead it is based on different labor market conditions that yield a situation where many firms face an increasing labor supply function.

In chapter 2.3 we focus on the effects of minimum wages on economic growth. In comparison to the many comparative static approaches, only a few studies analyze the effects of minimum wages on economic growth. Therefore, we must first present a very short overview of recent developments in the theory of endogenous growth to point out various possibilities of implementing minimum wages in dynamic models. Second, we present the outcomes of the studies that implement minimum wages in a model of endogenous growth.

In chapter 2.4 we present an overview of recent empirical results. This overview is based on the different methodological settings of the studies. Finally, we summarize the main results in chapter 2.5.

2.2   MINIMUM WAGES AND COMPARATIVE STATICS

2.2.1   The "Textbook Theory"

"An introductory textbook without a discussion on minimum wage laws might not be like a day without sunshine, but would certainly rank with a morning without caffeine" (Brown 1988, 134). Although it is general economic knowledge, we refer briefly to the "textbook theory" of minimum wages to point out the important drawbacks of this approach. A simple model with i identical households, j identical firms, one good for consumption, and working hours as the only endogenous factor of production, is discussed. Furthermore, all the standard basic assumptions of perfect competition are valid.[1]

To derive the supply function of working hours, assume that household i's twice differentiable and quasi-concave utility function is given by $U_i = U_i(C_i, F_i)$, where F_i describes leisure or "free" time and C_i

consumption. Households face a time constraint, normalized by one, that will be divided between time for working, H_i, and leisure time. The value of the household's consumption, pC_i, may not exceed total income that only originates from working effort, wH_i, where p describes the exogenous price for goods and w is the exogenous nominal wage. Substitute for leisure time into the budget constraint and reformulate to obtain that $C_i = w(1-F_i)/p$. We denote the Lagrange multiplier by λ_i and additionally assume the existence of an interior solution to describe the maximization problem simply by

$$\max_{} L_i = U_i(F_i, C_i) + \lambda_i(w - wF_i - pC_i). \tag{2.1}$$

The first order conditions (FOCs) for leisure time and consumption are given by $\partial U_i / \partial C_i = \lambda_i$, and $\partial U_i / \partial F_i = \lambda_i w / p$. Combining these FOCs yields the well-known result that the ratio of the marginal utilities from leisure and consumption – the marginal rate of substitution between these two variables – must equal the real wage. Including the FOC for the shadow price we obtain three equations with three unknown variables, namely C_i, F_i and λ_i. From these three equations – of course here only in general representation – it is possible to express leisure time as a function of the real wage. Additionally, the use of the time constraint helps to calculate H_i^s, the supply function for working hours, which comes out as

$$H_i^s = H_i^s(w/p). \tag{2.2}$$

Assume that the substitution effect induced by an exogenous rise in wages exceeds the income effect to guarantee that we obtain an upward sloping supply curve for working hours. Thus the supply function for the market, derived by the horizontal addition of the individual's supply functions, is also increasing.

The demand for working hours follows from the standard profit maximization behavior of the firms. For the sake of simplicity, we assume that firms produce output, Y_j, using only working hours as the input, $Y_j = Y_j(H_j)$. The production function is twice differentiable and exhibits positive and decreasing marginal productivity. Total costs are given by wH_j. The profit maximization problem is then described by,

$$\max_{} \pi_j = pY_j(H_j) - wH_j, \tag{2.3}$$

where π_j denotes profits. The FOC for labor, $p * \partial Y_j / \partial H_j = w$, states that the value of the marginal product of working hours must be identical to the wage. In this setting, the firm's demand for working hours, H_j^d, is identical to the inverse of the marginal product of working hours for given real wages, or

$$H_j^d = H_j^d (w / p) . \tag{2.4}$$

Based on the production technology, we focus a downward sloping demand curve for working hours for the single firm. The demand function for the market, derived by the horizontal addition of the firm's demand functions, is also decreasing.

Finally, the equilibrium condition of the "labor" market simultaneously determines equilibrium working hours and equilibrium nominal wage. The introduction of a binding minimum wage in this simple model will not affect the maximization problem of the firm, but definitely must yield "unemployment" in working hours. Furthermore, assuming a suitable rationing rule, this unemployment in working hours clearly leads to unemployment measured in persons. The effect of minimum wages on unemployment should be greater if the minimum wage is high in relation to the equilibrium wage, and if the elasticities of demand and supply for labor are high.

However, aside from general criticisms of the underlying neoclassical approach that will not be discussed in this book, we must mention the important shortcomings of this argumentation. First, the model is based on completely flexible working time that stands in contrast to existing different "regular" working time regimes. Second, without additional assumptions we are not able to predict the influence of the minimum wage on the average wage sum, because it simply depends on the specific elasticity of factor demand. Thus the aggregate wage sum could increase, decrease or stay identical. Third, no form of market power – neither of firms nor workers – exists. And fourth, neither does any form of economic friction.

More importantly, it seems that all results are derived within a partial equilibrium framework. This means that any possible effects on the labor market or other segments of the economy must be ignored. For instance, an increase in the aggregate wage sum caused by the implementation of a minimum wage could lead to a higher demand for goods, which in turn could induce a higher demand for labor. Or, as a second example, the increase of minimum wages in one low-paid sector could induce wage drifts in non-covered sectors. Hence, drawing conclusions from this micro-based partial equilibrium model and using them in macroeconomic argumentation, as is often done in political discussions, is a simple case of fallacy of composition. Finally, the model is completely static in nature and excludes the analysis of the possible long range effects of minimum wages.

2.2.2 The "Textbook theory," Wage Bargaining and Macroeconomics

We find an interesting application of the micro-based "Textbook theory" in the macroeconomic oriented discussion. As mentioned in chapter one, bargaining results following a "right to manage" or a "monopoly" behavior of the union lead to exactly the same results as are described by the "Textbook theory." However, taking the macroeconomic context into account, the unions' wage claims could change significantly.

We find an ongoing discussion on the importance of different institutional settings of wage bargains. Hence, different levels of bargaining strongly influence the wage claims of the unions, leading to different relative minimum wages and employment effects. This discussion is based on Calmfors und Driffills (1988), who claimed that a "humpshape" between minimum wages and the degree of centralization of wage bargaining exists on the empirical level.[2] The lowest wages are achieved without unions (the equilibrium wage) and, surprisingly, through very centrally organized unions and wage bargains. The situation "between," especially with decentralized wage bargains on the firm's level, would achieve the worst result, namely very high relative minimum wages. The basic reason for this result is that centrally organized unions take macroeconomic performance into account, which yields productivity-oriented wage claims. Thus, the union is not only oriented on the "partial equilibrium on the labor market," as is proposed by the simple bargaining models presented in the introduction.

Based on Calmfors und Driffills (1988) we find a newer discussion, where it is not the grade of centralization, but the grade of coordination that becomes the prevailing argument, and where other macroeconomic policies, especially monetary policy, are also analyzed (see for instance Soskice 1990, Crouch and Traxler 1995, Traxler 1999 and 2002, Traxler and Kittel 2000, and Traxler et al. 2001).

However, according to the mechanisms leading to employment effects of minimum wages, all these theoretical arguments are crucially based on the "Textbook theory", as reflected in the problems discussed in the previous chapter.

2.2.3 Minimum Wages and Monopsony Power

In its simplest version, the theory of monopsony power states that labor supply derived under perfect competition is confronted with the labor demand of a single firm (Stigler 1946). We therefore need not repeat the derivation of the supply function of working hours. However, the firm's problem changes significantly: it is no longer a price taker on the labor market. Thus, for profit maximization the firm must consider the effects of a change in wages and employment.

Assume that the firm may not pay different wages to different workers. In this case the market supply curve for working hours is identical to the average cost curve for working hours. Given the positive slope of this function, the marginal costs (marginal expenditures) for working hours must be higher than the average ones, showing that a marginal increase in working hours – and therefore in wages – not only induces additional marginal payments for this last hour, but for all other working hours as well.

We use a production function identical to those of the preceding chapter, $Y = Y(H)$, and note that the nominal wage no longer is exogenous.[3] As an additional maximization constraint it follows that $w = w(H)$, with $\partial w / \partial H > 0$, and the profit maximization problem turns out to be

$$\underset{\text{max}}{\pi} = pY(H) - w(H)H \,. \tag{2.5}$$

From the FOC for working hours we see that

$$p\frac{\partial Y}{\partial H} = \frac{\partial w}{\partial H}H + w(H) \,. \tag{2.6}$$

Thus the value of the marginal product must be identical to the marginal expenditures for additional employment of the factor. As a result, the value of the marginal product must be less than the wage rate. From this decision rule it follows that a unique demand function for the factor no longer exists, as the firm chooses exactly the corresponding optimal number of working hours and wages on the supply function for working hours. Thus, given the upward sloping supply curve for working hours, the monopsonist will pay less and will reduce working hours in comparison to the outcome of perfect competition. Adding a suitable rationing rule, these results are also valid for employment.

In this framework, the effect of the implementation of a minimum wage higher than the optimal wage rate of the monopsonistic firm is not clear. When the minimum wage is lower than the wage level determined by the intersection of marginal product and marginal expenditures, it definitely increases employment, but it decreases employment when the minimum wage is higher. But of course, all criticisms pointed out in the "textbook theory" are also valid for the monopsony case.

For a long time the possible positive employment effects of minimum wages were ignored based on the argument that monopsony buyers are extremely rare in the labor market. However, as mentioned in the introduction, in the recent discussion a kind of revival of the monopsony model has taken place. This is based on two different arguments. First, new empirical evidence with no or even positive effects of minimum wages on employment has been found, as shown later in more detail. Second, the developments of economic theory in other areas of research have influenced the discussion of the effects of minimum wages. Of course, to achieve the qualitative outcome described above, the "classic" form of monopsony with a single firm on the factor market is not required, as the theoretical argument is valid for every labor market where firms face an upward sloping labor supply function. Precisely this situation has been pointed out by recent developments in the theory of industrial organization and in the theory of labor economics. These are mostly based on empirical evidence which shows that firms do not take wages as exogenous.[4]

The first cause of this situation is that, in an "oligopsony" type market, firms exhibit profit functions that are functions of the employment of other firms, founded on heterogeneous preferences and differences in the firm's structure (Penrod 1995). Second, the "moving costs" of the workers may lead to monopsony power if wages increase (Black and Loewenstein 1991). A third reason is found in monopsonistic competition, where a large number of firms compete for workers and where the various non-wage characteristics of the jobs give each employer market power in choosing wages (Bhaska and To 1998). The fourth reason can be found in "equilibrium search." The seeking time of employees yields a finite number of households supplying labor (Albrecht and Axel 1984). Fifth, efficiency wage models have proposed a positive relation between wages and effective work. Because of their importance for a theoretical discussion on the effects of minimum wages, we will later describe the argumentation of the search and the efficiency wage approach in more detail.

2.2.4 Simple "Two-Sector Models"

In both models described above, the effects of minimum wages on other economic activities or sectors have not been analyzed. For instance, to discuss the possibility of wage drifts induced by the minimum wage and of possible employment effects in sectors that are not directly influenced by minimum wage legislation, we have to add at least one additional economic sector. Hence, two-sector models distinguish between two different sectors of economic activity. These sectors can differ by the coverage of the minimum wage, by properties of the economic agents or by different production technologies. The following presentation is oriented along these basic model settings.

Assume that the minimum wage is implemented in only one of two economic sectors. Then the minimum wage not only affects the market where it is implemented, but of course it also changes the relative prices of the economy, influencing participation decisions by changing the reservation wage or by inducing unemployment that may induce labor flows between the two sectors. We find two different types of such models, where the distinction is based on the characteristics of the employees. In models based on the work of Welch (1974), two different types of markets exist in an economy with homogenous labor supply, where only one is covered by the minimum wage. In models based on the work of Kosters and Welch (1972) the existence of heterogeneous labor is assumed.

The idea behind the model by Welch (1974), who analyzed a two-sector model based on homogenous labor, may be shown simply by assuming the existence of two different production technologies producing two different kinds of output in the two sectors. For the sake of simplicity we assume that the firm's maximization problems are similar to equation 2.3. Denote the variables according to the different sectors by the subscripts one and two to describe the maximization problems by

$$\max_{} \pi_z = p_z Y_z(H_z) - w_z H_z, \text{ with } z = 1, 2. \tag{2.7}$$

Note that subscripts one and two for working hours only describe the position on one of the two labor markets and not different forms of "labor." In accordance with the different production technologies in the two sectors, the maximization problems lead to two distinct demand functions with different wage elasticities for working hours. The household's supply of working hours is formally identical to equation 2.4, but randomly supplied on both labor markets. Without implementation of the minimum wage we obtain an identical equilibrium wage on both labor markets. The introduction of a minimum wage in the covered sector creates unemployment in this sector, leading to increased labor supply in the uncovered sector, which in turn induces a lower equilibrium wage rate and higher employment compared to the situation before. The aggregate employment effect depends on the different elasticities of labor demand in the two sectors and can be positive, negative or zero.

This model has been adapted in different ways, for instance by Mincer (1976) and Gramlich (1976), who additionally introduced different forms of risk aversion of the households. In these cases, in accordance with the "textbook theory," the implementation of minimum wages clearly must reduce employment in the low-skilled sector, and exhibits smaller effects on the employment of highly skilled persons, reducing the possibility of an overall positive effect on employment.

The idea of a two-sector model with heterogeneous labor, used for instance by Card and Krueger (1995), may be represented by adding heterogeneous "labor" to equation (2.3). Let $H_{1,j}$ describe low-skilled and $H_{2,j}$ high-skilled work and use identical indexes for the respective wage rates, and assume that there exists no possibility for households to change sectors. Therefore, the maximization problem results in

$$\pi_j = pY_j(H_{1,j}, H_{2,j}) - w_1 H_{1,j} - w_2 H_{2,j}. \tag{2.8}$$

max

Profit maximization yields that the ratio of the two marginal products must be identical to the relative wages, or

$$\frac{\partial Y_j / \partial H_{1,j}}{\partial Y_j / \partial H_{2,j}} = \frac{w_1}{w_2}. \tag{2.9}$$

Given standard production technologies and hence the standard signs and strength of the induced substitution and output effects in this setting, the implementation of a minimum wage in the low-skilled sector clearly leads to a decrease in employment.

Finally, assume the existence of a heterogeneous labor force that is determined by the level of the worker's skills and that there exists complete coverage, but that the minimum wage legislation is only binding at the bottom end of the income distribution (Grossmann 1983, Brown, Gilroy and Kohen 1983). Hence, we can not exactly speak of "two-sector" models, but the underlying economic intuition is very similar. The employment effect involved is simply based on the different elasticities of substitution between the different forms of labor. Thus, we obtain similar results to those in the model described above.

However, aside from the exceptions already discussed, the general criticism pointed out for the "textbook theory" is also valid for this class of models.

2.2.5 Monopsony Type Market Outcomes

A special focus must be located on two-sector models that exhibit similar outcomes to the monopsony case, namely models based on the existence of efficiency wages or search behavior, both yielding an upward sloping supply function of labor for the single firm.

The theory of *efficiency wages* states that a firm has obvious reasons (increasing productivity) for paying more than the equilibrium wage. The adaptation of the "shirking" variant (Shapiro and Stiglitz 1984) through the implementation of minimum wages and an additional economic sector yields the possibility for positive effects on employ-ment, as pointed out by Jones (1987). Rebitzer and Taylor (1991 and 1995) yield positive employment effects only in the short run and negative effects in the long run.

To point out the underlying economic intuition of the efficiency wage models, assume that the homogenous household's utility is positively influenced by income and negatively influenced by working effort. Additionally, we adapt equation (2.3) from the "textbook the-ory" by the existence of labor efficiency units that depend positively on the wage rate, $e_j = e_j(w_j)$, with $\partial e_j / \partial w_j > 0$. Furthermore, introduce "efficient labor" L_j, defined as $L_j = e_j(w_j)H_j$, as the factor of production. Correspondingly, households not only supply working hours, but also efficient labor. This means that the firm must maximize with respect to wages and working hours, and the maximi-zation problem turns out as

$$\pi_j = pY_j(L_j) - w_jH_j, \text{ where } L_j = e_j(w_j)H_j. \qquad (2.9)$$
$$\text{max}$$

Increasing the wage on the one hand increases labor costs and on the other hand increases working effort, inducing higher revenues. If the net effect for the firm is positive, this will lead to an endogenously set wage that is higher than the equilibrium wage of a standard system. Moreover, this may yield to involuntary unemployment.

Based on this basic concept and on the work of Shapiro and Stiglitz (1984), Jones (1987) assumed that households have an incentive to shirk, because working effort negatively influences utility. Furthermore, he assumed the existence of two types of firms, one acting in a primary sector where costs for supervision occur and one in the secondary market, where supervision creates no costs. In the primary sector, shirking may partially be reduced by supervision and catching a shirking household yields dismissal. Dismissed households may find work in the secondary sector or may become unemployed. In the secondary sector the wage is determined by perfect competition. Thus, the opportunity costs of shirking may be expressed as a function of the possibility of being caught, the wage differential and the unemployment rate, and any change in opportunity costs influences the amount of effort supplied in the primary sector. In this setting, the introduction of a binding minimum wage in the secondary sector on the one hand leads to lower opportunity costs for dismissed persons who find a new job, and on the other hand increases the opportunity costs in the case of becoming unemployed. Thus, there exists the possibility that overall opportunity costs will increase, which would lead to less shirking and higher output, and to the possibility for higher employment in the "shirking" sector, which may outdo the employment losses in the covered sector.

In an *equilibrium search* model, firms may partially set the wage level. The firm's possibility to attract workers depends on the relative wages compared to that of the other firms. Firms with relatively higher wages face a larger supply of labor and are able to attract higher qualified labor. Lang and Kahn (1998) model the labor market as a one-shot game with multiples stages where firms set wages to attract applicants, influencing the probability of filling their vacancies. To increase the probability of getting a job, low-wage workers have to consider that other workers may apply for the same job, setting their wage in such a way that high-wage workers will not apply. The implementation of a minimum wage disturbs this decision rule, because then both high and low-wage workers will apply for the same former low-wage job, increasing low-wage employment and decreasing high-wage employment. The authors show that the aggregate effect on employment is positive if the minimum wage is sufficiently low. Swinnerton (1996) proposes that the sign of the employment effect of minimum wages crucially depends on the level of the minimum wage, the induced change of the intensity of job search, and the probability of job offers. The outcome of this model depends on the different labor productivities of the firms and on the imperfect information of the unemployed, who tend to search for a job randomly and sequentially.

In a bilateral search model with heterogeneous workers Burdett and Mortenson (1989) also point out that an increase in minimum wages may attract more and better applicants to low-wage jobs.[5] The basic economic intuition of this model is that identically productive individuals accept every job offer where the wage exceeds the current wage or the reservation wage, respectively. Given equilibrium unemployment caused by search costs, the implementation of a minimum wage does not influence employment, because all offers above the reservation wage were already acceptable even before the implementation of the minimum wage occurred.

Finally, models of *monopsonistic competition* analyze the long term employment implications of minimum wages. Bhaskar and To (1999) account for firm exits in the long run and yield ambiguous employment effects. We find a positive employment effect of the minimum wage according to the standard theory of monopsony and a negative employment effect because of decreasing profits which lead to the exit of firms. Walsh (2003) extends the model of Bhaskar and To (1999) and yields unambiguously positive employment effects

However, identically to the "simple two-sector models" described above, the general criticisms pointed out for the "textbook theory" are – excluding the exceptions mentioned – also valid for this class of models.

2.3 MINIMUM WAGES AND ECONOMIC GROWTH

2.3.1 A Short Overview of the History and Newer Developments in the Theory of Economic Growth

The theory of economic growth is not a theory on the advances towards potential output, but on the evolution of potential output itself.[6] The foundations of modern growth theory date back to Alfred Marshall and Joseph Schumpeter. Marshall (1890) introduced the concept of increasing returns at the market level, yet non-increasing returns at the firm level. Joseph Schumpeter (1912) argued that the right to earn profits depends only on the potential to innovate, invent, or imitate new products or production processes. However, Harrod (1939) and Domar (1946) dynamized the static Keynesian system under the focus of steady state growth and stressed, similarly to classical economics, that investment, not innovation, is crucial for economic growth. But in the long run only very specific economic situations would permit a balancing of the "knife-edge-problem," which would lead to non-stable outcomes of the model.

Solow (1956) in macroeconomic argumentation and later Cass (1965) and Koopmans (1965), based on the work of Ramsey (1928) in micro-based models, solved the "knife-edge-problem." They all stressed the importance of technological change. Technological change is the one and only force that generates economic growth. For a long time these theories were extremely successful, but had the very important drawback that technological change and therefore growth itself was not explained. Nevertheless, the big advantage of the neo-classical growth theories was to focus on the question of the influence of technological change. Proposals for growth policy, such as subsidies for R&D, increasing human capital and specific structural policy laid the foundation for the development of the theory of "endogenous growth."

A new and ongoing area of economic research, partially using the ideas of Schumpeter and Marshall and the formal background of the exogenous theory of growth, was introduced by Romer (1986).[7] In spite of the identical aim, namely the explanation of changes in technology itself, the theoretical discussions have been very contradictory. While a first wave of perfect competition models (e.g. Romer 1986 and Lucas 1988) stressed the importance of external effects in human capital accumulation, leading to non-decreasing returns in accumulative factors of production, a second wave of papers stressed the importance of innovative activity in imperfectly competitive markets (e.g. Romer 1990, Grossman and Helpman 1994), based on a non-declining incentive to invest in innovative products and production processes, leading to a permanent positive growth rate of output. Thus, in both types of models the path of long-run development of an economy becomes endogenous. Permanent changes in economic parameters can now alter the economic rate of growth permanently, while temporary shocks only induce level shifts. Thus, both types of models explain changes in the capacity frontier itself.

The theory of endogenous economic growth was applied to a broad field of research areas,[8] such as growth and inequality (e.g. Aghion, Caroli and Garcia-Penalosa 1999, Deininger and Squire 1997), inflation and growth (e.g. Bruno and Easterly 1998), population dynamics and growth (e.g. Brander and Dowrick 1994, Ehrlich and Lui 1997), trade and growth (e.g. Grossman and Helpman 1991, Ben-David 1996, Murat and Pigliaru 1998), and fiscal policy and growth (e.g. Zagler 1999b). Evans, Honkapohja and Romer (1998) even propose a theoretical argument indicating that cycles and growth are interrelated, combining the theory of business cycles and the theory of economic growth. However, until now, the "new growth theory" has been insufficient in that no comprehensive general theory of endogenous growth has been developed, resulting in competition among different theoretical and therefore political proposals.

Despite the enormous success of theoretical economics, the empirical findings of the new growth theory remain unsatisfactory or at least controversial and debatable. For example, one of the central questions of economic growth, the question of economic convergence, is extremely controversial from an empirical perspective. Following the old neoclassical exogenous theory of growth, in the long run all countries should grow at the same rate, and many authors (e.g. Barro and Sala-I-Martin 1995) find empirical evidence that supports this thesis, and not the predictions of the new approaches. However, there exist substantial methodological problems in the estimation and interpretation of growth regressions.[9]

2.3.2 Employment, Minimum Wages and Economic Growth

Although the theory of endogenous growth and the theory of labor economics have been heavily exploited in past and recent years, for a long time relatively little has been published on common problems.[10] Because of the general assumption that labor markets stand in equilibrium, the "mainstream" part of the theory of endogenous growth has ignored the possibility of labor market frictions such as sticky wages, minimum wages, efficiency wages, and search costs. However, in the last decade we find interesting approaches which combine the two fields of research. For example, Bean and Pissarides (1993) introduced frictional unemployment into an endogenous growth model. In their model new members of the labor force have to be matched to a job vacancy. An increase in the exogenous rate of factor productivity increases economic growth, but on the other hand it also increases the rate of job creation, thus driving down the unemployment rate. Aghion and Howitt (1998) focused on structural change and pointed out that endogenous growth will affect unemployment. Zagler (1999a) proposed an efficiency wage model with a monopolistically competitive manufacturing sector and a competitive innovation sector where the unemployment rate exhibits a negative impact on long-run growth, as it reduces the innovative capacity of the economy. For an overview of the recent publications and for investigations of the interaction between changes in the level of unemployment and changes in the economic rate of growth we recommend Zagler (2004).

However, all these attempts only deal with general aspects of labor markets and not specifically with minimum wages. Only a small number of publications dealing with minimum wages exist, all focusing on the effects of minimum wages on human capital accumulation. All these studies assume existing external effects in human capital accumulation, typical of the first wave of growth models described in the chapter above, which have to generate an inefficient outcome of the market. Thus, taking the external effects properly into account, in this kind of model the planner's solution must generate a higher rate of growth than the market's outcome. This gives rise to the possibility that policy measures like the implementation of a minimum wage may increase economic growth by internalizing parts of the external effect.

Basic work on the effects of minimum wages on human capital in a static setting, which may be considered the precursor of the dynamic models, dates back to the early seventies. In a model where workers achieve skills by taking wage cuts necessary to finance training Rosen (1972), for example, argues that minimum wages induce lower human capital formation, because they increase the opportunity costs for training. However, Acemoglu and Pischke (1999), in a two period model, point out that if the assumption of perfectly competitive labor markets is relaxed, minimum wages can increase the stock of human capital of affected workers by inducing firms to train their unskilled employees. Arulampalam, Booth and Bryan (2002) present empirical support for this thesis. For the UK they found no evidence that the minimum wage reduces training, and some evidence that it increases it. Acemoglu and Pischke (1999) found qualitatively similar empirical results for the US case.

For the dynamic analysis we have to emphasize the contribution to endogenous growth theory where minimum wages in particular have been implemented, namely the work of Cahuc and Michel (1996) and of Raven and Sorenson (1995, 1999). The model by Raven and Sorenson (1995) is an overlapping generation model with an intergenerational externality that leads to too little accumulation of human capital. Hence, an "optimal" level of minimum wages could yield increased accumulation of skills and thereby induce higher economic growth. Raven and Sorenson (1999) proposed a model with similar underlying economic intuition. They assumed that skills are generated through the schooling and training of unskilled workers, leading to different effects of the minimum wage on these two elements, with a net effect depending on whether training or schooling dominates.

The contribution by Cahuc and Michel (1996) is based on a very similar setup. It will be presented in more detail to point out the underlying dynamics. The basic model setup is that of an overlapping generation model with production, a continuum of different individuals, and two sectors where an identical good is produced by firms with two different production technologies, one using skilled, the other unskilled work. Households live for three periods, where in the first period they decide to become skilled or unskilled, in the second they supply labor and earn different wages according to the level of their skills, and in the third they are retired. They maximize Neumann-Morgenstern utility which is a function of income and the probability of being employed. As in all similar endogenous growth models, economic growth is only driven by human capital accumulation. Positive externalities of human capital yield an inefficient (too low) accumulation of human capital. The implementation of a binding minimum wage in the unskilled sector induces that the proportion of skilled workers in the economy becomes a function of the unemployment rate. Based on this model, Cahuc and Michel show that there exists the possibility that a high rate of minimum wage growth yields more households that decide to become skilled because they are afraid of unemployment, thereby internalizing part of the externality, increasing skills accumulation, and increasing economic growth.

However, in the Cahuc and Michel's model unemployment still exists in the steady state. Exactly this point seems problematic, as a higher rate of growth must induce a higher demand for the level of all factors of production, and therefore also labor.

Furthermore, the implementation of unemployment in the individual's utility function to our point of view only partially helps to avoid the methodological problems of the existence of a non-market-clearing market in a general equilibrium model. This will be discussed in chapter three from a more general point of view.

2.4   THE EMPIRICAL EVIDENCE

Largely empirical analyses of the employment effects of minimum wages focus on the effects on youth, because young people generally have fewer skills and less experience, which should result in a higher sensitivity to changes in the minimum wage.

We find two waves of empirical studies analyzing the effect of minimum wages on employment. The first wave of studies dates from the 70s and shows clear negative effects. For an overview of this literature we recommend Brown, Gilroy and Cohen (1982). Beginning in the 80s, the second wave of empirical studies obtained strongly contradictory results. [11] We find studies yielding clearly negative evidence (e.g. Neumark and Wascher 1995), no effects whatsoever (e.g. Card 1992), differing outcomes (e.g. Dolado et al. 1996), and clearly positive employment effects (e.g. Card and Krueger 1995).

Three different methods have generally been used for the empirical analysis of minimum wages (OECD 1998). Studies that employ time series analysis generally regress data for the demographic group analyzed (for instance employed youth workers) on an indicator for the minimum wage and a set of control variables, on the one hand based on simple economic reasoning and on the other hand on underlying economic models that use the structural time series approach. Studies using pooled cross-sectional or longitudinal data have the opportunity to draw on additional information, such as relative minimum wages across different individuals, industries, regions or countries. Often a "difference in difference" approach (Zavodny 1998) is used, comparing the employment level before and after a minimum wage increase. Hence, the results are based on "natural experiments" which could be analyzed with traditional econometric methods or qualitative interviews. [12] In addition we find studies based on the so-called Meyer and Wise Approach. [13] Here, the actual income distribution for the case that no minimum wage exists is estimated using incomes above the minimum wage. Based on this estimation, the employment effect of minimum wages is calculated as the difference between the estimated and actual employment.

However, to our knowledge no empirical studies have tested the effects of minimum wages, in particular with respect to economic growth, as is proposed by the few theoretical models presented in the preceding chapter.

In the following we present an overview of newer results. Table 2.1 summarizes results from time series analysis. Table 2.2 presents the results from studies that use pooled, cross-sectional data or data from longitudinal studies. Both tables present the analyzed country, the time horizon of the respective analysis, and the main results concerning the

Table 2.1   Results from Time Series Analysis, Selected Studies

Authors	Countries	Time Horizon	Main Results	Unexpected Result
Bazen and Martin (1991)	France	1963/68–1986	Negative employment elasticities; not robust for youths, zero for adults.	Yes/?
Ragacs (1993a)*	Austrian Ind.	1969–90	Negative employment elasticities in the short run.	No
Ragacs (1993b)*	Austrian Ind.	1969–90	No effects in the long run.	Yes
Benhayoun (1994)	France	1975–91	No significant effect on youth employment.	Yes
Koutsogeorgopopoulou (1994)	Greece	1962–87	Employment elasticities negative for men and positive for women.	?
Card and Krueger (1995)	US	1954–93	No significant effect on teenage employment.	Yes
Maloney (1995)	New Zealand	1985–94	Negative effect on youth employment and positive on youth unemployment.	No
Mare (1995)*	New Zealand	1985–94	Increased employment of youth, but positive business cycle at the same time.	?
Deere et. al (1995)	US	1985–93	Negative effect on teenage employment.	No
Bell (1995)	Mexico, Columbia	1984–90	Significant negative for Columbia, insign. for Mexico; negative employment effects for low-skilled.	?

Table 2.1   Continued

Authors	Countries	Time Horizon	Main Results	Unexpected Result
Bazen and Marimoutou (1997)	US	1954–93	Negative effect on teenage employment.	No
Card and Krueger (1998)*	US, fast food restaurants	1992–93	Little or no negative effect on employment.	?/Yes
Dickens and Machin (1999)*	UK	1975–92	No negative effect on employment.	Yes
Baker et al.. (1999)*	Canada	1975–93	Contradictory results.	?
Bazen and Marimoutou (2002)*	US	1954–99; Subsamples	Negative effect on teenage employment.	No

Source:

Own compilations from table 2.B.1 from OECD (1998). Additions are marked with an asterisk.

Evaluation of "unexpected results" by the author.

employment effects of minimum wages. Furthermore, the column labeled "unexpected result" points out the qualitative results as a shortcut. "No" stands for results concerning the traditional textbook theory. "Yes" points out missing negative or even positive employment effects and a question mark indicates contradictory results.

As seen in both tables, the empirical outcome of the recent studies is strongly contradictory – independently of the methodology used – and partially supports the newer theoretical results presented in the chapter above. This has led to a broad discussion on the methodological setting and "the best" empirical method for measuring the empirical effects of minimum wages, and to a methodological discussion in almost every one of the recent studies (e.g. Dickens, Machin and Manning 1994, Teulings 1988, and Skinner et al. 2002). This discussion has by no means been resolved, but it at least points out the possibility that some of the older studies that show clearly negative em-

Table 2.2   Results from Pooled Data, Cross-Sectional Analysis and Longitudinal Approaches, Selected Studies

Authors	Countries/ Data	Time Horizon	Main Results	Unexpected Result
Card (1992)	US, population survey	1987–89	No signif. reduction in employment.	Yes
Neumark and Wascher (1992)	US, 50 states and districts	1973/77–1989	Signif. negative effect on teenage and young adult empl.	No
Card and Krueger (1994)*	US, fast food restaurants	about 1992	Employment increased.	Yes
Machin and Manning (1994)	UK, wage councils	1979–90	Positive relationship between mw. and employment.	Yes
Card and Krueger (1995)	US, state data	1987–89	No signif. reduction in employment.	Yes
Neumark and Wascher (1995)	US, population survey	1979–92	Employment of low-skilled is reduced.	No
Currie and Fallik (1996)	US, population survey	1979–87	Probability to be employed after being affected by the minimum wage decreases.	No
Dolado et al. (1996)	France, survey data	1981/85 – 85/89	No substantial effect on employment.	Yes
Bazen and Skourias (1997)	France, 38 industrial sectors	1980–84	Signif. negative effects on youth employment.	No
Burkhauser et al. (1997)	US, data from population and income surv.	1990–92	Signif. negative effects on teenagers, insign. effects on prime-age workers.	?
Baker et al. (1997)	Canada	1975–93	Signif. negative effects on teenagers.	No
Abowd et al.(1997)	US, population surv. France, lab. force survey	1981–1987/89	Youths paid at minimum wage have lower empl. probabilities.	No

Table 2.2 Continued

Authors	Countries/ Data	Time Horizon	Main Results	Unexpected. Result
Chapple (1997)	New Zealand, time series and panel data	1985–97 1980–97	Negative employment effects.	No
Card and Krueger (1998)*	US, fast food restaurants	1992–93	Little or no negative effects on employment.	Yes
Orazem and Mattila (1998)	US, Iowa	1990–92	Minimum wages lower employment opportunities.	No
OECD (1998)*	Nine OECD countries	1975–96	Sign. negative for teenage employment, no effect for adults.	?
Lang and Kahn (1998)*	US, population survey, food service	1988–91	Little up to no effects on employment level; shifts employment from adults to youths.	Yes
Burkhauser et al.. (2000)*	US, population survey	1979–97	Significant small reduction in employment.	No
Neumark and Wascher (2000)*	US, fast food restaurants	1992	Reduction in Employment.	No
Card und Krueger (2000)*	US, fast food restaurants	1992–97	No reduction in Employment.	Yes
Stewart (2002)*	UK, three surveys	1997–99	Empl. growth not sign. lower in low-wage areas.	Yes
Neumark and Wascher (2003)*	17 OECD countries	1975– 2000	Empl. loss for youths; strongest in countries with least regul. labor markets.	No

Source:
Own compilations from table 2.B.1 from OECD (1998).

Additions are marked with an asterisk. Evaluation of "unexpected results" by the author.

ployment effects of minimum wages may simply be missspecified. In particular, older time series often neglected to consider the stationarity and co-integration properties of analyzed variables, which may lead to spurious regression results.

The two different waves of studies ("the first and the second") differ not only in the qualitative but also in the quantitative result. Comparing the different employment elasticities of the studies immediately appears problematic because of the very different methods of estimation. However, a simple qualitative discussion is possible. Compared to the first wave of studies, the more newly estimated elasticities are much smaller, independently of the direction of the employment effect.[14] In the seventies the employment effects of a 10 percent increase of the minimum wage were on average between minus 1–3 percent. In many of the newer studies the elasticities (whether positive or negative) are quite often insignificant.

To summarize, the ongoing discussion gives rise to at least some reservation for the simple adaptation and use of the "textbook theory" in political discussion. But finally, to conclude this section, we must mention an argument which could reduce the importance of recent contradictory empirical results. Of course, in many cases there exists no way of comparing the minimum wage level with the "original" equilibrium wage, in particular if the minimum wage is the result of bargaining behavior. Those findings yielding missing negative employment effects of the minimum wage may therefore simply be explained by situations where the minimum wage is very close to the equilibrium wage.

2.5   SUMMARY OF THE MAIN RESULTS

We have presented an overview of the theoretically expected employment effects of minimum wages proposed by the standard textbook theory, by the theory of monopsony, by simple models based on two different economic sectors, and by alternative approaches yielding monopsony power as a market outcome. Many of these models provide a theoretical foundation for "unexpected," hence positive, employment results of minimum wages. Furthermore, after a short description of the developments in the "new" theory of endogenous growth, we have presented an overview of the theoretical discussion of the effects of minimum wages on economic growth. The few existing models which have implemented minimum wages into an endo-

Table 2.3   Minimum Wages and Employment: Theory

	Possibility for:	
	No reduction in employment	Increasing employment
The "textbook model"	No	No
Wage bargaining:		
• "Right to manage" and "Monopoly" behavior	No	No
• Efficient Bargains	Yes	Yes
Two-Sector models:		
• Two-Sector models with homogenous labor	Yes	No
• Two-Sector models with heterogeneous labor	Yes*	No
"Monopsony":		
• Only one firm	Yes	Yes
• Firms are not price takers in the labor market	Yes	Yes
Example: Efficiency wages	Yes*	Yes*
Example: Equilibrium search	Yes	Yes
Endogenous growth (human capital):		
• Training off the job	Yes	No
• Training on the job	No	No

*) *Employment reduction for low skilled workers*

genous growth model have also found an "unexpected" result, namely a possible increase in the rate of growth. Table 2.3 summarizes the theoretical results.

The standard "textbook version" of the theory of minimum wages is contradicted by empirical studies that find no, or even positive, effects of minimum wages on employment. From tables 2.1 and 2.2 it follows that the contradictory results are independent of the country analyzed; in particular the contradictory results for France and the US must be mentioned. At first glance, this provides support for alternative "monopsony market outcome" models based on efficiency wages or search behavior. However, newer support for the standard model can also be found, leading to a broad discussion on empirical methodology that provides an explanation for the varying results and the estimation methods used.

However, alternative explanations could also be found. Recent contributions to the theory of minimum wages may reveal that some of these empirical studies do not estimate all effects of minimum wages. First, we have to point out that the underlying estimated models are only partial equilibrium models, ignoring the possible effects of minimum wage on other economic sectors. Furthermore, and almost as importantly, we must consider the underlying static concept. Newer theoretical approaches in the theory of endogenous growth indicate that there should also exist long term effects of minimum wages which have not been covered by empirical analysis.

3
Minimum Wages and "General Equilibrium": Methodological Problems

3.1 INTRODUCTION: WALRASIAN AND "NON-MARKET-CLEARING" EQUILIBRIA

As illustrated in chapter two, the theoretical analysis of the effects of minimum wages in microeconomic literature is generally conducted in a partial equilibrium and comparative static context. We have pointed out that this procedure appears methodologically problematic, and that implementation in a general equilibrium system seems desirable. This undertaking raises theoretical problems, which will be covered in this chapter.

To outline these problems, we start by examining a simple general Walrasian system which includes a labor market. Due to Walras' Law, which states that the sum of excess demands must always be zero, a disequilibrium in one market always causes imbalances in other markets. The implementation of a binding minimum wage must also create this effect. At first sight, it is difficult for one to identify in which other market and to what extent the disequilibrium prevails. This is an aspect that can and must be completely ignored by partial equilibrium literature. Additionally, in contrast to the traditional discussion of policy measures in general equilibrium models, where parameter changes are carried out ex post and can meet maximization behavior, the exogenous introduction of minimum wages happens ex ante and therefore does not give the economic agents a chance to react.

These problems are meaningful in several ways. First of all, it seems useful from a simply methodological point of view to discuss the effect of minimum wages in a general equilibrium model and not just in a partial equilibrium framework. Second, it seems appropriate to implement the change in behavior of economic agents relating to the introduction of a minimum wage in order to identify the possible effects on markets other than the labor market, because many economic arguments on minimum wages can not be substantiated by traditional partial equilibrium comparative static models. Take for instance demand stimulants or even growth effects that stem from employees earning incomes higher than the minimum wage. Third, the possible dynamic effects of minimum wages should be analyzed using the framework of endogenous growth theory. The foundation of these growth models is that of a general equilibrium model.

Hence, this book aspires to create a model that closely follows general Walrasian equilibrium economics; a model in which the effects of exogenous minimum wages can be endogenized, but which still displays a clear, determined equilibrium after a minimum wage has been implemented. We believe that adapting the work of Malinvaud (1985), who formulated micro-based, general "non-market-clearing equilibrium models," seems appropriate for this aim. Using these models, the effect of the minimum wage on the maximization considerations of households and the possible effects on the aggregated demand for goods can be captured in both the static and the dynamic case.

"Non-market-clearing equilibrium models" were mainly created to analyze Keynesian unemployment or underemployment equilibria in micro-based settings. Likewise, they can also be enlisted for analyzing classical unemployment – that is, unemployment caused by wages that "are too high." The underlying direction of this theory was and is Keynesian-oriented and the emphasis on real money effects makes this apparent (compare e.g. Dreze 1991). Our interest here lies only in adapting the formal basic structure of the models, while we continue to move in a Walrasian-oriented economy with no real money effects in the analysis.

An important distinction must be made between market-clearing and non-market-clearing equilibria. First, let us examine the basics of Walrasian general equilibrium theory.[1] It is characterized by an always attainable general equilibrium. The agents' economic activities are driven only by price signals. Consequently, the general equilibrium is obtained solely through price adjustments. Additionally, disequilibrium can only exist in the short run, respectively in a model economy with simultaneous "adjustment" only in infinitely short time. In this case, as previously mentioned, the sum of the excess demands in all markets must be equal to zero. Finally, both supply and demand functions in all markets are derived under the assumption that transactions are always identical to supply and demand.

The central argument of the "non-market-clearing equilibrium theory" is that transactions are not always identical to supply, respectively demand.[2] There is a distinction between notional (corresponding to Walrasian economics) and effective supply, respectively demand. Short-term price rigidities up to fixed prices – which are unthinkable in Walrasian economics – account for this. Given these disequilibria on the individual markets, price adjustment mechanisms that would allow the model to adjust into Walrasian equilibrium no longer exist.

As a result, economic agents make quantity adjustments, not price adjustments. This stands in contrast with Walrasian economics. Representatives of the "non-market-clearing equilibrium theory" assume that, although markets must not be cleared in every case, they still reach equilibrium outcomes in the sense that they are unambiguous and stable. But in contrast to Walrasian economics, these equilibria do not let every economic individual conduct his/her desired transaction.

However, the basic model structure essentially corresponds to the structure of the Walrasian (micro-based) economy, which is particularly noticeable in the special case of missing market rigidities: in this case the models are identical, and the Walrasian equilibrium can be considered to be a special case of the "non-market-clearing equilibrium theory."

Thus, this examination works within the framework of micro-based "non-market-clearing equilibrium theory," and not in the field of Post-Keynesian approaches, where disequilibrium conditions are not clearly defined, or respectively stable. Here, the equilibrium itself is questioned and these models are not based on basic Walrasian (micro-funded) assumptions (e.g. see Davidson 1994).

Furthermore, the simple and general foundations of a comparative static "non-market-clearing equilibrium model" will be described. This will serve as a basis for further analysis.

3.2 "NON-MARKET-CLEARING" GENERAL EQUILIBRIUM

First, we provide an illustration of the basic assumptions and notations used. Next, the necessary conditions for the existence of an equilibrium are presented. This is followed by a discussion of the situation outside the equilibrium and the path towards the equilibrium; and finally, minimum wage effects within this model setting are discussed in general terms. The specific considerations for this presentation are essentially based on the work of Malinvaud (1985).[3]

3.2.1 Basic Ideas and Assumptions

There exist N consumers where the index $i\,(i=1,...N)$ describes the ith consumer. There are n producers with the index j, $(j=1...n)$, and r commodities with the index h, $(h=1,...r)$. The rth good serves as money. Hence, there exist $r-1$ goods markets, where all goods are exchanged for money. Money is treated like every other good; therefore it does not have any special properties such as liquidity aspects. But it is essential that the money market is the only one that is always cleared. In this sense, money is treated as the numéraire.

Prices of goods and factors are relative and considered to be fixed, assuming a short-run view. The distinction between consumers and producers can be made exclusively through the nature of their economic function. When a household demands goods, it is a consumer; when a household supplies labor, it is a producer. Firms are consumers in the factor markets and producers in the goods markets.

We distinguish between supply and demand on the one side and buying and selling on the other. Two types of net buyings and net sellings are possible: $a_{i,h}$ stands for the net purchase of good h by consumer i (negative with sales), and $b_{j,h}$ stands for the net sale of good h by the producer j (negative with buying). As previously mentioned, the net purchases and sales are different from the net demand and supply, where $u_{i,h}$ stands for the net demand of the consumer i for good h and $v_{j,h}$ stands for the net supply of the producer j of good h (valid for all goods except money). Desired demands are designated as notional demand, factual demands as effective demand.

If we examine sales and purchases and designate the sales price of good h (in monetary units) with p_h, the assumptions above prove that consumer i's monetary sale must be identical to the purchase sum of all non-monetary goods. We obtain that

$$a_{i,r} = -\sum_{h=1}^{r-1} p_h a_{i,h}, \tag{3.1}$$

and that monetary sales of the producer are identical to the purchase sum of all non-monetary goods, or

$$b_{j,r} = -\sum_{h=1}^{r-1} p_h b_{j,h}. \tag{3.2}$$

Thus, only two-sided market transactions for money are carried out.

3.2.2 Existence of Equilibrium

Three conditions are valid for the existence of any equilibrium, from which one can derive both rationed and non-rationed equilibria (Malinvaud 1985, 18 f.):

- First, we must yield the balancing of purchases and sales for each commodity, which is

$$\sum_{i=1}^{N} a_{i,h} = \sum_{j=1}^{n} b_{j,h}, \quad \text{for } h = 1,...r-1. \tag{3.3}$$

- Second, no one can be forced to purchase or sell more than s/he wants. Therefore, for all consumers i it is valid that

$$\begin{cases} u_{i,h} \geq a_{i,h} & \text{for all } h < r \text{ such that: } a_{i,h} > 0, \\ u_{i,h} \leq a_{i,h} & \text{for all } h < r \text{ such that: } a_{i,h} < 0. \end{cases}$$

In the first case the consumer acts as a buyer, in the second as a seller. To summarize, we obtain that

$$\left| a_{i,h} \right| \leq \left| u_{i,h} \right| \text{ and } a_{i,h} u_{i,h} \geq 0 \text{ for all } h < r. \tag{3.4}$$

Additionally it is valid for every producer j that

$$\left| b_{j,h} \right| \leq \left| v_{j,h} \right| \text{ and } b_{j,h} v_{j,h} \geq 0 \text{ for all } h < r. \tag{3.5}$$

Part two of equations (3.4) and (3.5) states that purchases only happen with net demand and sales only happen with net supply. The first part of the two equations states simply that sales and purchases are limited by the "short-side" of the market. Therefore, it is valid for every individual and for every good purchases cannot surpass demand and that sales cannot surpass supply. Hence, there are five logical positions for an individual (Rothschild 1981, 74): S/he may not take part in the market, be a rationed seller (sales are smaller than the demand), a rationed buyer (purchases are smaller than the demand), and a non-rationed buyer or seller (the purchases, respectively sales correspond to supply, respectively demand).

- Third, either the buyers or the sellers in a market may be rationed, but not both. This is illustrated in the following, where α and β stand for some consumer, respectively producer:

$$
\begin{cases}
\text{If } u_{\alpha,h} > a_{\alpha,h} \geq 0 \text{ or } v_{\beta,h} < b_{\beta,h} \leq 0, \\[4pt]
\text{then for all } i \text{ and } j \text{ it must be valid, that,} \\[4pt]
(u_{i,h} - a_{i,h}) \geq 0 \text{ and } (v_{j,h} - b_{j,h}) \leq 0 \text{ (Seller's market);} \\[10pt]
\text{If } u_{\alpha,h} < a_{\alpha,h} \leq 0 \text{ or } v_{\beta,h} > b_{\beta,h} \geq 0, \\[4pt]
\text{then for all } i \text{ and } j \text{ it must be valid, that,} \\[4pt]
(u_{i,h} - a_{i,h}) \leq 0 \text{ and } (v_{j,h} - b_{j,h}) \geq 0 \text{ (Buyer's market).}
\end{cases}
\tag{3.6}
$$

Hence in the case of the appearance of a rationed seller, there cannot be a rationed buyer and vice versa. Therefore, the following three market conditions are possible: a balanced market (equilibrium in a Walrasian sense), a seller's market and a buyer's market. Next, use the concept of aggregate excess demand (D_h) to give an easier presentation of this condition. Excess demand is defined as

$$
D_h = \sum_{i=1}^{N} u_{i,h} - \sum_{J=1}^{n} v_{j,h}.
\tag{3.7}
$$

D_h is positive if the total of all desired purchases is larger than desired sales, and vice versa. Use the information given by equation (3.3) to find out that

$$
D_h = \sum_{i=1}^{N} (u_{i,h} - a_{i,h}) - \sum_{J=1}^{n} (v_{j,h} - b_{j,h}).
\tag{3.8}
$$

Remember that equation (3.6) states that in a seller's market, $(u_{i,h} - a_{i,h}) \geq 0$ and $(v_{j,h} - b_{j,h}) \leq 0$. Note that in the case of a positive excess demand $(u_{i,h} - a_{i,h})$ and D_h are clearly positive.[4] If producers want to sell, $v_{j,h}$ is positive too, and we yield that $D_h v_{j,h}$ definitely is greater than zero. We know that in this case, $(u_{i,h} - a_{i,h}) > 0$ and $(v_{j,h} - b_{j,h}) \leq 0$. Because no one may be forced to sell more than s/he wants, the solution $(v_{j,h} - b_{j,h}) < 0$ is not possible from a logical point of view, and we yield that $b_{j,h} = v_{j,h}$. Similar argumentation is valid for a buyer's market; hence we are able to reduce the third property to

$$
\begin{cases}
a_{i,h} = u_{i,h} & \text{if } D_h u_{i,h} \leq 0, \\[4pt]
b_{j,h} = v_{j,h} & \text{if } D_h v_{j,h} \geq 0,
\end{cases}
\tag{3.9}
$$

where the first line of equation (3.9) describes a buyer's market and the second line describes a seller's market. The "short side" asserts itself in every market, and the "long side" is rationalized.

Equations (3.3), (3.4), (3.5) and (3.9) together describe an unambiguous equilibrium. It is clear that this model bears reference to the Walrasian equilibrium theory. It illustrates only a special case, namely $D_h = 0$, where both sides can fulfill their desires. However, the situation is different outside of the equilibrium where there is no longer a price adjustment mechanism that leads to Walrasian equilibrium.

3.2.3 Perceived Constraints, Disequilibrium and Movements to Equilibrium

For the ongoing analysis the following assumption must be valid:[5]

A1   There exist only three markets: a labor, a capital, and a goods market.

A2   Consumers and producers distinguish themselves in households and firms, where households appear as producers in the labor and capital market, and as consumers in the goods market. Firms appear as producers in the goods market and as consumers in the labor and capital markets.

A3   The number of households and firms is large enough to speak of perfect competition.

A4   The only market that experiences exogenous limitations is the labor market, and this limitation is only for households in their property as a producer. Hence only the wage is fixed and the other prices are flexible.

A5   At the beginning of the maximization period, households own a certain start-up endowment, $e_{i,h}$.[6] This may not cover the range of goods h, as stated here for the sake of simplicity, but must guarantee the possibility of at least one trade activity. The consumption of every household in a given period is labeled as $C_{i,h}$. Therefore it must be valid that

$$C_{i,h} = e_{i,h} + a_{i,h},\qquad(3.10)$$

where a_{ih} can be both positive and negative, but it must be guaranteed that consumption is positive.

A6   Producers maximize monetary income (firms: "profit," households: "income") from selling non-monetary goods, $-b_{j,r}$ stands for the purchase of money through producers.

A7　In contrast to actual purchases, $a_{i,h}$, in the market h, purchase limitations of consumers are marked as $\overline{a}_{i,h}$. No one can buy more than the observed rationing allows, hence it is valid for consumers that

$$\left|a_{i,h}\right| \le \left|\overline{a}_{i,h}\right|. \tag{3.11}$$

A8　Purchase limitations of producers in the market h are marked as $\overline{b}_{j,h}$. Here, too, no one can sell more than observed rationing allows, which is

$$\left|b_{j,h}\right| \le \left|\overline{b}_{j,h}\right|. \tag{3.12}$$

A9　The actual observation of rationing or missing rationing happens directly through the impossibility of fulfilling the desires and subsequently through their fulfillment. This is summarized by

$$\begin{cases} \overline{a}_{i,h} = a_{i,h} & \text{if } \left|a_{i,h}\right| < \left|u_{i,h}\right| & \text{with rationing,} \\ \left(\overline{a}_{i,h} - a_{i,h}\right) \ge 0 & \text{if } a_{i,h} = u_{i,h} & \text{without rationing.} \end{cases} \tag{3.13}$$

　　The first line of equation (3.13) describes perceived constraints. From the second line of (3.13), it follows that one knows that the market either finds itself in equilibrium or in success supply.

A10　The conditions described by equations (3.11) – (3.13) also exist for producers in similar form.

A11　All the activities of the agents in one market first only illustrate attempts to fulfill the corresponding desires. This does not happen independently of other markets where desires are also fulfilled or where the consumer is rationed. Therefore, after the first maximization process and the following possible rationing observation, further maximization processes occur, which can result in changed behavior in other markets. With the aid of this additional information, a "non-market-clearing equilibrium" will be reached. The adjustment process itself has not been analyzed. Its stability has to be additionally assumed.

A12　The abovementioned adjustment process takes place – corresponding to the Walrasian concept – in an infinitely short time period. Consequently, the "non-market-clearing equilibria" can immediately be analyzed.

3.3 CONCLUSIONS: GENERAL EFFECTS OF MINIMUM WAGES

Given the assumptions listed above, and assuming utility maximization for households, profit maximization for firms, and traditional properties of the respective utility and profit functions, the introduction of a minimum wage leads some households to observe a restriction in the labor market. The possible transactions no longer correspond to their desired transaction. Firms are not affected in their maximization decisions, except for the observation of a different wage rate. Consequently, an excess supply occurs in the labor market in the first step, and "classical unemployment," which is induced by wages that are too high and fixed, prevails.

Individuals who notice the rationing find out that they are on the short side of the market but have no information about how large the excess supply is in aggregate. It is now essential – and here lies the main difference to the pure Walrasian model – that these individuals must subsequently attempt to adjust their utility-maximizing behavior to the given situation. This also affects their activities in other markets as long as, given the additional information and limitation, a new utility maximum is obtained.

The effects on the other markets can only be analyzed when, contrary to the previous illustration, specific functional forms of the model have been assumed. However, it is essential that we are no longer in a system of markets with supply and demand functions that are given by the first maximization of all economic agents, and where a minimum wage simply induces the existence of different excess demands. Instead of this, unemployed households maximize given the information that they do not yield labor income, and employed households maximize given the information that their labor income has increased. Through the new maximization process, the position and the slope of the affected functions change until a new equilibrium (without excess demands in the Walrasian sense) appears. It may, however, exhibit other equilibrium quantities and prices, as shown in the following chapters.

These considerations are not valid for static models alone if we assume that in a dynamic model a binding minimum wage exists at every point in time. Chapter two showed that growth in the "new theory of growth" is either based on non-diminishing returns in accumulative production factors or non-diminishing incentives for innovative activities. Due to the previously mentioned minimum wage impacts, it seems probable that those markets where the actual growth process is generated will be influenced, as is shown in chapters six and seven.

To summarize, this chapter may help to formulate static and dynamic models and maximization problems which consider that involuntarily unemployed households recognize that their income is reduced and employed households recognize that their income increases. Both react to their situations logically. This will be further analyzed in the following chapters.

Part II:
Minimum Wages and Comparative Statics

4

Supporting the Partial Equilibrium Results

4.1 THE BASIC MODEL SETUP

As mentioned in the introduction, this chapter presents a simple static general Walrasian model, which has been modified to become a "non-market-clearing" equilibrium model through the introduction of a minimum wage. The analysis is based completely on the considerations of chapter three. However, the analysis is expanded by specific assumptions on the profit and utility maximization behavior of the economic agents. These assumptions will also serve as a foundation for the dynamic enlargement throughout our examination (without, respectively with the minimum wage). Thus, this model is illustrated in more detail than later models, even though the underlying mechanics are much simpler.

4.1.1 Basic Ideas and Macroeconomic Relations

A model is set up with three markets: a goods, a labor, and a capital market, and captures the effect of the introduction of a nominal minimum wage.[1] There exist one homogenous consumer good and two homogenous production factors (labor and physical capital). The price of capital will be set as the numéraire in order to analyze the price effects of the minimum wage on the good's market, but to facilitate an intuitive illustration, it will be upheld throughout a large part of the illustration.

Because the model is comparative static in nature, savings and investments are equal to zero. It is also assumed that no depreciation on capital exists. Hence, very simple macroeconomic relations are valid. The entire produced output is consumed, $Y = C$, monetary income, M,[2] of the household will be used only for consumption, $M = C$, and output equals income, $Y = M$.

51

The aggregate consumption of goods consists of the consumption of N identical households. Any household i ($i=1...N$) buys the amount C_i of consumer goods and sells working hours, H_i. Households own physical capital and rent it to firms, therefore obtaining capital income from capital ownership in the amount of rK_i, where K_i equals the capital stock of the individual i and r is the rental price of capital. There exist F identical firms. Every firm j ($j=1...F$) produces output, Y_j with a technology of constant returns to scale using labor, h_jL_j, where L_j describes the number of employed persons and h_j average working hours, and capital as factor inputs. This takes place under the condition of perfect competition. Hence, given the production technology and the assumption of perfect competition, economic profits have to be zero. To further simplify the analysis, it is assumed that population is normalized to one. Therefore the aggregate consumption expenditures, the creation of income and the creation of the aggregate output are simply given by

$$C = \sum_{i=1}^{N} pC_i, \quad M = \sum_{i=1}^{N} \left(wH_i + rK_i\right) \text{ and } Y = \sum_{j=1}^{F} pY_j,$$

where p is the price of goods and w is money wages. Note that these rules for aggregation are only valid for the notional system. In the case of the introduction of a minimum wage, we additionally have to distinguish between the income and consumption of employed and unemployed households.

We denote the undisturbed system as a notional system or "Walrasian Economy" and the system in which the minimum wage has been implemented as the "effective" case. Given the assumptions presented in chapter three, we note that both systems may be solved directly "in equilibrium." However, by using this methodology the important economic behaviors of the different systems are not captured. For instance, if we only achieve the result that the effective equilibrium output is smaller than the notional equilibrium output, the reasons for this would be difficult to analyze. They could be found in smaller supply of goods, smaller demand for goods or in both. Hence, all relevant supply and demand functions for both systems will be pointed out in order to also capture these effects.

We will then describe the maximization problems of firms and households. Chapter 4.2 analyzes the "Walrasian Economy" as a benchmark. The individual maximization results and the aggregation are presented, plus the different supply and demand functions for all endogenous variables, and finally, the market equilibrium. In chapter

4.3 the effects of minimum wages ("effective system") are discussed in an identical way. In chapter 4.4 we compare the outcomes of the two systems and summarize the main results.

4.1.2 Maximization Problems

Firms produce with Cobb-Douglas production technology and constant returns to scale,

$$Y_j = AK_j^{\alpha}(h_j L_j)^{1-\alpha},$$ (4.1)

where A describes exogenous technological progress, which for the ongoing analysis will be normalized by one. It is to be seen that we assume that it is not possible to produce with working hours or "physical labor" alone. α and $(1-\alpha)$ describe the output elasticities for capital and labor. As mentioned above, the index j ($j=1...F$) stands for the number of firms, which will be discussed later when the necessary aggregation of the individual's functions is presented.

Firms maximize profit, which under perfect competition means that marginal revenues, given by the price, must equal marginal costs. They have neither start-up capital nor labor. Both must be demanded in each respective market. With the given wage and price of renting capital, they are confronted with total costs (TC_j) of

$$TC_j = rK_j + wh_j L_j.$$ (4.2)

The production function is linear-homogenous; hence the value of production is completely divided between the two factors. Furthermore, the relative factor input is independent to the output. Therefore the factor demand functions cannot be derived by the standard profit maximization method and we have to derive "conditional factor demands."[3] Thus, the cost minimization problem of the individual firm turns out as:

$$\begin{cases} \min_{L_j,K_j} TC_j = \min_{L_j,K_j} (rK_j + wh_j L_j), \\ \text{s.t.}: \ Y_j = K_j^{\alpha}(h_j L_j)^{1-\alpha}. \end{cases}$$ (4.3)

Taking K_j from equation (4.1) and substituting it into equation (4.2), and correspondingly substituting $h_j L_j$, reduces the minimization problem to two partial problems. Their solution will be illustrated later.

Households are homogenous, except in their position in the labor market (employed or unemployed). The utility function U_i is given by

$$U_i = \ln C_i + \mu \ln F_i, \tag{4.4}$$

with $0 < \mu \leq 1$. C_i denotes consumption, F_i denotes leisure time and μ designates the elasticity of consumption with respect to leisure time.[4] The utility function fulfills standard concavity conditions with $U_{i,C} > 0$, $U_{i,F} < 0$, $U_{i,CC} < 0$, and $U_{i,CC} < 0$. As can be seen, consumption and leisure are logarithmic, and the utility function is divisible between C_i and F_i, thus the cross derivatives of U_i are zero.

Employed households supply exactly one unit of "physical" labor, but optimize supplied working hours according to their maximization problems. In the case of employment, households obtain income from working hours, wH_i, and from capital ownership, rK_i, where H_i describes the number of working hours. Unemployed households do not supply working hours, but capital income allows for consumption even in the case of unemployment. Of course, this assumption does not appear to be very practice-oriented, but in contrast to an implementation of a tax and transfer system it keeps the analysis as simple as possible. We assume that renting capital causes transaction costs η, $\eta > 0$, one example being real estate agents, and that the supply of capital, K_i^s, is given by

$$K_i^s = \overline{K}_i \frac{r}{r + \eta}. \tag{4.5}$$

$\overline{K}_i$ equals an initial stock of capital that is identical for every individual and exogenously determined. The existence of transaction costs results in a capital supply function that increases with the interest rate. It is further valid that, $\lim_{r \to \infty}(.) \Rightarrow \overline{K}_i$, $\lim_{r \to 0}(.) \Rightarrow 0$, $\lim_{\eta \to \infty}(.) \Rightarrow 0$, and $\lim_{\eta \to 0}(.) \Rightarrow \overline{K}_i$. Hence we assume declining costs due to fixed costs.

For their maximization decisions, households take into consideration the traditional trade-off between working and leisure time. We normalize the entire day's time by one, which yields the time constraint $L_i + H_i = 1$. Hence L_i and H_i describe a part of the entire day as a percentage. The budget constraint of the household is that consumption expenditures may not exceed income, so for employed households it is given by $pC_i \leq wH_i + rK_i$, which for unemployed households reduces to $pC_i \leq rK_i$.

The introduction of an exogenous minimum wage $\overline{w}$, $(\overline{w} > w)$, leads to the possibility of a lack of identity from "wishes" and transactions, and the perceived restriction on the labor market leads to the complete loss of labor income, as it is assumed that no form of short-term employment exists. All other variables, such as the price of goods, quantity of output, etc. will also be influenced. This will be covered in greater depth during the illustration of the specific market demand and supply functions presented later.

Summarizing and knowing that the household's supply of capital in every case is given by equation (4.5), the household's maximization problem turns out as:

$$\max U_i = \ln C_i + \mu \ln F_i$$

s.t.:

$$\begin{cases} C1: F_i + H_i = 1 \\ C2: pC_i \le wH_i + rK_i \end{cases} \text{notional case,}$$

$$\begin{cases} C1: F_i + H_i = 1 \\ C3: pC_i \le \overline{w}H_i + rK_i \end{cases} \text{effective case, if employed,}$$

$$\begin{cases} C4: F_i = 1 \\ C5: pC_i \le rK_i \end{cases} \text{effective case, if unemployed.}$$

4.2   THE REFERENCE MODEL ("THE WALRASIAN ECONOMY")

4.2.1   Individual Maximization Decisions and Aggregation

We use the aforementioned constraints C1 and C2, and denote the Lagrange multiplier as λ_i, so that the maximization problem of the unrestricted individual in the Lagrange illustration of the Kuhn-Tucker problem is given by[5]

$$L_i = \ln C_i + \mu \ln F_i + \lambda_i \{w(1 - F_i) + rK_i - pC_i\}. \tag{4.6}$$

We obtain that:

$$\frac{\partial L_i}{\partial C_i} = \frac{1}{C_i} - \lambda_i p = 0,$$

$$\frac{\partial L_i}{\partial F_i} = \frac{\mu}{F_i} - \lambda_i w_i = 0.$$

The complementary slackness condition must also be analyzed. For the first case, $\lambda_i = 0$ and $w(1 - F_i) + rK_i - pC_i \geq 0$, we yield that $1/C_i = 0$ and $\mu / F_i = 0$. The result is that households would achieve an infinite amount of leisure time and consumption. This result is ruled out for leisure by the time constraint and for consumption by limited economic resources. For the second possibility, with $\lambda_i \geq 0$ and $w(1 - F_i) + rK_i - pC_i = 0$, the Lagrange case of identity returns, hence the third FOC is obtained as $w(1 - F_i) + rK_i = pC_i$.

Next, the notional system's demand and supply functions are derived. Note that in the Walrasian case every household must be employed. In order to distinguish the results of this chapter from those of the "effective case," all derived functions of the Walrasian system are denoted by the superscript "n," standing for "notional." Additionally, in order to simplify the analysis at this point, remember that the rental price for capital is used as the numéraire, which helps to omit the specific notation for this price. Hence the notional capital supply of households, $K_i^{S,n}$, is arrived at by simplifying equation (4.5) as

$$K_i^{S,n} = \frac{1}{1+\eta} \overline{K}_i \equiv \xi \overline{K}_i. \tag{4.5'}$$

Divide the FOC for leisure time by that for consumption to yield the standard result: the ratio between marginal utility from leisure and marginal utility from consumption must be equivalent to the real wage. The combination of this relationship with the budget constraint, the time constraint and equation (4.5') helps to calculate the supply function of working hours, $H_i^{S,n}$, which is given by[6]

$$H_i^{S,n} = 1 - \frac{\mu}{1+\mu}\left(1 + \xi \frac{\overline{K}_i}{w}\right). \tag{4.7}$$

At a higher wage leisure is valued less. With larger returns from capital ownership leisure is valued more and the effect on the supply of working hours is simply inverse. Note that the supplied working time cannot exceed the entire day's time, which is normalized by one. Thus, it must be guaranteed that $\mu(1+\mu)^{-1}(1 + \xi \overline{K}_i / w) \leq 1$, which is fulfilled if $\mu\xi\overline{K} \leq w$.[7] The non-wage income valued by μ must be smaller than the wage rate. Only under this condition do higher wages lead to an increase in labor supply. However, this assumption only states that a rule is obtained for the calibration of the capital stock, which is free at this moment.

Furthermore, from the three FOCs and equation (4.5'), the notional individual's demand function for goods, $C_i^{D,n}$, can be derived.[8] Hence it is obtained that

$$C_i^{D,n} = \frac{1}{1+\mu}\frac{\xi\overline{K}+w}{p},\tag{4.8}$$

which is consequently strictly positive. The demand for goods increases with a smaller price of the good, a higher nominal wage, a higher non-wage income, and a smaller valuation of leisure.

From the firm's problem and the use of the rental price for capital as the numéraire, one is able to yield the corresponding "conditional" factor demand functions of the single firm for labor volume, $(h_j L_j)^{D,n}$, and capital, $K_j^{D,n}$,[9]

$$(h_j L_j)^{D,n} = \left(\frac{\alpha}{1-\alpha}w\right)^{-\alpha} Y_j,\tag{4.9}$$

$$K_j^{D,n} = \left(\frac{\alpha}{1-\alpha}w\right)^{1-\alpha} Y_j,\tag{4.10}$$

which are valid for every output of the firm j.

By substituting the "conditional" demand functions (4.9 and 4.10) into equation (4.2), and then using the rental price for capital as the numéraire, we express the firm's cost function[10]

$$TC(w,r,Y_j) = \alpha^{-\alpha}(1-\alpha)^{\alpha-1}w^{1-\alpha}Y_j.\tag{4.11}$$

As can be seen, marginal costs correspond to average costs. They are constant and independent to the produced output reflecting standard properties of Cobb-Douglas production functions (compare e.g. Varian 1992).

For the specific case of Cobb-Douglas with constant returns to scale, no supply function in the traditional sense – meaning a supply function increasing with the price of goods – exists. However, profit maximization must lead to the equivalence of marginal revenue, which in perfect competition simply equals the price and marginal costs.

Thus, for the ongoing analysis we must add this relationship instead of the traditional supply function of goods

$$p^n = \alpha^{-\alpha} (1-\alpha)^{\alpha-1} w^{1-\alpha} . \tag{4.12}$$

With constant returns to scale, neither the output nor the number of firms is determined. The number of firms can be freely chosen. It will be set to one; hence all aggregated functions for the demand of factors and supply of goods are formally identical to those of the single firm. We additionally normalize the number of households to one in order to yield the same result for goods and capital demand and for the supply of working hours.

Finally, it must be remembered that, in the case of identical individuals, the entire population always has to find work. Therefore, $N = L = 1$, and the term for "physical labor" in the aggregate labor demand function of the firms is also omitted. The expression reduces only to a demand function for average working hours, h_j, which in this setting must be identical to the level of working hours, H_j.

4.2.2 Market Equilibrium

Based on the simplifications mentioned above, an overview of all aggregated functions is listed below. Additionally, all variables of the notional system are marked by the index "n" for better distinction to the effective case. The original numbering of the equations is kept, but has been marked with an apostrophe for the sake of clarity. Hence, we obtain that:

Demand for goods:

$$C^{D,n} = \frac{1}{1+\mu} \frac{\xi \overline{K} + w^n}{p^n} \tag{4.8'}$$

Profit maximization:

$$p^n = \alpha^{-\alpha} (1-\alpha)^{\alpha-1} w^{n^{1-\alpha}} \tag{4.12'}$$

Demand for w. hours:

$$H^{D,n} = \left(\frac{\alpha}{1-\alpha} w^n \right)^{-\alpha} Y^n \tag{4.9'}$$

Supply of w. hours:

$$H^{S,n} = 1 - \frac{\mu}{1+\mu} \left(1 + \frac{\xi \overline{K}}{w^n} \right) \tag{4.7'}$$

Demand for capital:

$$K^{D,n} = \left(\frac{\alpha}{1-\alpha} w^n \right)^{1-\alpha} Y^n \tag{4.10'}$$

Supply of capital:

$$K^{S,n} = \xi \overline{K}. \tag{4.5''}$$

The addition of the equilibrium conditions for goods, $(Y^n = C^n)$, working hours and capital markets concludes the model. Due to the production technology $(p = MC)$, the quantity of goods produced will only be determined by the demand for goods. Six variables for quantities as well as three prices correspond to six behavioral equations and three equilibrium conditions. Walras' law eliminates one equilibrium condition, so that five independent equations remain. The normalization of the renting price of capital reduces the model to an unequivocally solvable system.

In the ongoing analysis an asterisk will indicate equilibrium values. We equate demand and supply of goods and substitute for the wage, calculated from the equilibrium in the capital market, in order to calculate the equilibrium output quantity,[11] $C^{*,n}$,

$$C^{*,n} = \left(\frac{1-\alpha}{1-\alpha+\mu}\right)^{1-\alpha} (\xi \, \overline{K})^\alpha .$$

(4.13)

Substitute the above expression back into the equilibrium of the capital market to obtain the equilibrium wage,[12] $w^{*,n}$,

$$w^{*,n} = \frac{1-\alpha+\mu}{\alpha} \xi \, \overline{K} .$$

(4.14)

As can be directly seen, substitution of the equilibrium wage from equation (4.14) into the supply function of goods leads to the equilibrium price, $p^{*,n}$,

$$p^{*,n} = \alpha^{-1} \left(\frac{1-\alpha+\mu}{1-\alpha}\right)^{1-\alpha} (\xi \, \overline{K})^{1-\alpha} .$$

(4.15)

Finally, substituting the equilibrium wage from equation (4.14) and $C^{*,n}$ from equation (4.13) into the demand function for working hours permits the expression of equilibrium working hours,[13] $H^{*,n}$,

$$H^{*,n} = \frac{1-\alpha}{1-\alpha+\mu} .$$

(4.16)

Let us recall that equilibrium capital is directly determined by equation (4.5'') and that the rental price of capital is used as the numéraire. Hence, the equilibrium in the Walrasian system is clearly defined.

4.3   THE EFFECTS OF MINIMUM WAGES ("THE EFFECTIVE CASE")

It is first necessary to provide some introductory notes on notation. The minimum wage in the effective case will create unemployment. We denote equilibrium employment in the effective case by $L^{*,e}$, with $L^{*,e} < N \equiv 1$ and denote all individuals who experience a restriction in the labor market with index "u," where, $u = 1...(1 - L^{*,e})$. Additionally, note that households which are not constrained by the minimum wage yield completely identical maximization results and derived supply and demand functions, as they do in the notional case. However, their number is now restricted to $L^{*,e}$. In order to omit additional notations, simply assume that the index i in this case only denotes households which are not restricted, hence $i = 1...L^{*,e}$. Furthermore, to point out the differences of the notional system, all aggregated functions and all respective variables will be denoted by the superscript "e" for "effective case."

4.3.1   Individual Maximization Decisions and Aggregation

As shown above, u individuals experience a restriction in the labor market. Because of the introduction of the minimum wage, $\overline{w} > w^{n}$, they cannot obtain income from working, but their supply of capital stays formally identical to (4.5') in the notional case. Hence their maximization problem in the Lagrange illustration of the Kuhn-Tucker problem results in

$$L_{u} = \ln C_{u} + \lambda_{u}(rK_{u} - pC_{u}).$$

(4.17)

The derivative with respect to consumption must remain identical to that in the notional case, as becomes immediately clear. Hence the analysis of the complementary slackness condition is conducted identically, yielding the equality condition for the budget constraint. Working hours are no longer a factor in the maximization problem, because the supply of labor in the "restricted case" is by definition equal to zero. The corresponding goods demand function, C_{u}^{D}, follows directly from the budget constraint, the use of the rental price of capital as the numéraire and the use of the capital supply function,

$$C_{u}^{D} = \frac{\xi \overline{K}_{u}}{p^{e}}.$$

(4.18)

The demand for goods is therefore financed only by non-wage income. The demand increases along with non-wage income and decreases with an increase of the price of goods.

As pointed out in the introduction, households that are not restricted yield identical results, as in the notional system. Hence the supply function of working hours, the demand function for goods and the supply function of capital remain identical to equations (4.5), (4.6) and (4.5'), but are weighted by the number of employed households.

Firms are only in so far affected by the introduction of a minimum wage that they notice a higher exogenous wage rate, but for the firm's maximization problem the wage is always exogenously determined. Consequently, there is no further influence on the supply and demand functions, and the notional and effective functional forms are formally identical to that of the individual firm, given by equations (4.12), (4.9) and (4.10). However, when aggregating it should be noted that employment is no longer identical to population, but we also obtain formally identical functions in comparison to the notional case.

Aggregation of the functions of households yields more changes. Note that the unemployment rate is simply given by $(1 - L^{*,e})$. Hence the aggregate effective supply of working time, $H^{S,e}$, is reduced to the supply of employed households. Note that the exogenous capital stock, $\overline{K}$, is identical for all households and use the rental price for capital as the numéraire to find out that

$$H^{S,e} = L^{*,e}\left\{1 - \frac{\mu}{1+\mu}\left(\frac{\xi\,\overline{K}}{\overline{w}} + 1\right)\right\}.\tag{4.19}$$

Aggregate effective demand for goods consists of the individual demand of households without a limitation, $C_i^{D,b}$, following from equation (4.8) and those with a limitation, C_i^D, following from equation (4.18). Use the rental price of capital as the numéraire to show the effective aggregated demand of goods, $C^{D,e}$,

$$\begin{cases} C^{D,e} = L^{*,e}C_i^{D,n} + (1 - L^{*,e})C_u^D = \\[2mm] \quad = L^{*,e}\dfrac{1}{1+\mu}\dfrac{\xi\,\overline{K}_i + \overline{w}}{p^e} + (1 - L^{*,e})\dfrac{\xi\,\overline{K}_u}{p^e}. \end{cases}\tag{4.20}$$

Effective demand for goods is therefore positively influenced by the population (standardized to one) and the non-wage income. It is influenced negatively by the prices of goods and by μ. The effect of the minimum wage is not clearly established at first. It impacts the income of those who continue to be employed as well as the income of the unemployed. In addition, it impacts the marginal costs of the firms and thus the price of goods. This will be afforded further consideration later.

Finally, the effective aggregated supply function of capital remains identical to the notional case.

4.3.2 Market Equilibrium

To provide a better overview, all corresponding functions will be reviewed here. As in the notional case, population and the technology parameter of the production function have been standardized to one. The exogenous nominal minimum wage $\overline{w}$ also reappears. Remember that functions, respectively variables, which are now specifically determined by the exogenous wage rate, will be labeled in the index "e." The price for capital is used as the numéraire. Note also that the exogenous capital stock is identical for all households, which helps to omit the superscripts. The equation labeling retains the original numbering, but to keep the presentation clearer it has been marked by two apostrophes. This leads to:

Demand for goods:
$$\begin{cases} C^{D,e} = L^{*,e} \, \dfrac{1}{1+\mu} \, \dfrac{\xi \, \overline{K} + \overline{w}}{p^{e}} + \\[2ex] \qquad + (1 - L^{*,e}) \dfrac{\xi \, \overline{K}}{p^{e}} \end{cases} \qquad (4.18'')$$

Profit maximization:
$$p^{e} = \alpha^{-\alpha} (1-\alpha)^{\alpha-1} \overline{w}^{1-\alpha} \qquad (4.12'')$$

Demand for w. time:
$$H^{D,e} = \left(\frac{\alpha}{1-\alpha} \, \overline{w} \right)^{-\alpha} Y^{e} \qquad (4.9'')$$

Supply of w. time:
$$H^{S,e} = L^{*,e} \left\{ 1 - \frac{\mu}{1+\mu} \left(\frac{\xi \, \overline{K}}{\overline{w}} + 1 \right) \right\} \qquad (4.7'')$$

Demand for capital:
$$K^{D,e} = \left(\frac{\alpha}{1-\alpha} \, \overline{w} \right)^{1-\alpha} Y^{e} \qquad (4.10'')$$

Supply of capital:
$$K^{S,e} = \xi \, \overline{K}. \qquad (4.5''')$$

Consequently, supply of capital, minimum wage, price of goods and rental price of capital (the numéraire) exist unequivocally in the form of parameters. Labor and output quantities are still undetermined, and so is the unemployment rate. As in the notional system, we add the three equilibrium conditions for goods ($Y^e = C^{D,e}$), working hours and capital in order to solve the system. First, substitute from capital supply into capital demand to directly calculate the equilibrium output as

$$C^{*,e} = \xi\, \overline{K} \left(\frac{1-\alpha}{\alpha}\, \frac{1}{\overline{w}} \right)^{1-\alpha} .$$ (4.21)

Next, substitute equilibrium output into demand for working time and reformulate to yield equilibrium working hours by

$$H^{*,e} = \frac{1-\alpha}{\alpha}\, \frac{\xi\, \overline{K}}{\overline{w}} .$$ (4.22)

Finally, in order to calculate equilibrium employment, we substitute equilibrium working hours into the supply function of hours, and reformulate to obtain[14]

$$L^{*,e} = (1+\mu)\frac{1-\alpha}{\alpha}\, \frac{\xi\, \overline{K}}{\overline{w} - \mu \xi\, \overline{K}} .$$ (4.23)

Given that the assumption presented after deriving equation (4.7) in the notional case, must also hold for the minimum wage ($\mu \xi\, \overline{K} \le \overline{w}$), employment is strictly positive.

4.4 COMPARISON OF THE RESULTS AND CONCLUSIONS

Our further examination of the differences in the outcomes of the two systems centers on the position of the supply and demand function of goods, the equilibrium price of goods, the equilibrium nominal and real outputs, the equilibrium employment respectively unemployment and the factor demand functions. Income effects will also be analyzed.[15] It is not possible to solve several of the results analytically, because they often depend on the possible ratios of the different parameters, which permit specifically different analytical implications depending upon their calibration. In several cases we must therefore confine the analysis to a discussion of simulation results.

4.4.1 Calibration and Simulation Results

The parameters to be specified are: α, which describes the output elasticity with respect to physical capital; the elasticity between consumption and leisure time, μ, the fixed costs for supply of capital, η, the stock of physical, $\overline{K}$; and the minimum wage, $\overline{w}$. By assumption we know that $0 < \alpha < 1$, $0 < \mu \leq 1$, $\eta > 0$, and $0 < w < \overline{w}$. In the notional system "physical labor" is normalized to one, and in the effective system it is smaller than or identical to one. Furthermore, note that in order for our system to generate meaningful results it has to be fulfilled that $\mu \xi \overline{K} < w$, which is necessary to yield a positive supply of working hours (equation 4.5). We have therefore made all calibrations under this assumption.

In order to specify α, we use the common stylized fact that the share of labor in developed countries is between 2/3 and 70 percent of the GNP. For instance, in the Austrian case in the 1990s it was less than about 70 percent on average (WIFO 1999). Hence we fix α with 0.3. For the calibration of μ, we use the estimated results of 0.6 from Cooley and Prescott (1995, 21), calculated for the US case. The aggregated capital stock in developed countries is on average about four times that of the GNP. Several tests with different parameters lead to fixing the capital stock to the value of two and the fixed costs for supply of capital, η, to 0.1. We know that this calibration is arbitrary, therefore we controlled the simulation with different values for these two parameters. The result was that changes within the restrictions presented in the paragraph above yield qualitatively similar and robust results. Finally, in the notional case the minimum wage only had to be greater than the equilibrium nominal wage.

We not only simulate the equilibrium values, but are also interested in how the minimum wage effects the position of the good's demand function. In order to do this, we calculated the goods demand function of the notional and the effective system at the price level of the effective model. Finally, to capture income effects, the real wage and the wage bill were also calculated. Table 4.1 presents the simulation results for the notional and effective system.

Increases in the minimum wage have been presented in order to focus more precisely on the results, which will be discussed below. Of course, the simulation results only show different possible outcomes of the systems, hence in many cases in the following we are only able to derive simple conjectures.

Table 4.1   Simulation Results, Basic Model and Effects of Minimum Wages

	Notional System	*Effective System*		
Restriction for w:	$1.0909 < w$	$1.0875 < \bar{w}$	$1.0766 < \bar{w}$	$1.0718 < \bar{w}$
$w, \bar{w}$	7.8788	7.9	7.95	8.0
L	1	0.9969	0.9896	0.9825
C	0.7757	0.7743	0.7708	0.7675
p	7.8134	7.8277	7.8623	7.8969
w/p	1.0084	1.0090	1.0111	1.0131
Wage bill	0.5430	0.5420	0.5396	0.5372
Demand at p^e	0.7709		0.7708	
r	1	1	1	1

Calibration:
$\alpha = 0.3, \eta - 0.1, \mu = 0.6, \bar{K} = 2.$
Variables:
L: Number of employed households, C: Real consumption (output), H: Working hours, p: Price level, r: Rental price for physical capital, w: Nominal wage, *Wage bill*: $(1-\alpha)C$.

Demand at p^e describes the goods demand function of the notional and the effective system at a given price level of 0.78134.

4.4.2 Comparison of the Outcomes of the two Systems

In the following we summarize all relevant results.

Proposition 4.1
   The equilibrium price of goods, determining the supply function of goods, is larger in the effective case.
   Proof: Since the price level is determined solely by Marginal costs, which are independent from output, and since the marginal costs increase in the event of the introduction of a minimum wage, the price level must also increase. See also the simulation result presented in table 4.1.

Conjecture 4.2
   Real equilibrium output is smaller than the respective notional one.
   Argument: Compare the simulation result presented in table 4.1.

Conjecture 4.3
   The effective demand is smaller than the notional demand.
   Argument: Compare the simulation result (demand at p^e) presented in table 4.1.

Conjecture 4.4
  The introduction of a minimum wage leads to a "left shift" of both factor demand functions.
  Argument: Given the output dependency of both factor demand functions (note the decline of the equilibrium output described above) and that the minimum wage is greater than the notional one, conjecture 4.4 is evident directly from the corresponding functions.

Conjecture 4.5
  The effective real wage is higher than the nominal wage.
  Argument: Compare the simulation result presented in table 4.1.

Conjecture 4.6
  The introduction of a minimum wage leads to a reduction of the real incomes.
  Argument: Calculate the FOC for effective work $(h_j L_j)$ from the firm's profit maximization problem and aggregate to yield that $p(1-\alpha)K^\alpha (hL)^{-\alpha} = whL$. Under the condition of perfect competition and Cobb Douglas technology with constant returns to scale, it has to be valid that

$$\frac{whL}{p} = K^\alpha (1-\alpha)(hL)^{-\alpha} hL = (1-\alpha)Y .$$

Consequently, the real total wage sum is determined by the production technology and the quantity of output. This argument is also valid for the effective case. The price level changes because of the introduction of the minimum wage, and so does the position of the factor demand function. However, the price level is no longer important for the analysis. Hence the effect on the total wage income results solely from the relationship between notional and effective equilibrium output. Following conjecture 4.3, the total wage sum clearly decreases with the introduction of a minimum wage. See also the simulation results in table 4.1. The argument for the capital income is analogous.

Conjecture 4.7
  The wage share is identical in the effective and in the notional case.
  Argument: This can be shown through a simple expansion of the denominator from the fraction used to conjecture 4.6 by the corresponding output as a known technical property of the Cobb-Douglas production function.

All the effects on the price level and the real sector of the economy correspond to standard economic intuition. However, they have been determined endogenously. In contrast to the partial equilibrium analysis, all results can be unequivocally determined by merely setting up the specific model as a non-equilibrium model.

Two equally oriented effects can explain the decrease of equilibrium output (conjecture 4.2). On the supply side it is a rise of marginal costs and on the demand side it is a reduction of aggregate demand of goods (conjecture 4.3), based on reduced aggregate wage income. These effects are connected to a reduction in the employment level and the rise of involuntary unemployment. The rise in involuntary unemployment on the one hand results from a movement along the demand function for labor, as in the partial equilibrium model, and is on the other hand intensified by a shift of the demand function for labor itself (conjecture 4.4).

The increase in the price of goods caused by the introduction of a nominal minimum wage is nevertheless always smaller than the wage differential between the original equilibrium and minimum wages. Hence, the introduction of a nominal minimum wage results in the existence of a higher real wage (conjecture 4.5). The effects on total wage sum and wage share (conjectures 4.6 and 4.7) result mainly from the technical properties of the Cobb-Douglas production function. The only difference is that the effect on the total wage sum, which is a function of the equilibrium quantity of goods, can be precisely explained when compared to the partial equilibrium analysis.

Due to the production technology in the present setting, the producer's rent can be ignored for a welfare analysis. The consumer's rent is reduced because of the increase of the price of goods and the reduction of the demand for goods.

In summary, the equilibrium result is characterized by lower employment, lower equilibrium output, higher prices of goods, higher real wages, unchanged capital amount, falling income from labor and capital and unchanged rental price of capital, since it was used as the numéraire. In addition, involuntary unemployment appears. Finally, a reduction of the consumer's rent occurs. These results therefore correspond qualitatively to those of the partial equilibrium analysis.

5

Minimum Wages, Unemployment and the Creation of Human Capital

5.1 THE BASIC MODEL SETUP

This section expands the basic model presented in chapter four by stressing the importance of human capital. First, we assume that, instead of physical labor, human capital is used to produce output. This reflects the observation that economies with higher average skill levels are more productive than those with lesser skill levels. Second, drawing on the Lucas model (1988), we assume that the average level of human capital positively affects the production function of the individual firm. The intuition behind this idea is simple: it seems obvious that people who work among intelligent people are more productive than those who do not. However, Lucas assumed positive external effects in a dynamic model setting, an idea which can also be easily implemented in a static model, as will be shown in this chapter. Third, we assume that the household's process to generate skills is positively influenced by the degree of unemployment. The rationale is that fear of unemployment influences the educational decisions of the households. This is based on the household's belief that a higher level of education decreases the probability of losing a job.

To be more exact, Lucas assumed two different types of external effects. The first and crucial one for the dynamics of the model is an external effect in the household's production function of skills, meaning that a higher level of skills increases the accumulation of skills. The second external effect focuses on the production function of goods. A higher level of average skills in the economy helps the single firm to produce more output.

Two possibilities for the modeling of skills generation can be found in the literature. Following Lucas (1988), skills are exclusively generated by activities off the job, such as through learning and education of the households. An alternative possibility is to implement training on the job, based on the training activities of the firms (Arrow 1962). At first glance, both possibilities should yield very similar effects. Given a fixed time constraint, learning off the job both reduces working time and increases the marginal productivity of the households. Training on the job must also reduce working time and increase the marginal product. We can obtain different qualitative outcomes by specifying educational or training costs in different ways (Raven and Sorenson 1999), but these problems are not within the scope of this analysis. Therefore, in this and the following two dynamic models we decided to focus on the first possibility because it helps to keep the models as simple as possible.

The implementation of human capital affects the analysis in two ways. First, the firm's problem changes; and second, we must adapt the household's problem in order to consider that the supply of human capital is subject to economic reasoning. Despite these changes, the assumptions made in chapters three and four are still valid if not otherwise mentioned. Furthermore, with exception of the origin of income, all macroeconomic relations are completely analogous.

As mentioned above, production is based on human capital and for the single firm there exists a positive external effect of aggregated average skills. To keep the analysis simple, we ignore working hours. Hence in the notional and in the effective case the firm's production technology is defined as

$$Y_j = A K_j^{\alpha} (s_j L_j)^{1-\alpha} s^{\psi} , \tag{5.1}$$

where A is a shift parameter, normalized for the ongoing analysis to one. L_j is "physical" labor, K_j is physical capital and s_j is a measure for the average quality of labor used in the single firm, with $s_j = S_j / L_j$. S_j denotes the level of the quality of labor. The external effect from average human capital in the economy is described by s^{ψ}. For the single firm, this effect is exogenous, hence it does not interfere with the standard results of perfect competition and constant returns to scale – in particular the firm's size and the number of firms remain indeterminate. α and ψ are production parameters, identical to the respective output elasticities of factor inputs, with ψ indicating the output elasticity of the external effect. $s_j L_j$ is the "human capital" used in the production process of firm j, so we assume that it is impossible to produce with "physical" labor or skills alone. As one can see, the firm exhibits constant returns to scale in its own inputs, and increasing returns to scale to all inputs.

Total costs, TC_j, are given by

$$TC_j = rK_j + ws_j L_j,$$ (5.2)

where r describes the rental price for capital and w the wage. Denoting the price of goods with p, the firm's profit maximization problem consequently turns out as

$$\max_{\pi} = pK_j^{\alpha}(s_j L_j)^{1-\alpha} s^{\psi} - rK_j - ws_j L_j.$$

Households recognize that human capital – not physical labor – is used in production. We assume that each employed household supplies one unit of "physical" labor perfectly wage inelastic, and splits his/her time between leisure and education (learning) time. Time used for education, E_i, is necessary but not sufficient to generate new skills. These are generated by a "learning" or "production function" for skills, which is given by

$$S_i = \phi\, E_i, \text{ where } \phi = \frac{\beta}{L^{*,e}} \text{ and } \beta > 0.$$ (5.3)

The creation of skills is based on a productivity function, ϕ, and the time spent on learning. Furthermore, it is assumed that the productivity function depends on the level of equilibrium employment, $L^{*,e}$, and on a technology parameter, β. Normalization of the number of households to one helps to avoid explicitly implementing the unemployment rate in the production function. For the case of full-employment, it reduces to $\phi = \beta$, unemployment decreases $L^{*,e}$ and increases the function.[1] In the notional case, with an unemployment rate of zero, the production of skills depends only on the exogenous production parameter. Hence β can be interpreted as an indicator for the average learning efficiency, which is based on the educational system of an economy.

Considering existing unemployment, a second interpretation of β is possible. Given the empirical observations that people react to the probability of becoming unemployed, we can interpret β as a measure of fear of getting dismissed. However, both interpretations remain exogenous in this model setting.

Finally, we assume that unemployed households do not generate new skills, which may also be interpreted in two ways. First, in unemployment skills are reduced rather than increased. This argument is often used in the discussion of hysteresis effects on the labor markets. Second, it may express very pessimistic expectations of unemployed persons.

Identical to the basic model (chapter four), households yield utility from consumption and leisure ("free time"), F_i, or[2]

$$U_i = \ln C_i + \mu \ln F_i .$$
(5.4)

Because our model exhibits no time dimension at all, we are able to assume that households learn and work and get utility from leisure at the same "time," learning and using the new work skills simultaneously.[3] The time constraint is normalized by one,

$$F_i + E_i = 1 .$$
(5.5)

If employed, every household earns income through work and capital ownership. Consequently the budget constraint is given by

$$pC_i \leq wS_i + rK_i .$$
(5.6)

If rationing occurs it simplifies to

$$pC_i \leq rK_i .$$
(5.7)

We assume that the household's supply function for physical capital, $K_i^{S,n}$, is identical to that of chapter four, described by equation (4.3). Hence it is given by

$$K_i^{S,n} = \frac{r}{r+\eta} \overline{K}_i ,$$
(5.8)

The technical properties of this function are described in chapter four. Remember that the use of the rental price of capital as the numéraire and the definition of $\xi \equiv 1/(1+\eta)$ reduces it to

$$K_i^{S,n} = \xi \overline{K}_i .$$
(5.8')

In summary, the maximization problems in the notional and in the effective case turn out to be:

$$\max \ U_i = \ln C_i + \mu \ln F_i$$

s.t.:

$$\left\{ \begin{array}{l} \text{C1}: \ F_i + E_i = 1 \\[4pt] \text{C2}: \ S_i = \beta \, E_i \\[4pt] \text{C3}: \ pC_i \le wS_i + rK_i \end{array} \right\} \text{notational case,}$$

$$\left\{ \begin{array}{l} \text{C1}: \ F_i + E_i = 1 \\[6pt] \text{C4}: \ S_i = \dfrac{\beta}{L^{*,e}} E_i \\[6pt] \text{C5}: \ pC_i \le wS_i + rK_i \end{array} \right\} \text{effective case, if employed,}$$

$$\left\{ \begin{array}{l} \text{C6}: \ F_i = 1 \\[4pt] \text{C7}: \ S_i = 0 \\[4pt] \text{C5}: \ pC_i \le rK_i \end{array} \right\} \text{effective case, if unemployed.}$$

5.2   THE REFERENCE MODEL ("THE WALRASIAN ECONOMY")

5.2.1   Individual Maximization Decisions and Aggregation

With the exception of the external effect and the fact that the firm's production is based on skills rather than working hours, the maximization decisions of the firms yield exactly the same results as in chapter four. Hence the mathematical derivations will not be discussed further, but they can be found in the mathematical appendix, A8. From the FOCs of the firm's problem, the production function and the use of the rental price of capital as the numéraire, we yield the notional factor demand functions for capital, $K_j^{D,n}$, and for human capital, $(s_j L_j)^{D,n}$, for the single firm as:[4]

$$K_j^{D,n} = \left(\frac{\alpha}{1-\alpha} w \right)^{1-\alpha} Y_j s^{-\psi}, \tag{5.9}$$

$$(s_j L_j)^{D,n} = \left(\frac{\alpha}{1-\alpha} w \right)^{-\alpha} Y_j s^{-\psi}. \tag{5.10}$$

Note that the firm's problem is not solvable on the firm's level for s_j or L_j alone.

Profit maximization was also discussed in chapter four. Now the marginal costs of the firm are additionally influenced by the average level of human capital, or[5]

$$MC_j = P = \alpha^{-\alpha}(1-\alpha)^{\alpha-1}s^{-\psi}w^{1-\alpha}.$$
(5.11)

As can be seen and in contrast to the basic model, the external effect from average human capital enters into all three relevant functions. The effect of average skills on these functions depends on the relationship of skills and "physical labor." If it is greater than one, it on the one hand reduces the demand for human capital and physical labor, and on the other hand reduces the marginal costs of the single firm. The effect also works in the reverse direction when the relationship is smaller than one.

In the notional case, households maximize utility under recognition of the constraints C1–C3. We denote the Lagrange multiplier by λ_i, to describe the maximization problem in the Lagrange illustration of the Kuhn-Tucker problem by

$$L_i = \ln C_i + \mu \ln F_i + \lambda_i\{w\beta(1-F_i)+rK_i - pC_i\}.$$
(5.12)

We obtain that:

$$\frac{\partial L_i}{\partial C_i} = \frac{1}{C_i} - \lambda_i\, p = 0,$$

$$\frac{\partial L_i}{\partial F_i} = \frac{\mu}{F_i} - \lambda_i\, w\beta = 0.$$

Furthermore, identical to the basic model in chapter four, the complementary slackness condition must be discussed. For the first possibility, namely $\lambda_i = 0$ and $w\beta(1-F_i)+rK_i - pC_i \geq 0$, we yield that $1/C_i = 0$ and $\mu/F_i = 0$. Hence, households would achieve an infinite amount of leisure and consumption, which, identical to the basic model in chapter four, is ruled out for leisure by the time constraint and for consumption by limited economic resources. For the second possibility, with $\lambda_i \geq 0$ and $w(1-F_i)+rK_i - pC_i = 0$, we are back in the Lagrange case of identity.

From the FOCs for consumption and leisure time it follows that the ratio between the marginal utilities of leisure and consumption is equivalent to $w\beta/p$. In contrast to chapter four this demonstrates the influence of the production technology for skills. Calculating C_i from these FOCs, substituting into the budget constraint and use of equation (4.8') helps to calculate the "leisure supply function," $F_i^{S,n}$.[6] We obtain that

$$F_i^{S,n} = \frac{\mu}{1+\mu}\left(1 + \frac{\xi\,K_i}{\beta\,w}\right). \tag{5.13}$$

The respective "supply function of learning time" is given by $1-F_i$, and will not be discussed further. What we are more interested in is the supply function of skills. Note that $E_i = 1-F_i$. We express educational time from the expression above and substitute into the production function for skills to express the supply function of skills, $S_i^{S,n}$, as[7]

$$S_i^{S,n} = \frac{1}{1+\mu}\left(\beta - \mu\frac{\xi\,K_i}{w}\right). \tag{5.14}$$

Note that physical labor and skills are supplied jointly. According to the normalization of physical labor by one, the above function also becomes the supply function for human capital. Higher wages, lower capital premium and higher learning efficiency yield higher skills supply and hence higher human capital.

Calculating F_i from the relationship of the marginal utilities from leisure and consumption and substitution into the budget constraint helps to calculate the demand function for goods, $C_i^{D,n}$, which leads to[8]

$$C_i^{D,n} = \frac{1}{1+\mu}\frac{w\beta + \xi\,K_i}{p}, \tag{5.15}$$

again reflecting the effect of the production parameter β. Finally, we remember that the capital supply function is given by equation (5.8').

Due to the normalization of the number of households and firms, all functions for the economic agents correspond to the aggregated ones. We know, however, that aggregation leads to $s = S/L$. In the notional case $(L=1)$ it therefore follows that the expression for the aggregate demand for human capital, $S^{D,n}$, reduces to an expression for skills only which turns out as[9]

$$S^{D,n} = \left(\frac{\alpha}{1-\alpha}w\right)^{-\frac{\alpha}{1+\psi}} Y^{\frac{1}{1+\psi}}. \tag{5.16}$$

5.2.2 Market Equilibrium

All variables of the notional system are marked by the index "n" for better distinction of the effective case. In the following, the original equation numbers were unchanged when no relevant changes occurred, but they have been marked by an apostrophe to show that we are presenting the aggregated functions. Summing up yields:

Goods demand:

$$C^{D,n} = \frac{1}{1+\mu} \frac{w^n \beta + \xi \overline{K}}{p^n} \qquad (5.15')$$

Goods supply:

$$p^n = \alpha^{-\alpha} (1-\alpha)^{\alpha-1} w^{n\,1-\alpha} S^{n\,-\psi} \qquad (5.11')$$

Demand of human capital:

$$S^{D,n} = \left(\frac{\alpha}{1-\alpha} w^n \right)^{-\frac{\alpha}{1+\psi}} Y^{n\,\frac{1}{1+\psi}} \qquad (5.16)$$

Supply of human capital:

$$S^{S,n} = \frac{1}{1+\mu} \left(\beta - \mu \frac{\xi \overline{K}}{w^n} \right) \qquad (5.14')$$

Demand for "physical capital": $K^{D,n} = \left(\dfrac{\alpha}{1-\alpha} w^n \right)^{1-\alpha} Y^n S^{n\,-\psi} \qquad (5.9')$

Supply of "physical capital": $K^{S,n} = \zeta \overline{K}. \qquad (4.8'')$

Note that the supply of human capital is the implicit product of physical labor and skills, because the population size is normalized to one. The argumentation about the general and specific solution of the model is analogous to that of the basic model in chapter four and will not be discussed further. We have to calculate $S^{*,n}$, $w^{*,n}$, $p^{*,n}$, and $C^{*,n}$, which requires some technical work. Hence here we will only present the results:[10]

$$L^{*,n} = 1,$$

$$w^{*,n} = \frac{\omega \xi \overline{K}}{\beta}, \qquad (5.17)$$

$$S^{*,n} = \frac{\beta}{1+\mu} \left(1 - \frac{\mu}{\omega} \right), \qquad (5.18)$$

$$C^{*,n} = (\xi \overline{K})^\alpha \left(\frac{\beta}{1+\mu} \left(1 - \frac{\mu}{\omega} \right) \right)^{1-\alpha+\psi}, \qquad (5.19)$$

$$p^{*,n} = \frac{\alpha^{-\alpha}(1-\alpha)^{\alpha-1}\,\beta^{\,\alpha-1-\psi}(1+\mu)^{\psi}\left(\xi\,\overline{K}\omega\right)^{1-\alpha}}{(1-\mu/\omega)^{\psi}}, \qquad (5.20)$$

$$\text{where } \omega \equiv \frac{1-\alpha}{\alpha}\left(\frac{1}{1+\mu}\right)^{\frac{1}{1-\alpha}} + \mu \,.$$

Compared to the basic model, the learning efficiency parameter β enters into all calculated equilibrium values. It has a positive effect on output and human capital,[11] and a negative effect on the price of goods as well as and on the wage rate.

5.3   THE EFFECTS OF MINIMUM WAGES (THE "EFFECTIVE CASE")

As in chapter four, we must first present introductory notes on notation. Denote equilibrium employment in the effective case by $L^{*,e}$, with $L^{*,e} < N \equiv 1$ and denote all individuals who experience a restriction in the labor market (being unemployed), with the index "u," $u = 1...(1-L^{*,e})$. Households that do not perceive constraints on the labor market yield completely identical maximization results and derived supply and demand functions, as in the notional case. However, their number is now restricted to $L^{*,e}$. In order to omit additional notations, we simply assume that the index i denotes only unrestricted households, where $i = 1...L^{*,e}$. Furthermore, to point out the differences to the notional system, all aggregated functions and all respective variables will be denoted by the superscript "e" for "effective case."

5.3.1 Individual Maximization Decisions and Aggregation

Further employed households maximize under the constraints C1, C4 and C5. The maximization problem is – with the exception of the existence of unemployment influencing the "production function of skills" – formally identical to that of the notional case, because for the single household the level of employment is exogenous. Hence we yield identical outcomes of the maximization problem, with the exception that β must be replaced by $\beta/L^{*,e}$. As can be seen from the maximization problem and the results in the notional case, we yield for the supply functions of skills for employed households, $S_i^{S,e}$, that

$$S_i^{S,e} = \frac{1}{1+\mu}\left(\frac{\beta}{L^{*,e}} - \mu\frac{\xi\,\overline{K}_i}{\overline{w}}\right). \qquad (5.21)$$

The demand function for goods of employed households, $C_i^{D,e}$, is given by

$$C_i^{D,e} = \frac{1}{1+\mu}\frac{\overline{w}\dfrac{\beta}{L^{*,e}} + \xi\,\overline{K}_i}{p^e}. \qquad (5.22)$$

Supply of physical capital is formally identical to that of the notional case of the basic model (chapter four) in any case.

Furthermore, unemployed households finance their entire consumption only from capital income, hence they maximize under the constraints C5, C6 and C7. Therefore the maximization problem of the restricted individual in the Lagrange illustration of the Kuhn-Tucker problem turns out as

$$L_u = \ln C_u + \lambda_u\,(rK_u - pC_u). \qquad (5.23)$$

The optimal consumption follows from the complementary slackness condition, where, with identical argumentation to that in chapter four, we yield the Lagrangian case of identity. We use the rental price as the numéraire, and equation (4.8') to calculate the demand for goods of unemployed households, C_u^D, as

$$C_u^D = \frac{\xi\,\overline{K}_u}{p^e}. \qquad (5.24)$$

Next we will aggregate all relevant functions of the households. We know that skills are only supplied by employed households. Use equation (4.8') to obtain that

$$S^{S,e} = L^{*,e}\frac{1}{1+\mu}\left(\frac{\beta}{L^{*,e}} - \mu\frac{\xi\,\overline{K}}{\overline{w}}\right). \qquad (5.25)$$

Hence unemployment affects the individual and aggregate levels of skills.

The goods demand function, $C^{D,e}$, is given by the sum of the individual demand functions of employed and unemployed households, or

$$C^{D,e} = L^{*,e} \frac{1}{1+\mu} \frac{\overline{w}\beta\, L^{*,e^{-1}} + \xi\,\overline{K}_i}{p^e} + (1-L^{*,e})\frac{\xi\,\overline{K}_i}{p^e}. \qquad (5.26)$$

Goods supply and capital demand stay formally identical to the notional case, except that minimum wage and average skills enter into the functions. Finally, we reformulate the firm's aggregated demand function for human capital, $S^{D,e}$, as a "demand function for skills" alone, which is given by[12]

$$S^{D,e} = \left(\frac{\alpha}{1-\alpha}\,\overline{w}\right)^{-\alpha} Y^e \left(\frac{S^e}{L^{*,e}}\right)^{-\psi}. \qquad (5.27)$$

5.3.2 Market Equilibrium

Remember that functions respectively variables that are specifically determined by the exogenous wage rate will be labeled with an "*e*" in the index. The price for capital is used as the numéraire, and we know that $1/(1+\eta) \equiv \xi$. Furthermore, note that the exogenous capital stock is identical for all households, which helps to omit the superscripts. Some aggregated functions only change marginally, hence we still keep the original numbering, but denote it with two apostrophes. In summary, the relevant functions are given by:

Demand for goods:
$$C^{D,e} = L^{*,e}\,\frac{1}{1+\mu}\,\frac{\overline{w}\beta\, L^{*,e^{-1}} + \xi\,\overline{K}}{p^e} + \\ + (1-L^{*,e})\frac{\xi\,\overline{K}}{p^e} \qquad (5.26'')$$

Profit maximization:
$$p^e = \alpha^{-\alpha}(1-\alpha)^{\alpha-1}\,\overline{w}^{1-\alpha}\left(\frac{S}{L^{*,e}}\right)^{-\psi} \qquad (5.11'')$$

Demand of human cap.:
$$S^{D,e} = \left(\frac{\alpha}{1-\alpha}\,\overline{w}\right)^{-\alpha} Y^e \left(\frac{S^e}{L^{*,e}}\right)^{-\psi} \qquad (5.27)$$

Supply of human cap.:
$$S^{S,e} = L^{*,e}\,\frac{1}{1+\mu}\left(\frac{\beta}{L^{*,e}} - \mu\,\frac{\xi\,\overline{K}}{\overline{w}}\right) \qquad (5.25)$$

Demand for capital
$$K^{D,e} = \left(\frac{\alpha}{1-\alpha}\,\overline{w}\right)^{1-\alpha} Y^e \left(\frac{S}{L^{*,e}}\right)^{-\psi} \qquad (5.9'')$$

Supply of capital:
$$K^{S,e} = \xi\,\overline{K}. \qquad (5.8'')$$

Contrary to the basic model described in chapter four, we also get equilibrium values for physical labor and skills. Like the notional case, the calculation of the equilibrium values requires some technical work, and therefore only the results have been presented:[13]

$$L^{*,e} = \frac{1+\mu}{\mu\xi\,\overline{K}}\,\varphi, \qquad (5.28)$$

$$C^{*,e} = \left(\frac{\alpha}{1-\alpha}\,\overline{w}\right)^{\alpha}\left(\frac{(\mu\xi\,\overline{K})^2}{(1+\mu)^2\,\varphi}\left(\frac{\beta}{(1+\mu)\varphi} - \frac{1}{\overline{w}}\right)\right)^{\psi}, \qquad (5.29)$$

$$p^{*,e} = \alpha^{-\alpha}\left(\frac{\overline{w}}{1-\alpha}\right)^{1-\alpha}\left(\frac{(\mu\xi\,\overline{K})^2}{(1+\mu)^2\,\varphi}\left(\frac{\beta\overline{w}}{(1+\mu)\varphi} - \frac{1}{\overline{w}}\right)\right)^{-\psi}, \qquad (5.30)$$

$$S^{*,e} = \frac{1}{1-\alpha} - \frac{\xi\,\overline{K}}{\overline{w}}, \qquad (5.31)$$

where $\varphi \equiv \overline{w}\left(\dfrac{\beta}{1+\mu} - \dfrac{1}{1-\alpha}\right) + \xi\,\overline{K}$.

These results will be discussed in the following chapter.

5.4 COMPARISON OF THE RESULTS AND CONCLUSIONS

The implementation of a minimum wage induces two effects. First, the number of employed households decreases. Second, the amount of skills changes, although the direction of this change is not unique. One the one hand, fewer people supply skills, which reduces the aggregate skill amount. On the other hand, employed households have a greater incentive to produce more skills. This makes it possible for decreasing employment to be joined by lower or higher aggregated income and, depending on the direction of the effect on income, by higher or lower skills and output.

5.4.1 Calibration and Simulation Results

The following section compares the specific equilibrium outcomes of the notional and effective human capital model. As in chapter four, analytically unsolvable problems occur, because the results depend on the relationships of the parameters, and those relationships allow for specifically different analytical implications depending on their calibration. In order to generate meaningful results, it must be fulfilled that[14]

$$\begin{cases} w > \dfrac{\mu\xi\,\overline{K}L}{\beta} & \text{(from supply of skills to be} > 0\text{),} \\[2ex] \overline{w} > (1-\alpha)\xi\,\overline{K} & \text{(from equil. output, price and skills to be} > 0\text{).} \end{cases}$$

Basically, these restrictions result from the normalization of the available time budget and the population size to one. All calibrations were carried out without disturbing these restrictions. In the notional case L is normalized to one. In the effective case, unemployment simply weakens the first condition.

The calibration used for the results of table 5.1 is largely identical to that in chapter four, with two exceptions. We must calibrate the pro-

Table 5.1　Simulation Results: Basic Model and Effects of Minimum Wages

	Notional System	Effective System		
Restriction for w:	$0.83 < w$	$1.26 < \overline{w}$	$1.26 < \overline{w}$	$1.26 < \overline{w}$
$w,\ \overline{w}$	2.4816	2.50	2.51	2.55
L	1	0.3849	0.3758	0.3393
C	0.6447	1.3961	1.4124	1.1483
S	0.5623	0.7086	0.7114	0.7227
p	4.2270	1.2586	1.2466	1.1970
r	1	1	1	1
w/p	0.5870	1,9863	2,0134	2,1303
Wage bill	0.4513	0,9772	0,9886	0,8038

Calibration:

$\alpha = 0.3,\ \beta = 1.3,\ \mu = 0.6,\ \psi = 0.2,\ \overline{K} = 2,\ \eta = 0.1.$

Variables:

L: Employment, C: Real output, S: Skills, p: Price level, r: Rental price for physical Capital, w: Nominal wage, *Wage bill:* $(1-\alpha)C$.

ductivity parameter β from the "production function for skills," and the output elasticity of the external effect, ψ. For the analysis we simply assumed the output elasticity of the external effect, ψ, to be smaller than the direct output elasticity of physical capital and fixed it by 0.2. Lack of empirical observations led us to calibrate with different values for the parameter β, but we only present the results for a parameterization of 1.3. This is somewhat arbitrary, but small changes within the restrictions presented in the paragraph above do not interfere with the qualitative results.

Table 5.1 presents the simulation results for the notional and effective system. As one can see, the level of the minimum wage is arbitrarily assumed. Increases in the minimum wage have been presented to focus more precisely on the results, which will be discussed in the next section.

5.4.2 Comparison of the Outcomes of the two Systems

Of course, the simulation results only show possible outcomes of the systems, hence in many cases we have to present simple conjectures. We yield:

Conjecture 5.1
   The effective equilibrium price of goods is lower than the notional price.
   Argument: By simulation results presented in table 5.1.

Conjecture 5.2
   The real effective equilibrium output is higher than the notional one.
   Argument: By simulation results presented in table 5.1.

Proposition 5.3
   The effective demand function is positioned to the right of the notional one.
   Proof: By subtraction of the two goods demand functions at the goods price, which is induced by the implementation of the minimum wage. See the mathematical appendix, A14.

Conjecture 5.4
   The implementation of the minimum wage leads to unemployment.
   Argument: By simulation results presented in table 5.1.

Conjecture 5.5
   The implementation of a minimum wage leads to an outward movement of both factor demand functions.

Argument: Given that both factor demand functions are a function of output in combination with conjecture 5.2, the argument can be seen directly from the functional form of the functions.

Conjecture 5.6
The effective real minimum wage is higher than the notional one.
Argument: By simulation results presented in table 5.1.

Conjecture 5.7
The implementation of a minimum wage leads to an increase in the real aggregated wage income.
Argument: By simulation results presented in table 5.1 with identical argumentation as presented in chapter four, argument for conjecture 4.6.

Conjecture 5.8
In both cases the wage bill is identical.
Argument: Given by identical argumentation as presented in chapter four, argument for conjecture 4.7.

These results are generated by three changes to the basic model, presented in chapter four: First, we assumed that instead of labor, human capital is used to produce output. Second, we assume that there exists a positive external effect of human capital in production. Third, we assumed that the household's process to generate skills is positively influenced by unemployment. Hence we are interested in which of these changes is generated by the outcomes described above and we must therefore capture the influence of the external effect. In order to do this, we fixed the minimum wage by 2.55 somewhat higher than the equilibrium wage and changed the impact of the external effect. Table 5.2 presents the model's outcome for different elasticities of the external effect.

The external effect in production does not influence equilibrium skills, employment and nominal wage. All other partly counterintuitive effects to be seen from table 5.2 can be found in the specific calibration and normalization of the model, which partly leads to an average level of skills smaller than one, yielding the effects already described in the paragraph after equation (5.11).

We have to remember that the effect of average skills on the demand for human capital and physical labor, as well as on marginal costs, depends on the relationship between skills and "physical labor." If it is greater than one, it reduces the demand for human capital and physical labor, as well as the marginal costs of the single firm. The effect also

Table 5.2 Simulation Results: Effects of a Change in the
Production Parameter ψ

	Notional System		Effective System	
	$\psi = 0$	$\psi = 0.2$	$\psi = 0$	$\psi = 0.2$
Restriction for w	$0.83 < w$	$0.83 < w$	$1.26 < \overline{w}$	$1.26 < \overline{w}$
L	1	1	0.3625	0.3625
C	0.7778	0.6877	1.027	1.0898
S	0.5405	0.5405	1.9736	1.9736
p	3.0548	3.9637	3.5471	2.7284
w	2.5007	2.5007	2.55	2.55
w/p	0.7152	0.6324	0.7189	0.9346
Wage bill	0.5444	0.4814	0.7189	0.7629

Calibration:
$\overline{w} = 2.55$, $\alpha = 0.32$, $\beta = 0.8$, $\mu = 0.6$, $\overline{K} = 1.8$, $\eta = 0.1$

Variables:
L: Number of employed households, C: Real output, S: Skills, p: Price level,
w: Nominal wage; *Wage bill:* $(1-\alpha)C$

works in the reverse direction, if the relationship is smaller than one. We see that the model's general outcome is not driven by the external effect in production. Therefore the interrelation between minimum wages, unemployment and skills production must generate the main results.

To summarize, this chapter stressed the importance of human capital by expanding the basic model (presented in chapter four) by the implementation of human capital and by the existence of fear of becoming unemployed. We assumed that human capital, instead of physical labor, is used to produce output and that a positive external effect of human capital exists. Both assumptions are based on the empirical findings that a higher stock of human capital coincides with higher per capita output. The implementation of human capital affects the analysis in two ways. First, the firm's problem changes, and second we must adapt the household's problem to consider that the supply of human capital is subject to economic reasoning. However, the unexpected results arise from the effect of fear of becoming unemployed on the creation of human capital.

This model's outcome seems to contrast many of the standard arguments used in the discussion on the effects of a minimum wage. Except for one result, namely that the minimum wage induces unemployment, we yield qualitatively completely different results. In particular, we must note that output and labor income increase and that the good's price declines. This result is based on the changing supply of human capital forced by the implementation of the minimum wage and the existence of unemployment.

Part III:
Minimum Wages and Economic Growth

6
Minimum Wages, Human Capital and Growth

6.1 THE BASIC MODEL SETUP

6.1.1 Basic Ideas

This chapter focuses on the effect of a minimum wage on steady state economic growth and steady state employment. As in the model presented in chapter five, we stress the importance of human capital, but we focus on economic dynamics and use the setup of an infinite horizon model based on Lucas (1988). Differences to the static model are that human and "physical capital" can be accumulated over time, and that "infinitely living" households maximize their lifetime ("dynastic") utility subject to intertemporal budget constraints. In contrast to Lucas's original model, the households must decide on the optimal use of labor, leisure and educational time.[1]

Furthermore, we assume that there exist two different types of positive external effects. One is to be found in the skills accumulation equation of the households. This effect is crucial for the generation of positive steady state growth. The other can be found in the production of goods. Hence, as in all models in endogenous growth theory with occurring external effects, the economic agents do not properly take these effects into account. Therefore, the rate of growth generated by the market must be lower than that which would be achieved in the command optimum. This property is especially crucial for the outcome of the model by Cahuc and Michel (1996), where minimum wages increase economic growth by internalizing parts of the externality, as was shown in section two.

Among other questions in the previous two chapters we were interested in the effect of a nominal minimum wage on the price of goods, which lead to the normalization of the rental price of physical capital to one. In this chapter the price of goods is used as the numéraire in order to analyze the effects of minimum wages on the rental price for capital. The interest rate is a crucial element for the dynamic development of the economy. Hence in this chapter nominal and real wage, or minimum wage respectively, are identical.

We must also change the assumptions for the market for physical capital to generate a possibility for households to save parts of their income. Households are not owners of physical capital who rent this physical capital to firms, as in the preceding static models. Instead, they hold tradable ownership claims on capital ("assets"), which are supplied only on the market for "physical capital." This implies that they cannot borrow assets from other households. Assets are measured in real terms (in consumption units), which helps to assume that firms that need capital to produce output are able to use rented capital directly for production. Therefore we are able to omit different notation for capital used in production or used as a store of value.

A binding minimum wage, defined as a constant wage premium on the equilibrium wage, is implemented in the effective case at every point in time. This wage must, at least in the first period, create unemployment. Finally, for simplification, the growth rate of population is zero and the number of population is normalized to one.

Despite these changes in the model setup, all assumptions of chapter five are still valid if not otherwise mentioned, and if possible the designations of variables are also identical to those in section five. However, the basic macroeconomic relationships change significantly. In this chapter we will describe them and then present the basic maximization problems of firms and households. As in chapter five, we denote the Walrasian Economy as a notional system and the model with implemented minimum wage as the "effective" one.

In chapter 6.2 the Walrasian Economy is analyzed as a benchmark. This chapter first presents the individual maximization results and the aggregation of the respective variables. Next, relative relationships between the steady state rates of growth of all variables of the system, and the steady state rate of growth of the economy are calculated. Chapter 6.3 discusses the effects of the minimum wage in an identical way and also analyzes the steady state level of unemployment. Chapter 6.4 compares the outcomes of the two systems, provides reasons for the outcome of the effective system, and sums up the main results.

6.1.2 Macroeconomic Relations

As an initial condition the stocks of "physical capital" and of skills are still exogenous, but capital and skill supply in all following periods are endogenously determined by the maximization decisions of the households. Savings in period t are given by the change in the stock of capital in this period, $\dot{K}_t$. For the sake of simplification, no depreciation of the capital stock exists, hence investment, I_t, is identical to savings, or $I_t = \dot{K}_t$. Produced output, Y_t, at each point in time is consumed, C_t, or invested, hence $Y_t = C_t + I_t$, and the household's income,[2] M_t, is spent on consumption and savings, $M_t = C_t + \dot{K}_t$. Finally, produced output corresponds to income, or $Y_t = M_t$.

There exist N households and F firms and each household i earns income from working time, $H_{i,t}$, from skills, $S_{i,t}$, and from ownership claims on capital.[3] Without being distorted by the implementation of a minimum wage, the model must create full-employment; this will be seen in the analysis presented later on. We denote the interest rate by r_t and the wage by w_t, and use the price of goods as the numéraire and j as the index for firms to obtain for the notional system that:

$$M_t = \sum_{i=1}^{N} \left(w_t S_{i,t} H_{i,t} + r_t K_{i,t} \right) \qquad \text{origin of income at time } t,[4]$$

$$Y_t = \sum_{j=1}^{F} Y_{j,t} \qquad \text{origin of output at time } t,$$

$$C_t = \sum_{i=1}^{N} C_{i,t} \qquad \text{consumption at time } t,$$

$$\dot{K}_t = \sum_{i=1}^{N} \left(w_t S_{i,t} H_{i,t} + r_t K_{i,t} \right) - \sum_{i=1}^{N} C_{i,t} \qquad \text{savings at time } t.$$

Introducing a minimum wage at least in the first period will create unemployment. Hence in the "effective case" the equations above must be adapted by the respective variables for households without labor income.

6.1.3 Maximization Problems

The production technology for the single firm j at every point in time is given by

$$Y_{j,t} = A K_{j,t}^{\alpha} (s_{j,t} h_{j,t} L_{j,t})^{1-\alpha} s_t^{\psi} . \tag{6.1}$$

A represents technological progress and will be normalized to one, $Y_{j,t}$ denotes produced output of firm j at time t, $K_{j,t}$ is physical capital, $L_{j,t}$ describes employment in persons, and $h_{j,t}$ are average working hours. The average quality of labor of a person is measured by $s_{j,t}$, with $s_{j,t} = S_{j,t}/L_{j,t}$, where $S_{j,t}$ denotes skills. $s_{j,t}h_{j,t}L_{j,t}$ is an expression for the human capital that is used in the production process of firm j, hence we assume that production without one of the elements of human capital is impossible. Therefore, even if employment of persons, $L_{j,t}$, remains constant, an increase in average working time or in skills will increase output and a fixed number of workers will not be the source of diminishing returns.[5] s_t^ψ describes the external effect of average human capital in the economy. α $(0 < \alpha < 1)$, and ψ $(0 < \psi < 1)$ are production parameters which are identical to the respective output elasticities of the factor inputs, with ψ indicating the output elasticity of the external effect in production. Hence, as in the model presented in chapter five, the firm exhibits constant returns to scale in its own inputs, but increasing returns to scale for all inputs.

Total costs, $TC_{j,t}$, are given by $TC_{j,t} = r_t K_{j,t} + w_t s_{j,t} h_{j,t} L_{j,t}$. Remember that the price of goods is normalized to one. Consequently the firm's problem turns out as

$$\underset{\max}{\pi_{j,t}} = K_{j,t}^\alpha (s_{j,t}h_{j,t}L_{j,t})^{1-\alpha} s_t^\psi - r_t K_{j,t} - w_t s_{j,t} h_{j,t} L_{j,t} . \qquad (6.2)$$

Every household i maximizes lifetime utility U_i, with separable point-in-time felicity, $u_{i,t}$, which is of the log-linear Cobb-Douglas type

$$\begin{cases} U_i = \int_\tau^\infty u_{i,t}(C_{i,t}, F_{i,t}) e^{-\theta(t-\tau)} dt = \\[2em] \qquad = \int_\tau^\infty (\ln C_{i,t} + \mu \ln F_{i,t}) e^{-\theta(t-\tau)} dt. \end{cases} \qquad (6.3)$$

$C_{i,t}$ denotes consumption of household i at time t, $F_{i,t}$ is leisure or "free time" and θ, $(0 < \theta < 1)$, is the intertemporal rate of time preference. A higher intertemporal rate of time preference points out that later utils are preferred less compared to earlier ones. The elasticity between leisure time and consumption is denoted by μ, and τ is the starting point of time of the maximization problem. Hence, we assume that the utility of household i at time zero is the weighted sum of all future flows of utility presented by the felicity function.[6] As implicit in all infinite horizon models, the felicity function is multiplied by the family size to represent the adding up of all family members' utils. But because population is normalized to one and zero population growth is assumed, we can abstract from this term. However, implementing utils of later generations into the utility function could be interpreted as a form of altruism, which is reduced by the rate of intertemporal time preference, representing a higher degree of utility for earlier generations.

In contrast to the static problem, and in contrast to the original model of Lucas (1988), households have the possibility to optimize the relationship between working, $H_{i,t}$, leisure, and educational, $E_{i,t}$, time. The reason for this is that, in our model, involuntary unemployment may exist, leading to "involuntary leisure time." For employed households the entire sum of time used to work, to learn and for leisure at every point in time is identical to the exogenous time constraint, which is normalized to one, or

$$E_{i,t} + F_{i,t} + H_{i,t} = 1. \tag{6.4}$$

Therefore the use of the specific utility function presented above is not arbitrary. In steady state the utility function must generate constant relationships among the elements of the time constraint, which is guaranteed by the functional form of equation (6.3).[7]

In order to generate growth we need an incentive to create human capital. This incentive is based on a standard production or accumulation function for skills, which uses educational time – and hence forgone opportunity costs of leisure or working time – and the existing level of skills as key inputs, and turns out as

$$\dot{S}_{i,t} = \beta \, S_{i,t} E_{i,t}. \tag{6.5}$$

We assume that no physical capital is used for the production of skills, which reflects the empirical observation that education is very intensive in human capital.[8] As in the static model of chapter five, β ($\beta > 0$), is a production ("learning efficiency") parameter, which may indicate the degree of development of an economy, with higher β indicating a higher level of educational efficiency for the economy as a whole. We state the standard assumptions that time is required to produce skills, that it is easier to produce new skills if the level of existing skills, $S_{i,t}$, is higher, and that it is impossible to forget knowledge – so no depreciation for skills exists.

The influence of the level of skills on the production of new skills describes the second external effect of the model. Furthermore, we assume that unemployed households do not accumulate skills during times of unemployment. Reasons for this behavior were presented in chapter five. Finally, as a consistency condition, households must own some basic amount of skills; that amount is identical for all households, hence $S_{i,\tau} = \bar{S}_\tau > 0$. For consistency, we assume that for every household some identical initial amount of capital, $K_{i,t} = \bar{K}_t > 0$, also exists. Any positive change of assets is defined as savings, which is given by income minus consumption.

Due to the functional form of the production and the utility function, every household has to find work in the notational system. Thus, employed households earn income from human and physical capital,[9] and the intertemporal accumulation equation is given by,

$$\dot{K}_{i,t} = w_t H_{i,t} S_{i,t} + r_t K_{i,t} - C_{i,t}. \tag{6.6}$$

The intertemporal accumulation equation for households who become unemployed after the introduction of the minimum wage consequently reduces to

$$\dot{K}_{i,t} = r_t K_{i,t} - C_{i,t}. \tag{6.7}$$

Adding the necessary transversality conditions in optimal control theory, as will be discussed later, we sum up the maximization problem of the single household:

$$\max_i U_i = \int_\tau^\infty (\ln C_{i,t} + \mu \ln F_{i,t}) e^{-\theta(t-\tau)} dt$$

s.t.:

$$\begin{cases} C1: E_{i,t} + H_{i,t} + F_{i,t} = 1 & \text{notional,} \\ C2: \dot{S}_{i,t} = \beta S_{i,t} E_{i,t} & \left.\begin{array}{l}\text{or effective}\end{array}\right\} \\ C3: \dot{K}_{i,t} = w_t H_{i,t} S_{i,t} + r_t K_{i,t} - C_{i,t} & \text{case if employed,} \\ \\ C4: F_i = 1 & \\ C5: \dot{S}_{i,t} = H_{i,t} = 0 & \left.\begin{array}{l}\text{effective case,} \\ \text{if unemployed,}\end{array}\right\} \\ C6: \dot{K}_{i,t} = r_t K_{i,t} - C_{i,t} & \\ \\ C7: K_{i,\tau} = \bar{K}_\tau > 0 & \\ C8: S_{i,\tau} = \bar{S}_\tau > 0 & \left.\begin{array}{l}\text{in every case.}\end{array}\right\} \\ C9: \text{Transversality conditions} & \end{cases}$$

6.1.4 Technical Notes

As mentioned in the introduction, in the effective case a minimum wage is implemented at every point in time. This minimum wage is defined as a constant premium ε, $(\varepsilon < 0)$, on the equilibrium wage, w_t^*, hence $(1+\varepsilon)w_t^* \equiv \overline{w}_t$. In the first period the minimum wage must lead to involuntary unemployment, which influences the budget constraints and decisions of all households. This will be discussed later.

In contrast to chapters four and five we solve the dynamic models "in equilibrium," yielding that in the effective case one may substitute directly for the minimum wage into the respective FOCs. This will become clear when the specific solution of the model is presented. This is important in two ways. First, because of this substitution and the utility function used, the minimum wage will not appear in the steady state rate of growth or in the steady state level of employment. Second, we do not capture effects of changing minimum wages, so the outcome of the system is to be interpreted as a general result of the implementation of any minimum wage. Hence changes in the minimum wage itself (in ε, exactly) will not alter the model's steady state outcomes.

We assume that at the specific point of time when households become unemployed, they remain unemployed. It is possible, however, that they may find work in later periods. Moreover, households may lose their jobs not only in period zero (τ). We do not point out these two possibilities by additional notation; instead we assume that "point zero" is simply the beginning point of the state of becoming unemployed or employed. Hence, the initial conditions for capital and skills are to be reinterpreted. The initial amount of skills and capital will be exogenous at the period τ, but may be influenced by former capital and skills formation at later points in time (we assumed that depreciation for both of them does not exist). Hence, for the specific maximization problem at the specific moment that determines the situation on the labor market, they remain exogenous. We are only interested in the steady state outcome and do not analyze the transitional dynamics of the system. Therefore these changes will not interfere with our model's solution because independently to the beginning of the maximization process, the respective FOCs must yield identical results. This can be seen in the mathematical appendix, A15.[10]

To simplify the ongoing presentation, we use the current value Hamiltonian, $\hbar(.)$.[11] We denote the dynamic Lagrange multipliers or respective present value shadow prices of the next period stock for savings and skills with $v_{i,t}$ and $\lambda_{i,t}$. Hence the current value shadow prices are defined by $\tilde{v}_{i,t} \equiv v_{i,t} e^{\theta(t-\tau)}$, and by $\tilde{\lambda}_{i,t} \equiv \lambda_{i,t} e^{\theta(t-\tau)}$. The use of the current value Hamiltonian implies that the two first order conditions for the dynamic variables are given by $\dot{\tilde{v}}_{i,t} = -\partial h(.)/\partial K_{i,t} + \theta\, \tilde{v}_{i,t}$, and $\dot{\tilde{\lambda}}_{i,t} = -\partial h(.)/\partial S_{i,t} + \theta\, \tilde{\lambda}_{i,t}$. Remember that households maximize until infinity. Thus, two transversality conditions must be fulfilled to evaluate the optimum control problem in every case, namely that $\lim_{t\to\infty}(e^{-\theta(t-\tau)}\lambda_{i,t}K_{i,t}) = 0$, and that $\lim_{t\to\infty}(e^{-\theta(t-\tau)}v_{i,t}S_{i,t}) = 0$. Both conditions state that in infinity there is no possibility for being better off by reinvesting all income in accumulative factors and nothing in consumption. To state it technically, the integral in the Hamiltonian must converge.

6.2   THE REFERENCE MODEL (THE "WALRASIAN ECONOMY")

6.2.1   Individual Maximization Decisions and Aggregation

Maximization of the firm's problem, given by equation (6.2), yields three identical FOCs for the elements of human capital and one FOC for physical capital, which are given by:[12]

$$\frac{\partial \pi_{j,t}}{\partial s_{j,t}} = \frac{\partial \pi_{j,t}}{\partial h_{j,t}} = \frac{\partial \pi_{j,t}}{\partial L_{j,t}} = (1-\alpha)K_{j,t}^{\alpha}s_{j,t}^{-\alpha}h_{j,t}^{-\alpha}L_{j,t}^{-\alpha}s_t^{\psi} = w_t,$$

$$\frac{\partial \pi_{j,t}}{\partial K_{j,t}} = \alpha K_{j,t}^{\alpha-1}s_{j,t}^{1-\alpha}h_{j,t}^{1-\alpha}L_{j,t}^{1-\alpha}s_t^{\psi} = r_t.$$

Normalize the number of firms to one, note that due to full-employment "physical" labor is identical to population, which is also normalized to one, and aggregate to reduce the FOCs to:

$$(1-\alpha)K_t^{\alpha} S_t^{\psi-\alpha} H_t^{-\alpha} = w_t, \tag{6.8}$$

$$\alpha K_t^{\alpha-1} S_t^{1-\alpha+\psi} H_t^{1-\alpha} = r_t. \tag{6.9}$$

Households maximize utility considering the constraints C1–C3 and C7–C9. Hence the Hamiltonian for the single household turns out as

$$\begin{cases} \tilde{h}_i = \ln C_{i,t} + \mu \ln F_{i,t} + \tilde{v}_{i,t}(w_t H_{i,t} S_{i,t} + r_t K_{i,t} - C_{i,t}) + \\ \quad + \tilde{\lambda}_{i,t}\beta\, S_{i,t}(1 - H_{i,t} - F_{i,t}). \end{cases} \tag{6.10}$$

The shadow prices or Lagrange multipliers describe the price of the next period stock of the respective dynamic variable (capital respectively skills). Hence they show the first order increase in the utility function, if the constraint is relaxed marginally. The seven first order conditions (for $C_{i,t}$, $F_{i,t}$, $S_{i,t}$, $H_{i,t}$, $K_{i,t}$, $\tilde{\lambda}_{i,t}$ and $\tilde{\upsilon}_{i,t}$) are given by:

$$\frac{\partial \tilde{h}_i}{\partial C_{i,t}} = \frac{1}{C_{i,t}} - \tilde{\upsilon}_{i,t} = 0 \,,$$

$$\frac{\partial \tilde{h}_i}{\partial F_{i,t}} = \frac{\mu}{F_{i,t}} - \tilde{\lambda}_{i,t}\, \beta \, S_{i,t} = 0 \,,$$

$$\frac{\partial \tilde{h}_i}{\partial H_{i,t}} = \tilde{\upsilon}_{i,t}\, w_t\, S_{i,t} - \tilde{\lambda}_{i,t}\, \beta \, S_{i,t} = 0 \,,$$

$$\frac{\partial \tilde{h}_i}{\partial K_{i,t}} = \tilde{\upsilon}_{i,t}\, r_t = -\dot{\tilde{\upsilon}}_{i,t} + \theta\, \tilde{\upsilon}_{i,t} \,,$$

$$\frac{\partial \tilde{h}_i}{\partial S_{i,t}} = \tilde{\upsilon}_{i,t}\, w_t\, H_{i,t} + \tilde{\lambda}_{i,t}\, \beta \, (1 - H_{i,t} - F_{i,t}) = -\dot{\tilde{\lambda}}_{i,t} + \theta\, \tilde{\lambda}_{i,t} \,,$$

$$\frac{\partial \tilde{h}_i}{\partial \tilde{\upsilon}_{i,t}} = w_t\, H_{i,t}\, S_{i,t} + r_t\, K_{i,t} - C_{i,t} = \dot{K}_{i,t} \,,$$

$$\frac{\partial \tilde{h}_i}{\partial \tilde{\lambda}_{i,t}} = \beta \, S_{i,t}\, (1 - H_{i,t} - F_{i,t}) = \dot{S}_{i,t} \,.$$

The seven first order conditions, the transversality conditions, the initial conditions for skill and physical capital and the FOCs from the firm's problem describe the evolution of the model.

The first equation shows that the marginal utility from consumption must be equal to the shadow price from capital accumulation. The second equation states that the marginal utility from leisure must be identical to the product of the initial level of skills, skills production efficiency, β, and the respective shadow price. The third FOC shows that this last expression must be identical to marginal income from one working hour. The fourth equation, the first dynamic equation, describes the Euler equation or Keynes-Ramsey rule of optimal saving, whereas the fifth equation provides a condition for optimal skills generation. Finally, the two dynamic accumulation conditions are repeated.

All households must be employed in equilibrium. Individual and aggregated variables are therefore identical. We will change the notation to express this fact by simply canceling the index i. The two Lagrange multipliers denote shadow prices, hence they are not influenced by aggregation, but we change the notation in the same way for consistency. We substitute into the FOCs for the factor prices from equations (6.8) and (6.9) and reformulate to obtain that:

$$\frac{1}{C_t} = \tilde{\upsilon}_t, \tag{6.11}$$

$$\frac{\mu}{F_t} = \tilde{\lambda}_t \beta\, S_t, \tag{6.12}$$

$$\tilde{\upsilon}_t (1-\alpha) K_t^{\alpha} S_t^{1-\alpha+\psi} H_t^{-\alpha} = \tilde{\lambda}_t \beta\, S_t, \tag{6.13}$$

$$\tilde{\upsilon}_t \alpha K_t^{\alpha-1} S_t^{1-\alpha+\psi} H_t^{1-\alpha} = -\dot{\tilde{\upsilon}}_t + \theta\, \tilde{\upsilon}_t, \tag{6.14}$$

$$\tilde{\upsilon}_t (1-\alpha) K_t^{\alpha} S_t^{\psi-\alpha} H_t^{1-\alpha} + \tilde{\lambda}_t \beta (1 - H_t - F_t) = -\dot{\tilde{\lambda}}_t + \theta\, \tilde{\lambda}_t, \tag{6.15}$$

$$K_t^{\alpha} S_t^{1-\alpha+\psi} H_t^{1-\alpha} - C_t = \dot{K}_t, \tag{6.16}$$

$$\beta S_t (1 - H_t - F_t) = \dot{S}_t. \tag{6.17}$$

Thus we face a system of seven equations and seven variables in levels and four dynamic variables with the corresponding four equations of motion.

6.2.2 Steady State Rates of Growth

We will solve the model for the rate of growth in three steps. First, we calculate the relative rates of growth of consumption, physical capital and skills. Second, we show that the rate of growth for capital and consumption depends on the difference of the rate of growth of the two shadow prices. Third, we calculate the two shadow prices in parameters and the rate of growth.

The calculation of the *first step* for solving the model is based on equation (6.14), which describes the Keynes-Ramsey rule of optimal saving. We differentiate equation (6.11) with respect to time,

$$\dot{\tilde{\upsilon}}_t = -\frac{\dot{C}_t}{C_t^2}, \tag{6.18}$$

and equate with the Euler equation to yield that

$$\tilde{v}_t \alpha K_t^{\alpha-1} S_t^{1-\alpha+\psi} H_t^{1-\alpha} = \frac{\dot{C}_t}{C_t^2} + \theta \tilde{v}_t \, . \tag{6.19}$$

Substitute for the Lagrange multiplier from equation (6.11), rearrange, and denote the rate of growth of consumption by γ to reduce the expression to

$$\gamma = \alpha K_t^{\alpha-1} S_t^{1-\alpha+\psi} H_t^{1-\alpha} - \theta \, . \tag{6.20}$$

Next, we divide both sides of equation (6.16) by the capital stock and reformulate to get that $(\dot{K}_t + C_t) K_t^{-1} = K_t^{\alpha-1} S_t^{1-\alpha+\psi} H_t^{1-\alpha}$. Rearranging equation (6.20) in the form of $K_t^{\alpha-1} S_t^{1-\alpha+\psi} H_t^{1-\alpha} = \alpha^{-1}(\gamma + \theta)$ helps to combine these two results. The left side of the last expression equals the right side of the prior equation. Substitution and reformulation yields that

$$\frac{1}{\alpha}(\gamma + \theta) - \frac{\dot{K}_t}{K_t} = \frac{C_t}{K_t} \, . \tag{6.21}$$

We know that in steady state the left hand side of this equation is constant by definition. Assume that it is positive. Taking logarithms and derivatives with respect to time helps to express the relationship between the rates of growth of consumption and capital,[13] which is given by

$$\gamma = \frac{\dot{C}_t}{C_t} = \frac{\dot{K}_t}{K_t} = \alpha K_t^{\alpha-1} S_t^{1-\alpha+\psi} H_t^{1-\alpha} - \theta \, . \tag{6.22}$$

Hence physical capital and consumption grow at exactly the same rate γ. Next, we move the rate of time preference to the left side of the equation, which is then constant by definition in steady state. Divide by α, take logarithms and derivatives and remember that the rate of growth of capital is given by γ to get a condition that describes the relationships between the rates of growth of consumption, capital, skills and working hours by

$$\gamma(1-\alpha) = (1-\alpha+\psi)\frac{\dot{S}_t}{S_t} + (1-\alpha)\frac{\dot{H}_t}{H_t} \, .$$

In steady state the rate of growth of working hours is zero. Rearrange to express the rate of skills growth as

$$\frac{\dot{S}_t}{S_t} = \gamma \frac{1-\alpha}{1-\alpha+\psi}.$$

(6.23)

Hence the rate of skills growth is lower than that of capital and consumption, which reflects the existence of the external effect in production. We see that the rate of the economy's growth is driven only by the growth rate of skills if no external effect exists, and that the external effect has a positive effect on the rate of growth. This result is identical to the outcome of the original Lucas model (1988, 22).

The rate of growth of capital and consumption depends on the difference of the rates of growth of the two shadow prices. This will be shown in the *second step* in solving for the rate of growth. Taking the derivative of equation (6.12) with respect to time yields

$$\dot{\tilde{\lambda}}_t = -\frac{\mu}{\beta}(\frac{\dot{S}_t}{S_t^2 F_t}+\frac{\dot{F}_t}{F_t^2 S_t}).$$

We rearrange equation (6.15), substitute for $\dot{\tilde{\lambda}}_t$ from the equation above, and note that the rate of growth of leisure time in steady state is zero to obtain that

$$\tilde{\upsilon}_t(1-\alpha)K_t^\alpha S_t^{\psi-\alpha}H_t^{1-\alpha} = \frac{\mu}{\beta}\frac{\dot{S}_t}{S_t}S_t^{-1}F_t^{-1} - \tilde{\lambda}_t\beta(1-H_t-F_t)+\theta\tilde{\lambda}_t.$$

We divide by the Lagrange multiplier $\tilde{\lambda}_t$, note that by equation (6.17) the second term of the right side of the expression above is identical to the rate of growth of skills and substitute for this growth rate from equation (6.23) to get

$$\frac{\tilde{\upsilon}_t}{\tilde{\lambda}_t}(1-\alpha)K_t^\alpha S_t^{\psi-\alpha}H_t^{1-\alpha} = \frac{\mu}{\beta\tilde{\lambda}_t S_t F_t}\frac{1-\alpha}{1-\alpha+\psi}\gamma - \frac{1-\alpha}{1-\alpha+\psi}\gamma+\theta.$$

Substitute into the second term of the right side for $\beta\tilde{\lambda}_t S_t F_t$ from equation (6.12) and take further manipulations to reduce the expression to

$$\frac{\tilde{\upsilon}_t}{\tilde{\lambda}_t}K_t^\alpha S_t^{\psi-\alpha}H_t^{1-\alpha} = \frac{\theta}{1-\alpha}.$$

Next we take logarithms and derivatives and note that the rate of growth of working time in steady state is zero. This will show that the difference of the rate of growth of the two shadow prices may be described by a function of the rate of growth of skills and of capital, which is given by

$$\frac{\dot{\tilde{\upsilon}}_t}{\tilde{\upsilon}_t} - \frac{\dot{\tilde{\lambda}}_t}{\tilde{\lambda}_t} = (\alpha - \psi)\frac{\dot{S}_t}{S_t} - \alpha\frac{\dot{K}_t}{K_t}.$$

Again we substitute for the growth rate of skills from equation (6.23) and for the growth rate of capital from equation (6.22) and rearrange to reduce the expression to[14]

$$\gamma = \left(\frac{\dot{\tilde{\lambda}}_t}{\tilde{\lambda}_t} - \frac{\dot{\tilde{\upsilon}}_t}{\tilde{\upsilon}_t}\right)\frac{1-\alpha+\psi}{\psi}. \tag{6.24}$$

We mentioned above that the difference between the rates of growth of the shadow values helps to calculate the rate of growth of the economy, which will be done in the *third step* in solving the system. Therefore we must express the rates of growth of the two shadow prices in terms of parameters. From equation (6.14) we already know that $\dot{\tilde{\upsilon}}_t / \tilde{\upsilon}_t = \theta - \alpha K_t^{\alpha-1} S_t^{1-\alpha+\psi} H_t^{1-\alpha}$. The right hand side of this equation is identical to the negative of equation (6.22). Hence the rate of growth of the first shadow price is given by

$$\frac{\dot{\tilde{\upsilon}}_t}{\tilde{\upsilon}_t} = -\gamma. \tag{6.25}$$

To calculate the second Lagrange multiplier, we rearrange equation (6.15) and substitute by equation (6.17) to obtain that

$$\frac{\dot{\tilde{\lambda}}_t}{\tilde{\lambda}_t} = -\frac{\dot{S}_t}{S_t} - \frac{\tilde{\upsilon}_t}{\tilde{\lambda}_t}(1-\alpha)K_t^{\alpha}S_t^{\psi-\alpha}H_t^{1-\alpha} + \theta.$$

Then we use equation (6.13) for the ratio of the two shadow prices,

$$\frac{\tilde{\upsilon}_t}{\tilde{\lambda}_t} = \frac{\beta}{(1-\alpha)K_t^{\alpha}S_t^{\psi-\alpha}H_t^{-\alpha}},$$

and substitute by this expression and the rate of skills growth (6.23) to express the rate of growth of the shadow price as a function of working time. This turns out as

$$\frac{\dot{\tilde{\lambda}}}{\tilde{\lambda}_t} = -\gamma\frac{1-\alpha}{1-\alpha+\psi} - \beta H_t + \theta. \tag{6.26}$$

Therefore we are able to calculate the rate of growth of the second Lagrange multiplier if we express steady state working time in terms of parameters. We express working time from the time constraint, $H_t = 1 - F_t - E_t$, and substitute for F_t and E_t from equations (6.12) and (6.17) to yield that

$$H_t = 1 - \frac{\mu}{\tilde{\lambda}_t \beta S_t} - \frac{1}{\beta}\frac{\dot{S}_t}{S_t}.$$

Next, we substitute for $\tilde{\lambda}_t \beta S_t$ from equation (6.13) and for the rate of growth of skills, which is described by equation (6.23),

$$H_t = 1 - \frac{\mu}{\tilde{v}_t(1-\alpha)K_t^\alpha S_t^{1-\alpha+\psi} H_t^{-\alpha}} - \gamma\frac{1-\alpha}{\beta(1-\alpha+\psi)},$$

substitute for the Lagrange multiplier from equation (6.11), reformulate,

$$H_t = 1 - \frac{\mu H_t}{(1-\alpha)K_t^{\alpha-1}S_t^{1-\alpha+\psi} H_t^{1-\alpha}}\frac{C_t}{K_t} - \gamma\frac{1-\alpha}{\beta(1-\alpha+\psi)},$$

and substitute for the rate of growth from equation (6.20) to obtain that,

$$H_t = 1 - \frac{\alpha\mu H_t}{(1-\alpha)(\gamma+\theta)}\frac{C_t}{K_t} - \gamma\frac{1-\alpha}{\beta(1-\alpha+\psi)}.$$

Now we have to substitute for C_t/K_t from equation (6.21) and for the rate of growth of capital and consumption by equation (6.22). Reformulate, and define that $(1-\alpha+\psi) \equiv \Omega$ and $(1-\alpha) \equiv \Phi$. Hence we yield an expression in terms of parameters and H_t,

$$H_t = 1 - \frac{\mu\, H_t(\gamma+\theta-\alpha\gamma)}{(1-\alpha)(\gamma+\theta)} - \gamma\frac{\Phi}{\beta\,\Omega}. \tag{6.27}$$

Substitution of equation (6.27) into equation (6.26) would help to express the rate of growth of $\tilde{\lambda}_t$ in terms of parameters. However, for a more simple mathematical representation first remember all remaining relevant functions for the calculation of the economy's rate of growth. They are given by equations (6.26) and (6.27) and by equation (6.24), which states that the rate of growth may be expressed as a function of the rates of growth of the two Lagrange multipliers, and by equation (6.25) which describes the rate of growth of $\tilde{v}_t$.

To calculate the rate of growth of the economy, we substitute equations (6.25) and (6.26) into equation (6.24) and simplify to obtain that $H_t = \theta / \beta$.[15] Substitution for H_t into equation (6.27) helps to directly yield a quadratic equation as the solution of the system, which turns out as

$$\gamma^2 \frac{\Phi}{\Omega} + \gamma \left[\theta \left(\mu + \frac{\Phi}{\Omega} \right) - (\beta - \theta) \right] + \theta \left(\mu \frac{\Phi}{\Omega} - (\beta - \theta) \right) = 0 .$$

In order to exhibit an meaningful result we analyze the respective discriminate, which is given by

$$D = \left(\theta \left(\mu + \frac{\Phi}{\Omega} \right) - (\beta - \theta) \right)^2 - 4 \frac{\Phi}{\Omega} \theta \left(\mu \frac{\Phi}{\Omega} - (\beta - \theta) \right) > 0?$$

Note that a positive solution must always exist for $\beta / \theta > 1 + \mu / F$. For $\beta / \theta < 1 + \mu / F$ the possibility of a positive solution depends on the relative size of the parameters. We will not discuss this case because it is convenient to calibrate the time preference rate with values much smaller than one, and in particular smaller than the interest rate. This is a well-known restriction for a positive rate of growth. This can also be seen in equation (6.29) at the end of this page. Hence we are able to simply assume that $1 + \mu - \beta / \theta < 0$. It logically follows that $1 + \mu / F - \beta / \theta < 0$, and therefore the solution of the quadratic equation turns out as

$$\left\{ \gamma_{1,2} = \frac{(\beta - \theta) - \theta(\mu + \xi)}{2\xi} \pm \right.$$

$$\left. \pm \frac{\left[(\theta(\mu + \xi) - (\beta - \theta))^2 - 4\xi\theta \left(\frac{\mu\theta}{1-\alpha} - (\beta - \theta) \right) \right]^{\frac{1}{2}}}{2\xi} , \right. \tag{6.28}$$

$$\text{where } \xi \equiv \frac{1 - \alpha}{1 - \alpha + \psi} .$$

The system must generate at least one positive rate of growth. In order to capture the corresponding comparative static behavior, we could calculate the partial derivatives with respect to the parameters. The formal complexity of the expression would require some technical effort. However, it will be shown that this is not necessary. We are specifically interested in the effect of the "learning efficiency" parameter, β, the intertemporal rate of time preference, θ, and the elasticity of the external effect, ψ.

To capture the effect of the intertemporal rate of time preference, we recall equation (6.25), which states that $\dot{\tilde{v}}_t / \tilde{v}_t = -\gamma$. This expression is also crucial for the behavior of our system in time. We reformulate equation (6.14), substitute for the rate of growth from the expression above and resubstitute for the interest rate from the respective individual first order condition to yield

$$\gamma = r_t - \theta . \tag{6.29}$$

Hence the rate of growth is determined by the steady state interest rate and the rate of intertemporal time preference; less willingness to substitute intertemporally decreases the rate of growth.

In order to analyze the effect of the "learning efficiency" parameter and of the external effect, we substitute for the rate of growth of skills, which is given by equation (6.17) into equation (6.23) and rearrange to obtain that

$$\gamma = \beta(1 - H_t - F_t)\frac{1 - \alpha + \psi}{1 - \alpha} .$$

In steady state, educational time, as described by the term in brackets, is constant. Hence the rate of growth of the economy is positively influenced by the "learning efficiency" and the external effect.

Finally, based on the previously discussed equation (6.29) and on equation (6.23), which states that the rate of growth depends on skills accumulation, our model qualitatively generates the same outcome as the original Lucas model (1988).[16] However, our results are based on the individual's optimal choice of division between labor, working and leisure time.

6.3   THE EFFECTS OF MINIMUM WAGES ("THE EFFECTIVE CASE")

6.3.1   Individual Maximization Decisions and Aggregation

The number of employed persons in the notional system is identical to population, which was normalized to one. In the effective system we must distinguish between unemployed and employed households. The population is still normalized to one, but the minimum wage makes the number of employed individuals, L_t, at least in the first period smaller than one. In the following we denote the number of unemployed persons by $(1-L_t)$, all variables of employed persons by the index "e," and all variables of unemployed persons by the index "u." Subscripts denote the variables for individual households and superscripts denote aggregated variables.

For most of the respective variables that belong to *employed households* we yield very simple rules for aggregation, namely $K_t^e = L_t K_{e,t}$, $C_t^e = L_t C_{e,t}$, $S_t^e = L_t S_{e,t}$, $F_t^e = L_t F_{e,t}$, $E_t^e = L_t E_{e,t}$, and $H_t^e = L_t H_{e,t}$. Furthermore, we must also express the change of the dynamic individual variables $\dot{K}_{e,t}$ and $\dot{S}_{e,t}$ in terms of aggregated variables. This follows from the derivation of the levels of the individual variables with respect to time, which yields that $\dot{S}_{e,t} = S_t^e L_t^{-1}(\dot{S}_t^e / S_t^e - \dot{L}_t / L_t)$ and that $\dot{K}_{e,t} = K_t^e L_t^{-1}(\dot{K}_t^e / K_t^e - \dot{L}_t / L_t)$.

Furthermore, remember that the time constraint for the single household is given by $1 - H_{e,t} - F_{e,t} = E_{e,t}$. Substitute for the aggregated variables to obtain that $L_t - H_t^e - F_t^e = E_t^e$.. Finally, the shadow prices do not need to be aggregated, but we change the notation to simplify the presentation. Hence $\tilde{\upsilon}_t^e = \tilde{\upsilon}_{e,t}$ and $\tilde{\lambda}_t^e = \tilde{\lambda}_{e,t}$. Note that working time, educational time and skills are variables that belong only to employed households. That will be discussed later.

The conditions for the aggregation of the variables of *unemployed households* are simply given by $C_t^u = (1 - L_t)C_{u,t}$, $K_t^u = (1 - L_t)K_{u,t}$, $\dot{K}_{u,t} = K_t^u (1 - L_t)^{-1}(\dot{K}_t^u / K_t^u + \dot{L}_t /(1 - L_t))$, and by $\tilde{\upsilon}_t^u = \tilde{\upsilon}_{u,t}$. Because the number of households is normalized to one, any change in employment must be identical to the negative of the change in unemployment, or $\dot{K}_{u,t} = K_t^u (1 - L_t)^{-1}(\dot{K}_t^u / K_t^u - (1 - \dot{L}_t)/(1 - L_t))$.

Finally, we sum up capital stocks and the consumption of employed and unemployed households to yield the economy-wide levels, hence $C_t = C_t^e + C_t^u$ and $K_t = K_t^e + K_t^u$, note that the sum of changes of the variables for employed and unemployed households must be identical to the change of the respective aggregated values, hence $\dot{K}_t = \dot{K}_t^e + \dot{K}_t^u$, and $\dot{C}_t = \dot{C}_t^e + \dot{C}_t^u$.

The *firm's problem* is nearly identical to that of the notional case and leads to nearly identical FOCs. The difference is that labor may be below the full-employment level and that firms face the minimum wage.[17] To point this out, we do not introduce a new equation numbering; instead, we indicate the original equation numbers by an apostrophe. Hence the FOCs are given by:[18]

$$(1-\alpha)K_t^\alpha S_t^{e\,\psi-\alpha} H_t^{-\alpha} L_t^{\alpha-\psi} = \overline{w}_t, \qquad (6.8')$$

$$\alpha K_t^{\alpha-1} S_t^{e\,1-\alpha+\psi} H_t^{e\,1-\alpha} L_t^{\alpha-\psi-1} = r_t. \qquad (6.9')$$

Unemployed households do not aggregate human capital. Hence the income of $(1-L_t)$ unemployed persons is only given by $r_t K_t$. Unemployed households maximize utility given the constraints C4–C9 and C7–C9, which were presented in the "basic model setup." Therefore the individual's Hamiltonian reduces to

$$\tilde{h}_u(.) = \ln C_{u,t} + \tilde{\upsilon}_{u,t}(r_t K_{u,t} - C_{u,t}). \qquad (6.30)$$

We yield the following three FOCs:

$$\frac{\partial \tilde{h}_u}{\partial C_{u,t}} = \frac{1}{C_{u,t}} - \tilde{\upsilon}_{u,t} = 0,$$

$$\frac{\partial \tilde{h}_u}{\partial K_{u,t}} = \tilde{\upsilon}_{u,t} r_t = -\dot{\tilde{\upsilon}}_{u,t} + \theta \tilde{\upsilon}_{u,t},$$

$$\frac{\partial \tilde{h}_u}{\partial \tilde{\upsilon}_{u,t}} = r_t K_{u,t} - C_{u,t} = \dot{K}_{u,t}.$$

The first equation states that marginal utility from consumption must be equal to the shadow price from the capital accumulation equation, whereas the second describes the Keynes-Ramsey rule for optimal saving for unemployed households, and the third equation repeats the dynamic accumulation condition for capital.

We substitute for the aggregated values and for the interest rate from equation (6.9') and remember that working hours and skills are only supplied by employed households, to yield for the economy that:

$$\frac{1-L_t}{C_t^u} = \tilde{\upsilon}_t^u, \tag{6.31}$$

$$\tilde{\upsilon}_t^u \alpha K_t^{\alpha-1} H_t^{e^{1-\alpha}} S_t^{e^{1-\alpha+\psi}} L_t^{\alpha-\psi-1} = -\dot{\tilde{\upsilon}}_t^u + \theta \tilde{\upsilon}_t^u, \tag{6.32}$$

$$\begin{cases} \alpha K_t^{\alpha-1} H_t^{e^{1-\alpha}} S_t^{e^{1-\alpha+\psi}} L_t^{\alpha-\psi-1} \dfrac{K_t^u}{1-L_t} - \dfrac{C_t^u}{1-L_t} = \\[2em] = \dfrac{K_t^u}{1-L_t}\left(\dfrac{\dot{K}_t^u}{K_t^u} + \dfrac{(\dot{1-L_t})}{1-L_t} \right). \end{cases}$$

Furthermore, we note that in steady state, the rate of growth of unemployment is zero and reformulate the last equation to obtain that

$$\alpha K_t^{\alpha-1} H_t^{e^{1-\alpha}} S_t^{e^{1-\alpha+\psi}} L_t^{\alpha-\psi-1} - \frac{C_t^u}{K_t^u} = \frac{\dot{K}_t^u}{K_t^u}. \tag{6.33}$$

Employed households supply exactly one unit of "physical labor." They maximize, given the constraints C1–C3 and C6–C9, which are described in the "basic model setup."[19] Hence the Hamiltonian for the single employed household is given by

$$\begin{cases} \tilde{\hbar}_{e,t}(.) = (\ln C_{e,t} + \mu \ln F_{e,t}) + \\[0.5em] \qquad + \tilde{\upsilon}_{e,t}(\overline{w}_t H_{e,t} S_{e,t} + r_t K_{e,t} - C_{e,t}) + \\[0.5em] \qquad + \tilde{\lambda}_{e,t} \beta S_{e,t}(1 - H_{e,t} - F_{e,t}). \end{cases} \tag{6.34}$$

The maximization problem results in seven first order conditions (for $C_{i,t}$, $F_{e,t}$, $S_{e,t}$, $H_{e,t}$, $K_{e,t}$, $\tilde{\lambda}_{e,t}$ and $\tilde{\upsilon}_{e,t}$):

$$\frac{\partial \tilde{\hbar}_e}{\partial C_{e,t}} = \frac{1}{C_{e,t}} - \tilde{\upsilon}_{e,t} = 0,$$

$$\frac{\partial \tilde{\hbar}_e}{\partial F_{e,t}} = \frac{\mu}{F_{e,t}} - \tilde{\lambda}_{e,t} \beta S_{e,t} = 0,$$

$$\frac{\partial \tilde{\hbar}_e}{\partial H_{e,t}} = \tilde{\upsilon}_{e,t} \overline{w}_t S_{e,t} - \tilde{\lambda}_{e,t} \beta S_{e,t} = 0,$$

$$\frac{\partial \tilde{\hbar}_e}{\partial K_{e,t}} = \tilde{\upsilon}_{e,t} r_t = -\dot{\tilde{\upsilon}}_{e,t} + \theta \tilde{\upsilon}_{e,t},$$

$$\frac{\partial \tilde{h}_e}{\partial S_{e,t}} = \tilde{\upsilon}_{e,t}\,\overline{w}_t H_{e,t} + \tilde{\lambda}_{e,t}\beta(1 - H_{e,t} - F_{e,t}) = -\dot{\tilde{\lambda}}_{e,t} + \theta\,\tilde{\lambda}_{e,t},$$

$$\frac{\partial \tilde{h}_e}{\partial \tilde{\upsilon}_{e,t}} = \overline{w}_t H_{e,t} S_{e,t} + r_t K_{e,t} - C_{e,t} = \dot{K}_{e,t},$$

$$\frac{\partial \tilde{h}_e}{\partial \tilde{\lambda}_{e,t}} = \beta\,S_{e,t}\,(1 - H_{e,t} - F_{e,t}) = \dot{S}_{e,t}.$$

The economic interpretation of the first order conditions is identical to that of the "Walrasian Economy." Therefore it will not be repeated.

We substitute for the aggregated variables, the wage and the interest rate from equations (6.8' and 6.9'), note that the rate of growth of employment in steady state is zero and reformulate in order to express the FOCs in aggregated variables as:

$$\frac{L_t}{C_t^e} = \tilde{\upsilon}_t^e, \tag{6.35}$$

$$\frac{\mu\,L_t}{F_t^e} = \tilde{\lambda}_t^e \beta\,\frac{S_t^e}{L_t}, \tag{6.36}$$

$$\tilde{\upsilon}_t^e(1-\alpha)K_t^\alpha S_t^{e\,1+\psi-\alpha} H_t^{e\,-\alpha} L_t^{\alpha-\psi-1} = \tilde{\lambda}_t^e \beta\,\frac{S_t^e}{L_t}, \tag{6.37}$$

$$\tilde{\upsilon}_t^e \alpha K_t^{\alpha-1} S_t^{e\,1-\alpha+\psi} H_t^{e\,1-\alpha} L_t^{\alpha-\psi-1} = -\dot{\tilde{\upsilon}}_t^e + \theta\tilde{\upsilon}_t^e, \tag{6.38}$$

$$\begin{cases} \tilde{\upsilon}_t^e(1-\alpha)K_t^\alpha S_t^{e\,\psi-\alpha} H_t^{e\,1-\alpha} L_t^{\alpha-\psi-1} + \\[2mm] + \tilde{\lambda}_t^e \beta\left(1 - \frac{H_t^e}{L_t} - \frac{F_t^e}{L_t}\right) = -\dot{\tilde{\lambda}}_t^e + \theta\tilde{\lambda}_t^e, \end{cases} \tag{6.39}$$

$$\begin{cases} (1-\alpha)K_t^\alpha S_t^{e\,1+\psi-\alpha} H_t^{e\,1-\alpha} L_t^{\alpha-\psi-2} + \\[2mm] + \alpha K_t^{\alpha-1} S_t^{e\,1-\alpha+\psi} H_t^{e\,1-\alpha} L_t^{\alpha-\psi-1} \dfrac{K_t^e}{L_t} - \dfrac{C_t^e}{L_t} = \dfrac{K_t^e}{L_t} \dfrac{\dot{K}_t^e}{K_t^e}, \end{cases}$$

$$\beta\frac{S_t^e}{L_t}\left(1 - \frac{H_t^e}{L_t} - \frac{F_t^e}{L_t}\right) = \frac{S_t^e}{L_t} \frac{\dot{S}_t^e}{S_t^e}.$$

We rearrange the last two FOCs to obtain that

$$\begin{cases} (1-\alpha)K_t^\alpha S_t^{e^{1+\psi-\alpha}} H_t^{e^{1-\alpha}} L_t^{\alpha-\psi-1} + \\[2mm] +\alpha K_t^{\alpha-1} S_t^{e^{1-\alpha+\psi}} H_t^{e^{1-\alpha}} L_t^{\alpha-\psi-1} K_t^e - C_t^e = K_t^e \dfrac{\dot{K}_t^e}{K_t^e}, \end{cases} \tag{6.40}$$

$$\frac{\dot{S}_t^e}{S_t^e} = \beta\left(1 - \frac{H_t^e}{L_t} - \frac{F_t^e}{L_t}\right). \tag{6.41}$$

We will yield three rates of growth for consumption and for "physical capital," one for the employed, one for the unemployed's sub-system and one for the whole economy. Furthermore, we will get growth rates for skills and for the shadow prices. We know that in steady state all rates of growth for leisure, learning and working time and for employment must be zero. Note that it is impossible to solve for the outcome of the employed and unemployed's system separately, but from a methodological point of view this is not problematic, because all FOCs were determined from the individual's perspective.

   Including the two equations for aggregation of output and capital, we face a system of 12 equations and 13 variables in levels, namely ten structural variables, given by L_t, S_t^e, C_t, C_t^e, C_t^u, H_t^e, F_t^e, K_t, K_t^e, and K_t^u, and three Lagrange multipliers, namely $\tilde{v}_t^e$, $\tilde{v}_t^u$, and λ_t^e. In particular, within this system of equations, employment is not properly defined. However, we are able to solve this problem because we know that, as in the static models presented earlier, employment is determined by the factor demand function for human capital at every point in time. Therefore, it will be added to the system of equations. We will discuss this argument later. Furthermore, note that the number of variables in movement, which are given by $\dot{S}_t^e$, $\dot{K}_t^e$, $\dot{K}_t^u$, $\dot{\tilde{v}}_t^e$, $\dot{\tilde{v}}_t^u$, and $\dot{\tilde{\lambda}}_t^e$ corresponds to the number of intertemporal equations.

6.3.2 Steady State Rates of Growth

Because of the complexity of the system, the calculation of the economy's rate of growth in parameters requires some technical work. However, we present the complete necessary procedure in order to point out the whole dynamics of the system. We will calculate the steady state rate of growth of the system in three steps. First we use all possible information from the unemployed household's system. In the next step we use the additional information provided by the employed household's system to calculate the relationships between the rates of growth of consumption and capital of employed and unemployed households, the aggregated system, the two shadow prices and the level of skills. In the third and final step we calculate the rate of growth of the systems in terms of parameters. The way of solution for the rate of growth is different to that used for the solution of the notional system and will be described at the beginning of the third step.

As mentioned above, the *first step* points out all possible information from the unemployed's system. Equation (6.32) describes the Euler equation for unemployed households. Rearrangement yields that

$$\alpha K_t^{\alpha-1} H_t^{e^{1-\alpha}} S_t^{e^{1-\alpha+\psi}} L_t^{\alpha-\psi-1} = -\frac{\dot{\tilde{v}}_t^u}{\tilde{v}_t^u} + \theta \ .$$

Assume that the right side of this equation is greater than zero,[20] hence the right side of the equation in the steady state is constant. Taking logarithms and differences results in

$$(1-\alpha+\psi)\frac{\dot{S}_t^e}{S_t^e} + (1-\alpha)\frac{\dot{H}_t^e}{H_t^e} + (\alpha-\psi-1)\frac{\dot{L}_t}{L_t} = (1-\alpha)\frac{\dot{K}_t}{K_t} \ .$$

We describe the rate of growth of the aggregated capital stock by γ, remember that the change of working time and employment in steady state is zero and reformulate to calculate the relationship between the economy's rate of growth and skills' rate of growth, which turns out as

$$\gamma = \frac{\dot{K}_t}{K_t} = \frac{1-\alpha+\psi}{1-\alpha}\frac{\dot{S}_t^e}{S_t^e} \ . \tag{6.42}$$

With the exception that skills are only produced by employed households, this expression is identical to that of the notional case (equation 6.23). Hence we will not repeat the resulting economic causalities.

Next we differentiate equation (6.31) with respect to time to yield an expression for the change in the shadow price $\tilde{v}_t^u$,

$$-\dot{\tilde{v}}_t^u = \frac{\dot{L}_t C_t^u + \dot{C}_t^u(1-L_t)}{C_t^{u^2}} \ , \tag{6.43}$$

and equate with the Euler Equation (6.38) to get that

$$\tilde{v}_t^u \alpha K_t^{\alpha-1} H_t^{e^{1-\alpha}} S_t^{e^{1-\alpha+\psi}} L_t^{\alpha-\psi-1} = \frac{\dot{L}_t C_t^u + \dot{C}_t^u(1-L_t)}{C_t^{u^2}} + \theta \tilde{v}_t^u \; .$$

We substitute for the Lagrange multiplier from equation (6.31), note that in steady state the change of employment is zero, denote the rate of growth of consumption of unemployed households by γ^u, and reformulate to reduce the expression to[21]

$$\gamma^u = \alpha K_t^{\alpha-1} H_t^{e^{1-\alpha}} S_t^{e^{1-\alpha+\psi}} L_t^{\alpha-\psi-1} - \theta \; . \tag{6.44}$$

Rearranging equation (6.32) shows that the rate of growth of $\tilde{v}_t^u$ is the negative of γ^u, which is described by the equation above. Hence we have found a relationship between the shadow price's rate of growth and the rate of growth of the unemployed's system. This turns out as

$$\frac{\dot{\tilde{v}}_t^u}{\tilde{v}_t^u} = -\gamma^u \; . \tag{6.45}$$

Substitute the right side of equation (6.44) into the left hand side of equation (6.33) and rearrange to obtain that

$$\gamma^u + \theta - \frac{\dot{K}_t^u}{K_t^u} = \frac{C_t^u}{K_t^u} \; .$$

We assume that the left side of the equation is greater than zero.[22] Take logarithms and differences to show that consumption and capital grow at an identical rate, or

$$\frac{\dot{C}_t^u}{C_t^u} = \frac{\dot{K}_t^u}{K_t^u} = \gamma^u \; . \tag{6.46}$$

Substitute back to yield that the relation of consumption and capital of the unemployed households is only determined by the rate of intertemporal time preference. It simplifies to

$$\frac{C_t^u}{K_t^u} = \theta \; . \tag{6.47}$$

Finally, similar to the "Walrasian Economy," we substitute equation (6.45) into the Euler-Equation, resubstitute for the rate of interest from the firm's FOC and reformulate to yield that the rate of growth of the unemployed's system is crucially driven by the interest rate of the whole system, or

$$\gamma^u = r_t - \theta. \tag{6.48}$$

To summarize the results from the unemployed's system, we calculated the relationship of the rates of growth of aggregated skills and capital for the whole system as well as the relationships between the rates of growth of consumption, capital stock and shadow price of the unemployed households. Moreover we showed that the rate of growth of the subsystem depends on the outcome of the whole system.

Next, we use the additional information provided by the system of employed households. The *second step* in solving the system focuses on the relationships between the rate of growth of consumption and the capital of employed and unemployed households, the aggregated system, the two shadow prices and the level of skills. In many cases the proceeding is identical to the one used for the solution of the notional case. Note that equation (6.38) describes the Euler equation or Keynes-Ramsey rule of optimal saving for employed persons. Taking the derivative of equation (6.35) with respect to time leads to

$$\dot{\tilde{v}}_t^e = \frac{\dot{L}_t C_t^e - \dot{C}_t^e L_t}{C_t^{e^2}}. \tag{6.49}$$

Equate with the Euler Equation to yield that

$$\tilde{v}_t^e \alpha K_t^{\alpha-1} S_t^{e^{1-\alpha+\psi}} H_t^{e^{1-\alpha}} L_t^{\alpha-\psi-1} = -\frac{\dot{L}_t C_t^e - \dot{C}_t^e L_t}{C_t^{e^2}} + \theta \tilde{v}_t^e.$$

We substitute for the Lagrange multiplier from equation (6.35), note that in steady state the rate of growth of employment is zero, denote the rate of growth of the employed's system by γ^e, reformulate,[23]

$$\frac{\dot{C}_t^e}{C_t^e} = \alpha K_t^{\alpha-1} S_t^{e^{1-\alpha+\psi}} H_t^{e^{1-\alpha}} L_t^{\alpha-\psi-1} - \theta \equiv \gamma^e, \tag{6.50}$$

and use the information from equations (6.44) and (6.46) of the unemployed's system to obtain the relationship between the rate of growth of consumption of unemployed and employed households. This turns out to be simply $\gamma^u = \gamma^e$. Hence the rates of growth of consumption in both subsystems are identical.

Furthermore, we know that the change in aggregate consumption must be identical to the change in consumption of the two sub-systems, hence $\dot{C}_t = \dot{C}_t^e + \dot{C}_t^u$. We reformulate this expression to yield that $\dot{C}_t / C_t * C_t = \gamma^e C_t^e + \gamma^u C_t^u$. The rates of growth of consumption of employed and unemployed households are identical, which yields that $\dot{C}_t / C_t * C_t = \gamma^e (C_t^e + C_t^u)$. Knowing that $C_t = C_t^u + C_t^e$, we substitute to see that aggregate consumption grows at exactly the same rate as the two subsystems, or $\dot{C}_t / C_t = \gamma^e = \gamma^u$.

To find the relationships between all rates of growth of consumption and capital, we substitute from equation (6.44) into equation (6.37) to yield that

$$\tilde{\upsilon}_t^e \frac{1-\alpha}{\alpha}(\gamma+\theta)\frac{K_t}{H_t^e} = \tilde{\lambda}_t^e \beta \frac{S_t^e}{L_t},$$

and substitute for $\tilde{\upsilon}_t^e$ from equation (6.35), and for the right side of the above expression by equation (6.36), and reformulate to obtain that

$$\frac{C_t^e}{K_t} = \frac{1-\alpha}{\alpha\mu}(\gamma+\theta)\frac{F_t^e}{H_t^e}. \tag{6.51}$$

Note that the rates of growth of leisure time and working hours in steady state are constant. Taking logarithms and derivatives yields that $\gamma^e = \dot{K}_t / K_t$. Furthermore, with an argumentation similar to the one provided for the relationships of the different rates of growth of consumption, we obtain that the rate of growth of the capital stock of the employed's system is identical to γ.[24] To sum up, we have found that

$$\gamma = \gamma^e = \gamma^u = \frac{\dot{K}_t}{K_t} = \frac{\dot{K}_t^u}{K_t^u} = \frac{\dot{K}_t^e}{K_t^e} = \frac{\dot{C}_t}{C_t}. \tag{6.52}$$

Next, we express the rate of time preference from equations (6.38) and (6.44), equate and note that the rates of growth of the two subsystems and the economy are identical in order to yield the rate of growth of $\tilde{\upsilon}_t^e$, which is given by

$$\frac{\dot{\tilde{\upsilon}}_t^e}{\tilde{\upsilon}_t^e} = -\gamma. \tag{6.53}$$

In the following we will calculate the relative rate of growth of $\tilde{\lambda}_t^e$. From equation (6.36) it follows that $S_t^e = \mu\, L_t^2 (\beta F_t^e \tilde{\lambda}_t^e)^{-1}$. Difference with respect to time,

$$\dot{S}_t^e = \mu\, L_t \frac{2\dot{L}_t F_t \tilde{\lambda}_t^e - L_t \dot{F}_t^e \tilde{\lambda}_t^e - L_t \dot{\tilde{\lambda}}_t^e F_t}{\beta F_t^{e^2} \tilde{\lambda}_t^{e^2}},$$

and reformulate to yield that

$$\dot{S}_t^e = \mu\, L_t^2 \left(\frac{2\dot{L}_t F_t \tilde{\lambda}_t^e}{L_t \beta F_t^{e^2} \tilde{\lambda}_t^{e^2}} - \frac{\dot{F}_t^e \tilde{\lambda}_t^e}{\beta F_t^{e^2} \tilde{\lambda}_t^{e^2}} - \frac{\dot{\tilde{\lambda}}_t^e}{\beta F_t^e \tilde{\lambda}_t^{e^2}} \right).$$

We know that the rates of growth of leisure time and employment in steady state are zero, hence the equation reduces to

$$\dot{S}_t^e = -\frac{\mu}{\beta}\, \frac{L_t^2}{F_t^e}\, \frac{\dot{\tilde{\lambda}}_t^e}{\tilde{\lambda}_t^e}\, \frac{1}{\tilde{\lambda}_t^e}.$$

Divide this expression by S_t^e from equation (6.36) to yield that the rate of growth of the shadow price for skills accumulation has to be identical to the negative of the rate of growth of skills, or

$$\frac{\dot{S}_t^e}{S_t^e} = -\frac{\dot{\tilde{\lambda}}_t^e}{\tilde{\lambda}_t^e}. \tag{6.54}$$

Remember that the growth rate of skills is determined by equation (6.42).

The main results, which were derived in the second step of solving the system, are as follows:

$$\left\{ \begin{aligned} \gamma = \gamma^e = \gamma^u &= \frac{\dot{C}_t}{C_t} = \frac{\dot{K}_t}{K_t} = \frac{\dot{K}_t^u}{K_t^u} = \frac{\dot{K}_t^e}{K_t^e} = -\frac{\dot{\tilde{v}}_t^e}{\tilde{v}_t^e} = \\ &= -\frac{1-\alpha+\psi}{1-\alpha}\, \frac{\dot{\tilde{\lambda}}_t^e}{\tilde{\lambda}_t^e} = \frac{1-\alpha+\psi}{1-\alpha}\, \frac{\dot{S}_t^e}{S_t^e}. \end{aligned} \right. \tag{6.55}$$

Hence we have calculated the relationships between all relevant variables of the system. This helps to ignore the superscripts of the respective rates of growth for the ongoing analysis.

In the *third step* of solving the system, we will calculate the rate of growth of the system in terms of parameters. For mathematical reasons it is not possible to use the same methodology as was used for the analysis of the "Walrasian Economy," where we had to express the rate of growth as a function of the difference of the two shadow prices, because the additional variables in the effective model, especially the relationship of the level of consumption of employed households and the aggregate capital stock, makes this method of solution impossible. First, we show that it is possible to calculate two equations that express the relationship of consumption of employed households and the aggregate capital stock as a function for working hours, leisure time and employment. Second, we calculate steady state working and leisure time. Third, we calculate the rate of growth of the system in terms of parameters.

The first equation that expresses the relationship of consumption of employed households and the aggregate capital stock was already calculated above (equation 6.51). To calculate the second equation, which describes this relationship, we substitute from equation (6.44) and for the rate of growth of the capital stock of the unemployed households into equation (6.40) and reformulate to yield that

$$\frac{1-\alpha}{\alpha}(\gamma+\theta)K_t + \theta\, K_t^e = C_t^e.$$

Next, we substitute by the aggregate capital stock from equation (6.51) into the equation above and take further manipulations to obtain that[25]

$$\frac{C_t^e}{K_t^e} = \theta\left(1 - \frac{\mu\, H_t^e}{F_t^e}\right)^{-1}. \tag{6.56}$$

Note that, in contrast to equation (6.51), the denominator on the left side of this equation is not the aggregate stock of capital – as in equation (6.51), but the capital stock of employed households. Here we must anticipate the analysis that is provided later. We will then show that in steady state the economy must achieve full-employment. In steady state, the capital stock of employed households is identical to aggregate capital.[26] This helps to equate equations (6.51) and (6.56), and after some mathematical rearrangements we yield an expression in terms of working and leisure time and the rate of growth of the system that is given by[27]

$$\frac{F_t^e}{H_t^e} = \frac{\alpha\mu}{1-\alpha}\frac{\theta}{(\gamma+\theta)} + \mu \, .$$

(6.57)

To express working time in parameters, we rearrange equation (6.39) and substitute from equation (6.41) to see that

$$\frac{\dot{\tilde{\lambda}}_t^e}{\tilde{\lambda}_t^e} = -\frac{\dot{S}_t^e}{S_t^e} - \frac{\tilde{\upsilon}_t^e}{\tilde{\lambda}_t^e}(1-\alpha)K_t^\alpha S_t^{e\,\psi-\alpha} H_t^{e\,1-a} L_t^{\alpha-\psi-1} + \theta \, .$$

We then use equation (6.37) to express the relationship of the two shadow prices as $\tilde{\upsilon}_t^e / \tilde{\lambda}_t^e = \beta\, S_t^e((1-\alpha)K_t^\alpha S_t^{e\,1-\alpha+\psi} H_t^{e-\alpha} L_t^{\alpha-\psi})^{-1}$, and substitute for this expression and for the rate of growth of skills, given by equation (6.42), to turn out the rate of growth of $\tilde{\lambda}_t^e$ as a function of working time, the rate of growth and employment. We obtain that

$$\frac{\dot{\tilde{\lambda}}_t^e}{\tilde{\lambda}_t^e} = -\gamma\frac{1-\alpha}{1-\alpha+\psi} - \frac{\beta H_t^e}{L_t} + \theta \, .$$

From equation (6.55) we know that the negative of the rate of growth of $\tilde{\lambda}_t^e$ is identical to the first term of the left side of this equation. Hence we are able to express working time in terms of parameters and employment as

$$H_t^e = \frac{\theta}{\beta}L_t \, .$$

(6.58)

Compared to the "notional" system, working time consequently depends on the level of employment. To calculate leisure time, remember that from equations (6.41) and (6.42) we know that

$$\gamma\frac{1-\alpha}{1-\alpha+\psi} = \beta - \beta\frac{H_t^e}{L_t} - \beta\frac{F_t^e}{L_t} \, .$$

Substitute by H_t^e from equation (6.58) and reformulate to express working time as a function of parameters and employment which is given by

$$F_t^e = \frac{L_t}{\beta}\left(\beta - \theta - \gamma\frac{1-\alpha}{1-\alpha+\psi}\right) .$$

(6.59)

Finally, to calculate the rate of the system's growth, we substitute for working and leisure time, which are given by equations (6.58) and (6.59), into equation (6.57) and take further mathematical reformulations, which are to be found in the mathematical appendix, A21. The rate of growth turns out as

$$
\left\{
\begin{aligned}
\gamma_{1,2} &= -\frac{\left(\theta(\mu+\xi)-(\beta-\theta)\right)}{\xi} \pm \\
&\pm \frac{\left[\left(\theta(\mu+\xi)-(\beta-\theta)\right)^2 - 4\xi\theta\left(\frac{\mu\theta}{1-\alpha}-(\beta-\theta)\right)\right]^{\frac{1}{2}}}{\xi}
\end{aligned}
\right. ,
\tag{6.60}
$$

where $\xi \equiv 2\dfrac{1-\alpha}{1-\alpha+\psi}$.

Hence the rate of growth of the effective system is identical to the rate of growth of the notional system (equation 6.28). Therefore we will not discuss this function's properties further.

To close this section, as in the chapter of the "Walrasian economy," we substitute for the rate of growth into the Euler Equation, resubstitute for the rate of interest and reformulate to obtain that

$$
\gamma = r_t - \theta . \tag{6.61}
$$

Hence, as in the "Walrasian Economy" and the original Lucas model, the rate of growth is determined by the interest rate and the rate of intertemporal time preference.

6.3.3 Steady State Level of Employment

The firms' demand function for human capital must be binding at every point in time. This will help to calculate the steady state level of labor. To calculate the factor demand function for human capital, we use the standard profit maximization approach. We have therefore only presented the result; for the single firm it is given by[28]

$$
s_{j,t}^e h_{j,t}^e L_{j,t} = \left(\frac{1-\alpha}{\alpha}\frac{r_t}{w_t}\right)^{\alpha} Y_{j,t} s_t^{e-\psi} . \tag{6.62}
$$

Remember that skills and working time are supplied only by employed households, represented by the superscript "e". Furthermore, remember that the firm always faces a binding minimum wage. In equilibrium the minimum wage has to correspond to the FOC of the firm, which is repeated in terms of aggregated variables, or

$$(1-\alpha)K_t^{\alpha}S_t^{e\psi-\alpha}H_t^{e-\alpha}L_t^{\alpha-\psi} = \overline{w}_t . \tag{6.8'}$$

We substitute for the wage by equation (6.8') and for the interest rate from equation (4.8.9'), which is the FOC of the firm's problem for capital in aggregated variables, into the demand function for human capital, and reformulate to obtain that $Y_t = K_t^{\alpha}S_t^{el-\alpha+\psi}H_t^{el-\alpha}L_t^{\alpha-\psi-1}$.[29] Note that, in equilibrium, output is identical to consumption minus investment, $Y_t = C_t - \dot{K}_t$, and rearrange for mathematical reasons only to yield that $(C_t + \dot{K}_t)K_t^{-1}\alpha = \alpha K_t^{\alpha-1}S_t^{el-\alpha+\psi}H_t^{el-\alpha}L_t^{\alpha-\psi-1}$. We substitute this expression into equation (6.32), the Keynes-Ramsey rule for unemployed households, and remember that the rate of growth of capital is given by γ, to obtain that

$$\tilde{v}_t^u \alpha\left(\frac{C_t}{K_t}+\gamma\right) = -\dot{\tilde{v}}_t^u + \theta\tilde{v}_t^u . \tag{6.63}$$

From the analysis of the unemployed's system, we know that the derivative of equation (6.31) with respect to time yields equation (6.43), or, in reformulated form, $-\tilde{v}_t^u C_t^u = \dot{L}_t + \dot{C}_t^u C_t^{u-1}(1-L_t)$. Note that in steady state, the change in employment is zero and substitute for the rate of growth to yield that

$$-\dot{\tilde{v}}_t^u C_t^u = \gamma(1-L_t) . \tag{6.43'}$$

This analysis focuses on steady state variables, hence on variables that do not grow in per capita terms. Unlike the "Walrasian Economy," where employment was identical to one, per capita variables and variables in levels are not identical in the effective case. In order to calculate steady state employment, we will reformulate the variables of the necessary equations accordingly. We will denote per capita variables by small letters.[30]

We multiply equation (6.31) from the unemployed's system by consumption, divide it by L_t, use the new notation, and reformulate to see that

$$L_t = \frac{1}{\tilde{v}_t^u c_t^u + 1} . \tag{6.64}$$

We then express equation (6.63) in per capita terms,[31]

$$\tilde{v}_t^u \frac{c_t}{k_t}\alpha = -\dot{\tilde{v}}_t^u + \theta\tilde{v}_t^u - \tilde{v}_t^u \alpha\gamma , \tag{6.65}$$

and note that equation (6.43') in per capita terms is given by

$$-\dot{\tilde{v}}_t^u = \frac{\gamma}{c_t^u}\frac{1-L_t}{L_t} . \tag{6.66}$$

Next, substitute equation (6.66) into equation (6.65) and reformulate to see that[32]

$$\tilde{v}_t^u = \frac{\gamma}{c_t^u}\frac{1-L_t}{L_t}\frac{1}{\dfrac{c_t}{k_t}\alpha-\theta} . \tag{6.67}$$

Finally, we substitute equation (6.67) into equation (6.64) and rearrange to yield that $L_t = 1$.[33] Hence, in spite of the implementation of the minimum wage, in steady state the economy achieves full-employment. We will discuss the reasons for this outcome in the next chapter.

6.4 DISCUSSION OF THE RESULTS

As previously mentioned, the rates of growth of the reference model ("The Walrasian Economy") and of the effective system are identical, and the effective system also creates steady state full-employment. This result seems to be interesting in three ways:

- First, upon examining employment it stands in contrast to the previously-presented static models.
- Second, it stands in contrast to the implications of the model by Cahuc and Michel (1996), presented in chapter two. In contrast to this model, the introduction of the minimum wage state did not internalize the external effect of the economy which would increase the steady rate of growth. Hence the outcome of both the notional and the effective system stays below the optimal one.
- Third, given that there exists unemployment due to the existence of the minimum wage, at first sight we would expect a lower rate of steady state growth.

To point out this last argument, we repeat the skills accumulation equation (6.41) and combine it with equation (6.42), which states that the rate of growth of the system is driven by skills accumulation, and reformulate to see that

$$\gamma = \frac{\dot{S}_t^e}{S_t^e}\frac{1-\alpha+\psi}{1-\alpha} = \beta\left(1-\frac{H_t^e}{L_t}-\frac{F_t^e}{L_t}\right)\frac{1-\alpha+\psi}{1-\alpha}.$$

As to be seen, a ceteris paribus decrease in employment should decrease the steady state rate of growth. However, this argument is comparatively static in nature and ignores possible changes of the optimal working and leisure time decisions of the still-employed households.

The following section discusses reasons for steady state full-employment in the effective case, and the underlying economic causalities that lead to the identical rate of growth. We will see that the existence of steady state full-employment is founded on the dynamic setting of the model, which allows for intertemporal adjustments to react properly to the minimum wage. More specifically, employed households recognize that their income frontier becomes less restricted. Hence they maximize utility with respect to this additional information. Every positive change in educational time, or a decrease in the sum of working and leisure time, which could be the result of this new maximization behavior, will lead to a positive influence on the rate of growth. That induces reduced unemployment. In the following we discuss the underlying processes in more detail.

To capture the effect of the minimum wage on aggregate skills accumulation we first analyze the effects that lead to an increase of the individual's skill accumulation for situations outside the steady state. Second, we show how these effects will lead to steady state full-employment and finally we discuss why the steady state rates of growth are identical in the notional and effective cases. For all three cases we will not point out the transitional dynamics of the system and only present causality arguments.

Until now, we analyzed the steady state behavior of the system. For an easier interpretation of the situation *outside the steady state* we will repeat the first three original FOCs for the employed individual household, which follow from equation (6.34):

$$\frac{\partial \tilde{h}_e}{\partial C_{e,t}} = \frac{1}{C_{e,t}} - \tilde{\upsilon}_{e,t} = 0,$$

$$\frac{\partial \tilde{h}_e}{\partial F_{e,t}} = \frac{\mu}{F_{e,t}} - \tilde{\lambda}_{e,t}\beta\, S_{e,t} = 0\,,$$

$$\frac{\partial \tilde{h}_e}{\partial H_{e,t}} = \tilde{\upsilon}_{e,t}\overline{w}_t S_{e,t} - \tilde{\lambda}_{e,t}\beta\, S_{e,t} = 0\,.$$

We denote marginal utility from consumption by $MU^C_{e,t}$ and marginal utility from leisure by $MU^F_{e,t}$ and substitute to yield that $MU^C_{e,t} = \tilde{\upsilon}_{e,t}$ and $MU^F_{e,t} = \tilde{\lambda}_{e,t}\beta\, S_{e,t}$. We substitute for $\tilde{\lambda}_{e,t}\beta\, S_{e,t}$ from the third FOC into the expression for marginal utility from leisure time to obtain that $MU^F_{e,t} = \tilde{\upsilon}_{e,t}\overline{w}_t S_{e,t}$, and divide this expression by the equation for marginal utility from consumption to get

$$\frac{MU^F_{e,t}}{MU^C_{e,t}} = \overline{w}_t S_{e,t}\,. \tag{6.68}$$

Hence, the ratio between marginal utility of leisure time and marginal utility of consumption for every point in time is given by the product of the minimum wage and the level of skills. The level of skills at point t is fully determined by forgone skills accumulation. Therefore, it will not be influenced by exogenous changes in the minimum wage at this point in time. The implementation of the minimum wage increases the relationship between the marginal utilities of leisure and consumption, which induces that for the household leisure time relative to consumption becomes less important in terms of opportunity costs.[34] The change in this relationship, however, provides no clear answer for the effect on educational time. We only know that $E_{e,t} = 1 - F_{e,t} - H_{e,t}$, and that marginal utility from leisure time relative to marginal utility from consumption decreases. This could on the one hand lead to an increase in working time in this period in order to immediately increase consumption, or it could on the other hand increase working time in order to increase future income and thus future consumption. Hence, the effect of minimum wages on educational time remains unclear at the moment.

Furthermore, the analysis of the effect of the minimum wage on the ratio of the two shadow prices helps to answer this question. From the third FOC it follows that

$$\frac{\tilde{\lambda}_{e,t}}{\tilde{\upsilon}_{e,t}} = \frac{\overline{w}_t}{\beta}\,. \tag{6.69}$$

Hence the ratio between the shadow prices for skills and capital accumulation depends on the minimum wage, and it is therefore higher than in the notional system. Recall that the shadow prices describe the marginal value of an increment in skills and capital accumulation, respectively, at time t. Hence the value of additional skills, $\tilde{\lambda}_{e,t}$, relative to the value of additional savings, $\tilde{\upsilon}_{e,t}$, will increase. The only possibility to react on this situation is to give up working time in order to increase educational time.

To summarize, leisure and working time will decrease, which must lead to increased educational time. According to the skills accumulation equation, this must foster the skills accumulation of the still employed households, which induces an increase of the growth rate for all points in time outside of the steady state. We call this effect the "skills effect."

Recall the production technology, hence $Y_{j,t} = K_{j,t}^{\alpha}(s_{j,t}h_{j,t}L_{j,t})^{1-\alpha}s_t^{\psi}$. It exhibits constant returns to scale on the firm's level and increasing returns to scale for the economy. Hence a higher rate of growth creates a permanently higher demand for all factors of production, and therefore also for "physical labor." The rate of growth of working time in steady state is zero and labor is the only remaining factor of human capital that is limited. Hence in steady state the additional use of labor must stop at full-employment, and the "skills effect" stops.

6.5   CONCLUSIONS

We implemented a minimum wage in a Lucas type model of endogenous growth where, unlike the original model, the household must decide for optimal use of labor, leisure and educational time, and where the implementation of minimum wage is analyzed in a "non-market-clearing" general equilibrium model. We implemented a minimum wage for every point in time. As a result, the effective system's rate of growth is identical to that of the notional one. Furthermore, even if a minimum wage exists, in steady state the system achieves full-employment. Hence the minimum wage has no impact on steady state employment and steady state growth.

Reasons for this can be found in the skills accumulation equation, the changed economic behavior of the employed households and in the production technology. Neglecting the effects of minimum wages, the outcome of the system is qualitatively identical to that of the reference model of Lucas (1988). This result appears interesting for three reasons:

- First, looking at employment, it stands in contrast to the static models presented earlier in chapter four.
- Second, it stands in contrast to the implications of the model by Cahuc and Michel (1996) presented in chapter two. The minimum wage, in particular, does not internalize parts of the externality which would lead to increased skills accumulation and economic growth.
- Third, given that outside the steady state there exists unemployment caused by the implementation of the minimum wage, at first sight we would expect a lower rate of steady state growth.

Based on these long term steady state results, the long run effects of minimum wages appear to have been overrated in political discussion. The minimum wage simply has no long term negative effect on the rate of growth and the level of employment. However, only a steady state analysis has been provided in this chapter. In the short run unemployment still exists.

7
Minimum Wages, Unemployment and Growth

7.1 THE BASIC MODEL SETUP AND THE WALRASIAN ECONOMY

7.1.1 The Basic Model Setup

In chapter six, the economy exhibits two external effects: one in the production of skills, the other in the production of goods. Both lead to an inefficient outcome of the market solution. This gives rise to the possibility that economic measures like the implementation of minimum wages may increase economic growth. However, this effect did not occur in our specific model setting, hence the minimum wage did not change steady state employment and growth.

The economic intuition behind the model presented in this chapter is quite different. First, we omit the assumption of external effects in production. Second, we also emphasize the importance of human capital, but focus on the underlying ideas of the static model presented in chapter five. The outcome of that model depends solely on the existence of a fear of becoming unemployed. In particular, we stated that employed households acting in an economy with involuntary unemployment think that more education and the related increase in skills reduces the probability of becoming unemployed. This chapter builds upon the same intuition, but in a dynamic model setting similar to that of chapter six. Therefore all basic assumptions – including the macroeconomic relations presented in chapter six – are still valid if not otherwise mentioned.

Furthermore, the reaction of employed households on unemployment enters into the "production function of skills" which is represented by

$$\dot{S}_{i,t} = \phi_t S_{i,t} E_{i,t}, \quad \text{where } \phi_t = \frac{\beta}{L_t^\varphi}, \quad \text{and } \beta > 0, \ \varphi > 0. \tag{7.1}$$

Hence the household's creation of new skills is based on a productivity function ϕ_t, and educational time. As in chapter five, normalizing the number of households to one helps to avoid an expression for the unemployment rate in the productivity function. Full-employment reduces the function to $\phi_t = \beta$, and any existence of unemployment, hence any reduction in employment, must increase it.[1] The interpretation of β is identical to that presented in chapter five and will not be discussed further. The parameter φ simply acts as a measure of the fear of becoming dismissed.

Otherwise, we hold the same assumptions as in chapter six to be true, so the household's problem can be presented directly without further discussion. We obtain that:

$$\max_{i} U_i = \int_{\tau}^{\infty} (\ln C_{i,t} + \mu \ln F_{i,t})e^{-\theta(t-\tau)}\,dt$$

s.t.:

$$
\begin{cases}
C1: E_{i,t} + H_{i,t} + F_{i,t} = 1 \\[4pt]
C2: \dot{S}_{i,t} = \beta L_t^{-\varphi} S_{i,t} E_{i,t} \\[4pt]
C3: \dot{K}_{i,t} = w_t H_{i,t} S_{i,t} + r_t K_{i,t} - C_{i,t} \\[10pt]
C4: F_i = 1 \\[4pt]
C5: \dot{S}_{i,t} = H_{i,t} = 0 \\[4pt]
C6: \dot{K}_{i,t} = r_t K_{i,t} - C_{i,t} \\[10pt]
C7: K_{i,\tau} = \overline{K}_\tau > 0 \\[4pt]
C8: S_{i,\tau} = \overline{S}_\tau > 0 \\[4pt]
C9: \text{Transversality conditions}
\end{cases}
\quad
\begin{aligned}
& \left.\vphantom{\begin{matrix}1\\1\\1\end{matrix}}\right\} \text{notional,} \\
& \quad\; \text{or effective} \\
& \quad\; \text{case if employed,} \\[6pt]
& \left.\vphantom{\begin{matrix}1\\1\\1\end{matrix}}\right\} \text{effective case,} \\
& \quad\; \text{if unemployed,} \\[10pt]
& \left.\vphantom{\begin{matrix}1\\1\\1\end{matrix}}\right\} \text{in every case.}
\end{aligned}
$$

It can be seen that the only difference to the model presented in chapter six arises from the changed condition C2.

Firms produce with identical cost constraints and technology as in chapter six, but without the existence of external effects. Hence the firm's problem, which was given by equation (6.2), reduces to

$$\max_{j} \pi_j = K_{j,t}^{\alpha}(s_{j,t}h_{j,t}L_{j,t})^{1-\alpha} - r_t K_{j,t} - w_t s_{j,t} h_{j,t} L_{j,t}. \tag{7.2}$$

In the effective case, also identically to chapter six, a constant wage premium on the equilibrium wage determines the minimum wage. Finally, all equations used for the aggregation of the variables are completely identical to those in chapter six and we use the same notation. Therefore, in many cases we only refer to the results and methodology used in chapter six in order to keep the presentation as short as possible.

7.1.2 The Reference Model ("The Walrasian Economy")

The solution of the Walrasian system reduces to the outcome of chapter six, which was given by equation (6.28), without the external effect in production of goods. Assuming that $1+\mu(1-\alpha)-\beta/\theta<0$, as was discussed in chapter six, the rate of growth turns out as[2]

$$\left\{ \gamma_{1,2} = \frac{(\beta-\theta)-\theta(\mu+1)}{2} \pm \right.$$

$$\left. \pm \frac{\left[(\theta(\mu+1)-(\beta-\theta))^2 - 4\theta\left(\frac{\mu\theta}{1-\alpha}-(\beta-\theta)\right)\right]^{\frac{1}{2}}}{2} \right. \tag{7.3}$$

Identically to chapter six, we could show that this system creates qualitatively identical results to those in the original model by Lucas (1988). In particular, the rate of growth is driven by skills accumulation and is determined by the difference between the interest rate and the intertemporal rate of time preference. However, we do not point out these arguments in detail here and only refer to the argumentation of chapter six which can analogously be adapted for this special case.

7.2   THE EFFECT OF MINIMUM WAGES: ("THE EFFECTIVE CASE")

7.2.1   Individual Maximization Decisions and Aggregation

Remember that the index "u" denotes variables for unemployed households and the index "e" denotes variables for employed households. Subscripts denote individual variables, whereas superscripts stand for the aggregated ones. The firm's problem leads to[3]

$$\frac{\partial \pi_{j,t}}{\partial s^e_{j,t}} = \frac{\partial \pi_{j,t}}{\partial h^e_{j,t}} = \frac{\partial \pi_{j,t}}{\partial L_{j,t}} = (1-\alpha)K^{\alpha}_{j,t} s^{e^{-\alpha}}_{j,t} h^{e^{-\alpha}}_{j,t} L^{-\alpha}_{j,t} = \overline{w},$$

$$\frac{\partial \pi_{j,t}}{\partial K_{j,t}} = \alpha K^{\alpha-1}_{j,t} s^{e^{1-\alpha}}_{j,t} h^{e^{1-\alpha}}_{j,t} L^{1-\alpha}_{j,t} = r_t.$$

We rearrange, normalize the number of firms to one, split up average skills and average working time after maximization, and aggregate to obtain two identical FOCs for the elements of human capital and one for physical capital, which turn out as:

$$(1-\alpha)K^{\alpha}_t S^{e^{-\alpha}}_t H^{e^{-\alpha}}_t L^{\alpha}_t = \overline{w}_t, \tag{7.4}$$

$$\alpha K^{\alpha-1}_t S^{e^{1-\alpha}}_t H^{e^{1-\alpha}}_t L^{\alpha-1}_t = r_t. \tag{7.5}$$

The individual FOCs of *unemployed* households are completely identical to the FOCs for unemployed households in chapter six. Hence we will not repeat them. The way to express the FOCs in aggregated variables is similar to that used for the derivation of equations (6.31), (6.32) and (6.33) in chapter six. However, substitution by the aggregated variables and the interest rate from equation (7.5) into the FOCs of the individuals, and reformulation yields different results because in this model no external effect in production exists. We yield that:

$$\frac{1-L_t}{C^u_t} = \widetilde{\upsilon}^u_t, \tag{7.6}$$

$$\widetilde{\upsilon}^u_t \alpha K^{\alpha-1}_t H^{e^{1-\alpha}}_t S^{e^{1-\alpha}}_t L^{\alpha-1}_t = -\dot{\widetilde{\upsilon}}^u_t + \theta\widetilde{\upsilon}^u_t, \tag{7.7}$$

$$\alpha K^{\alpha-1}_t H^{e^{1-\alpha}}_t S^{e^{1-\alpha}}_t L^{\alpha-1}_t - \frac{C^u_t}{K^u_t} = \frac{\dot{K}^u_t}{K^u_t}. \tag{7.8}$$

Every *employed* household supplies exactly one unit of "physical labor," hence the Hamiltonian for the single employed household is given by

$$\begin{cases} \widetilde{\hbar}_i(.) = (\ln C_{e,t} + \mu \ln F_{e,t}) + \\ \qquad + \widetilde{\upsilon}_{e,t}(\overline{w}_t H_{e,t} S_{e,t} + r_t K_{e,t} - C_{e,t}) + \\ \qquad + \widetilde{\lambda}_{e,t}\,\beta\,S_{e,t} L^{-\varphi}_t (1 - H_{e,t} - F_{e,t}). \end{cases} \tag{7.9}$$

The maximization problem results in seven first order conditions (for $C_{i,t}$, $F_{e,t}$, $S_{e,t}$, $H_{e,t}$, $K_{e,t}$, $\tilde{\lambda}_{e,t}$, and $\tilde{\upsilon}_{e,t}$):

$$\frac{\partial \tilde{h}_e}{\partial C_{e,t}} = \frac{1}{C_{e,t}} - \tilde{\upsilon}_{e,t} = 0 ,$$

$$\frac{\partial \tilde{h}_e}{\partial F_{e,t}} = \frac{\mu}{F_{e,t}} - \tilde{\lambda}_{e,t} S_{e,t} \frac{\beta}{L_t^\varphi} = 0 ,$$

$$\frac{\partial \tilde{h}_e}{\partial H_{e,t}} = \tilde{\upsilon}_{e,t} \overline{w}_t S_{e,t} - \tilde{\lambda}_{e,t} S_{e,t} \frac{\beta}{L_t^\varphi} = 0 ,$$

$$\frac{\partial \tilde{h}_e}{\partial K_{e,t}} = \tilde{\upsilon}_{e,t} r_t = -\dot{\tilde{\upsilon}}_{e,t} + \theta\, \tilde{\upsilon}_{e,t} ,$$

$$\frac{\partial \tilde{h}_e}{\partial S_{e,t}} = \tilde{\upsilon}_{e,t}\, \overline{w}_t H_{e,t} + \tilde{\lambda}_{e,t} \frac{\beta}{L_t^\varphi} (1 - H_{e,t} - F_{e,t}) = -\dot{\tilde{\lambda}}_{e,t} + \theta\, \tilde{\lambda}_{e,t} ,$$

$$\frac{\partial \tilde{h}_e}{\partial \tilde{\upsilon}_{e,t}} = \overline{w}_t H_{e,t} S_{e,t} + r_t K_{e,t} - C_{e,t} = \dot{K}_{e,t} ,$$

$$\frac{\partial \tilde{h}_e}{\partial \tilde{\lambda}_{e,t}} = S_{e,t} \frac{\beta}{L_t^\varphi} (1 - H_{e,t} - F_{e,t}) = \dot{S}_{e,t} .$$

As in chapter six, we substitute for the aggregated variables and for the factor prices, which are given by equations (7.7) and (7.8), and reformulate to obtain that:

$$\frac{L_t}{C_t^e} = \tilde{\upsilon}_t^e , \tag{7.10}$$

$$\frac{\mu\, L_t}{F_t^e} = \tilde{\lambda}_t^e \frac{\beta}{L_t^\varphi} \frac{S_t^e}{L_t} , \tag{7.11}$$

$$\tilde{\upsilon}_t^e (1-\alpha) K_t^\alpha S_t^{e^{1-\alpha}} H_t^{e^{-\alpha}} L_t^{\alpha-1} = \tilde{\lambda}_t^e \frac{\beta}{L_t^\varphi} \frac{S_t^e}{L_t} , \tag{7.12}$$

$$\tilde{\upsilon}_t^e \alpha K_t^{\alpha-1} S_t^{e^{1-\alpha}} H_t^{e^{1-\alpha}} L_t^{\alpha-1} = -\dot{\tilde{\upsilon}}_t^e + \theta \tilde{\upsilon}_t^e , \tag{7.13}$$

$$\begin{cases} \tilde{\upsilon}_t^e (1-\alpha) K_t^\alpha S_t^{e^{-\alpha}} H_t^{e^{1-\alpha}} L_t^{\alpha-1} + \tilde{\lambda}_t^e \frac{\beta}{L_t^\varphi} \left(1 - \frac{H_t^e}{L_t} - \frac{F_t^e}{L_t} \right) = \\[2ex] = -\dot{\tilde{\lambda}}_t^e + \theta \tilde{\lambda}_t^e , \end{cases} \tag{7.14}$$

$$\begin{cases} (1-\alpha)K_t^{\alpha}S_t^{e\,1-\alpha}H_t^{e\,1-\alpha}L_t^{\alpha-1}+\alpha K_t^{\alpha-1}S_t^{e\,1-\alpha}H_t^{e\,1-\alpha}L_t^{\alpha-1}K_t^e- \\[2ex] -C_t^e = K_t^e\,\dfrac{\dot{K}_t^e}{K_t^e}, \end{cases} \tag{7.15}$$

$$\frac{\beta}{L_t^{\varphi}}\left(1-\frac{H_t^e}{L_t}-\frac{F_t^e}{L_t}\right)=\frac{\dot{S}_t^e}{S_t^e}. \tag{7.16}$$

In addition to the equations for aggregation of output and capital, we face a system of 12 equations and 13 variables, namely ten structural variables in levels, L_t, S_t, C_t, C_t^e, C_t^u, H_t, F_t^e, K_t, K_t^e, and K_t^u, and three Lagrange multipliers in levels, namely $\tilde{v}_{e,t}$, $\tilde{v}_{u,t}$, and $\tilde{\lambda}_{e,t}$. Hence, as in chapter six, we must add the demand function for human capital in order to calculate steady state employment. Furthermore, we see that the number of variables in movement corresponds to the number of intertemporal equations. Similar to chapter six, the complexity of the system requires some technical work to calculate the steady state rate of growth and the steady state level of unemployment. In cases where the procedure differs from chapter six, we will present the whole derivation, but we will only refer to the method of solution used in chapter six if it is identical.

7.2.2 Steady State

We will solve the system in three distinct steps. First, as in chapter six, we obtain all possible information from the system of the unemployed households. Second, we calculate the relationships between the rates of growth of all relevant variables. Based on this information, we are able to calculate the steady state rate of growth for the whole system as a function of parameters and employment, and the level of steady state employment in the third step.

The general way of solution for the system of *unemployed household* is formally completely identical to that of chapter six.[4] We therefore only present the results, which turn out to be:

$$\frac{\dot{K}_t}{K_t}=\frac{\dot{S}_t^e}{S_t^e}\equiv\gamma, \tag{7.17}$$

$$\frac{\dot{L}_tC_t^u+\dot{C}_t^u(1-L_t)}{C_t^{u\,2}}=-\dot{\tilde{v}}_t^u, \tag{7.18}$$

$$\gamma^u = \alpha K_t^{\alpha-1} H_t^{e^{1-\alpha}} S_t^{e^{1-\alpha}} L_t^{\alpha-1} - \theta,$$ (7.19)

$$\frac{\dot{\tilde{\upsilon}}_t^u}{\tilde{\upsilon}_t^u} = -\gamma^u,$$ (7.20)

$$\frac{\dot{C}_t^u}{C_t^u} = \frac{\dot{K}_t^u}{K_t^u} = \gamma^u,$$ (7.21)

$$\frac{C_t^u}{K_t^u} = \theta.$$ (7.22)

In contrast to equation (6.42) from chapter six, we obtain that physical capital and skills grow at exactly the same rate reflecting that no external effect in production exists. From equation (7.5) we know that $\alpha K_t^{\alpha-1} H_t^{e^{1-\alpha}} S_t^{e^{1-\alpha}} L_t^{\alpha-1} = r$, hence by substitution into equation (7.19) and similar to the preceding chapter, we yield that the rate of growth of the unemployed's system is determined by the difference of the rate of growth of the economy and the intertemporal rate of time preference.

In the *second step* in solving the model, we calculate the relation between the different rates of growth of the relevant variables. Equation (7.13) from the system of *employed households* describes the Euler equation or Keynes-Ramsey rule. We differentiate equation (7.10) with respect to time to get

$$\dot{\tilde{\upsilon}}_t^e = \frac{\dot{L}_t C_t^e - \dot{C}_t^e L_t}{C_t^{e^2}},$$ (7.23)

and equal with the Euler Equation to yield that

$$\tilde{\upsilon}_t^e \alpha K_t^{\alpha-1} S_t^{e^{1-\alpha}} H_t^{e^{1-\alpha}} L_t^{\alpha-1} = -\frac{\dot{L}_t C_t^e - \dot{C}_t^e L_t}{C_t^{e^2}} + \theta \tilde{\upsilon}_t^e.$$

Next, we substitute for the Lagrange multiplier from equation (7.10), rearrange, and note that in steady state the rate of growth of employment is zero to obtain that[5]

$$\frac{\dot{C}_t^e}{C_t^e} \equiv \gamma^e = \alpha K_t^{\alpha-1} S_t^{e^{1-\alpha}} H_t^{e^{1-\alpha}} L_t^{\alpha-1} - \theta.$$ (7.24)

By substituting the equilibrium interest rate we also – not surprisingly – find for the employed household's system that the rate of growth is identical to the difference of the interest rate and the intertemporal rate of time preference.

Using equations (7.24) and (7.21) we obtain that the growth rates of consumption for unemployed and employed households are identical and that this rate of growth is equal to the rate of growth of the capital stock of employed households. Furthermore, we know that the change in aggregate consumption must be identical to the change of consumption of the two subsystems, or $\dot{C}_{t_1} = \dot{C}_t^e + \dot{C}_t^u$. Reformulate this relationship to yield that $\dot{C}_t C_t^{-1} C_t = \dot{C}_t^e C_t^{e^{-1}} C_t^e + \dot{C}_t^u C_t^{u^{-1}} C_t^u$, and substitute by the identical rates of growth to obtain that $\dot{C}_t C_t^{-1} C_t = \gamma^e (C_t^e + C_t^u)$. Finally, remember that aggregate consumption is simply defined as the sum of consumption of employed and unemployed households to show that the rates of growth of consumption of the unemployed and the employed households and of the whole economy are identical, or $\dot{C}_t / C_t = \gamma^e = \gamma^u$.

In order to calculate the ratio of the steady state rates of growth of aggregate consumption and the aggregate capital stock, we only refer to the analysis provided in chapter six (calculation of equation 6.52). We obtain the identical result, namely that $\dot{K}_t / K_t = \dot{C}_t / C_t$. Based on similar considerations as presented above, we yield that the growth rates of the capital stock of the unemployed and the employed households and of the whole economy are identical, and that this rate of growth is identical to that of consumption.

In order to calculate the relationship between the shadow prices of unemployed households we reformulate equation (7.11), and remember from equation (7.1) that $\phi_t = \beta L_t^\varphi$, to obtain that

$$\tilde{\lambda}_t^e = \frac{\mu}{\phi_t} \frac{L_t^2}{F_t^e S_t^e} .$$

In steady state the change in working time must be zero. Taking the derivative of equation (7.11) with respect to time yields the steady state change in time of $\tilde{\lambda}_t^e$. After some reformulations it simplifies to[6]

$$\dot{\tilde{\lambda}}_t^e = -\frac{\mu}{\phi_t} \frac{\dot{S}_t^e}{S_t^e} \frac{L_t^2}{F_t^e S_t^e} .$$

Rearrange equation (7.14) and substitute for $\dot{\tilde{\lambda}}_t^e$ to obtain that

$$
\begin{cases}
\tilde{\upsilon}_t^e (1-\alpha) K_t^\alpha S_t^{e^{-\alpha}} H_t^{e^{1-\alpha}} L_t^{\alpha-1} = \\
\\
= \dfrac{\mu}{\phi_t} \dfrac{\dot{S}_t^e}{S_t^e} \dfrac{L_t^2}{F_t^e S_t^e} - \tilde{\lambda}_t^e \phi_t \left(1 - \dfrac{H_t^e}{L_t} - \dfrac{F_t^e}{L_t} \right) + \theta \tilde{\lambda}_t^e
\end{cases}
$$

Furthermore, we substitute for the growth rate of skills from equations (7.17) and (7.16), rearrange,

$$
\frac{\tilde{\upsilon}_t^e}{\tilde{\lambda}_t^e} (1-\alpha) K_t^\alpha S_t^{e^{-\alpha}} H_t^{e^{1-\alpha}} L_t^{\alpha-1} = \gamma \frac{\mu}{\phi_t \tilde{\lambda}_t^e} \frac{L_t^2}{F_t^e S_t^e} - \gamma + \theta ,
$$

substitute into the second term for $\phi_t \tilde{\lambda}_t^e S_t^e F_t^e$ from equation (7.11), and reformulate to reduce the expression to

$$
\frac{\tilde{\upsilon}_t^e}{\tilde{\lambda}_t^e} K_t^\alpha S_t^{e^{-\alpha}} H_t^{e^{1-\alpha}} L_t^{\alpha-1} = \frac{\theta}{1-\alpha} .
$$

Taking logarithms and differences and remembering that the rate of growth of working time in steady state is zero yields that the difference of the rate of growth of the two shadow prices may be described by a function of the rate of growth of skills and of capital, or

$$
\frac{\dot{\tilde{\upsilon}}_t^e}{\tilde{\upsilon}_t^e} - \frac{\dot{\tilde{\lambda}}_t^e}{\tilde{\lambda}_t^e} = \alpha \left(\frac{\dot{S}_t^e}{S_t^e} - \frac{\dot{K}_t}{K_t} \right) .
$$

We remember that the rate of growth of skills and of capital is identical to directly obtain that the rates of growth of the two shadow prices must also be identical. Hence $\dot{\tilde{\upsilon}}_t^e / \tilde{\upsilon}_t^e = \dot{\tilde{\lambda}}_t^e / \tilde{\lambda}_t^e$.

Next, from equation (7.13) we get an expression for the rate of growth of $\tilde{\upsilon}_t^e$ which is given by $\dot{\tilde{\upsilon}}_t^e / \tilde{\upsilon}_t^e = \theta - \alpha K_t^{\alpha-1} S_t^{e^{1-\alpha}} H_t^{e^{1-\alpha}} L_t^{\alpha-1}$. Furthermore, from equation (7.24) we know that the rate of growth is given by $\gamma = a K_t^{\alpha-1} S_t^{e^{1-\alpha}} H_t^{e^{1-\alpha}} L_t^{\alpha-1} - \theta$. Substitute to obtain that the rate of growth of $\tilde{\upsilon}_t^e$ is identical to that of the economy, or

$$
\frac{\dot{\tilde{\upsilon}}_t^e}{\tilde{\upsilon}_t^e} = -\gamma . \tag{7.25}
$$

In summary, the relationships between the relevant rates of growth of the system turn out as

$$\begin{cases} \gamma = \dfrac{\dot{C_t}}{C_t} = \dfrac{\dot{C_t^e}}{C_t^e} = \dfrac{\dot{C_t^u}}{C_t^u} = \dfrac{\dot{K_t}}{K_t} = \dfrac{\dot{K_t^e}}{K_t^e} = \dfrac{\dot{K_t^u}}{K_t^u} = \dfrac{\dot{S_t^e}}{S_t^e} = \\[2em] \qquad = -\dfrac{\dot{\tilde{v}_t^e}}{\tilde{v}_t^e} = -\dfrac{\dot{\tilde{v}_t^u}}{\tilde{v}_t^u} = -\dfrac{\dot{\tilde{\lambda}_t^e}}{\tilde{\lambda}_t^e}. \end{cases}$$

Hence all variables in levels grow with exactly identical rate γ. This helps to ignore the different indications of the rates of growth for the remaining analysis.

In the following we focus on the *third step* in solving the system, namely the representation of the rate of growth in terms of parameters and employment and the analysis of steady state employment. We use equation (7.14) to calculate for the rate of growth and substitute for the rate of growth of skills and the shadow price to obtain that

$$\frac{\tilde{v}_t^e}{\tilde{\lambda}_t^e}(1-\alpha)K_t^\alpha S_t^{e^{-\alpha}} H_t^{e^{1-a}} L_t^{\alpha-1} = \theta.$$

Then we use equation (7.12) to express the ratio of the two shadow prices,

$$\frac{\tilde{v}_t^e}{\tilde{\lambda}_t^e} = \frac{\beta}{(1-\alpha)K_t^\alpha S_t^{e^{-\alpha}} H_t^{e^{-\alpha}} L_t^{\alpha-\varphi}},$$

substitute into the equation above and rearrange in order to express working time as a function of employment. We yield that

$$H_t^e = \frac{\theta}{\beta} L_t^{1+\varphi}.$$

For an easier presentation we remember that $\phi_t = \beta L_t^{-\varphi}$. Then we reformulate the aggregated time constraint, which is given by $F_t^e = L_t - H_t^e - E_t^e$, substitute for H_t^e, for E_t^e from equation (7.16), and for F_t^e from equation (7.11) to get that

$$\frac{\mu L_t^2}{\tilde{\lambda}_t^e \phi_t S_t^e} = L_t - \frac{\theta\,L_t}{\phi_t} - \gamma\frac{L_t}{\phi_t}.$$

Reformulate, and substitute for $\tilde{\lambda}_t^e S_t^e L_t^{-1}$ from equation (7.12) to obtain that

$$\gamma = \phi_t - \frac{\mu \phi_t}{\tilde{v}_t^e (1-\alpha) K_t^\alpha S_t^{e1-\alpha} H_t^{e-\alpha} L_t^\alpha} - \theta \ .$$

Next, we substitute for $\tilde{v}_t^e$ by equation (7.10) and rearrange to yield that

$$\gamma = \phi_t - \frac{\mu \phi_t H_t^e L_t^{-1}}{(1-\alpha) K_t^{\alpha-1} S_t^{e1-\alpha} H_t^{e1-\alpha} L_t^{\alpha-1}} \frac{C_t^e}{K_t} - \theta \ .$$

From equation (7.24) we know that $\alpha K_t^{\alpha-1} S_t^{e1-\alpha} H_t^{e1-\alpha} L_t^{\alpha-1}$ is identical to $\gamma + \theta$, and again remember that working time is given by $\theta_{,t} \phi_t^{-1}$. Substitute for both expressions and rearrange to see that

$$\gamma = \phi_t - \frac{\alpha \mu \theta}{(1-\alpha)(\gamma+\theta)} \frac{C_t^e}{K_t} - \theta \ . \tag{7.26}$$

Hence it is possible to calculate the rate of growth in terms of employment (which is an element of ϕ_t) and parameters if we express the ratio of consumption of employed households and the stock of physical capital, which will be done next. Note that the rate of growth of effective capital is given by γ. Divide equation (7.15) by K_t and rearrange to yield that

$$\begin{cases} (1-\alpha) K_t^{\alpha-1} S_t^{e1-\alpha} H_t^{e1-\alpha} L_t^{\alpha-1} + \alpha K_t^{\alpha-1} S_t^{e1-\alpha} H_t^{e1-\alpha} L_t^{\alpha-1} \dfrac{K_t^e}{K_t} - \\[2ex] -\dfrac{K_t^e}{K_t} \gamma = \dfrac{C_t^e}{K_t} \ . \end{cases}$$

Remember that from equation (7.24) we already know that $\alpha K_t^{\alpha-1} S_t^{e1-\alpha} H_t^{e1-\alpha} L_t^{\alpha-1}$ is identical to $\gamma + \theta$. Substitute and rearrange to get that

$$\frac{C_t^e}{K_t} = \frac{1-\alpha}{\alpha}(\gamma+\theta) + \frac{K_t^e}{K_t}\theta \ .$$

Similar to chapter six, at this point we have to anticipate the analysis that is provided later in this chapter, where we will show that in steady state the economy must also achieve full-employment. Hence in steady state, the capital stock of employed households is identical to aggregate capital.[7] This reduces the expression to

$$\frac{C_t^e}{K_t} = \frac{1-\alpha}{\alpha}(\gamma+\theta)+\theta \,. \tag{7.27}$$

In order to calculate the rate of growth, substitute for C_t^e / K_t from this equation into equation (7.26) and carry out some mathematical reformulations to obtain that[8]

$$\gamma^2 + \gamma(\theta(2+\mu)-\phi_t)+\theta\left(\frac{\mu\theta}{1-\alpha}+\theta-\phi_t\right)=0 \,.$$

We see that the discriminant of the solution is positive if $1+\mu(1-\alpha)-\phi_t / \theta < 0$. This condition is identical to that discussed in chapter six except that the level of unemployment – included in ϕ_t – enters into it. After some simple reformulations which enable an easier comparison to the notional system we yield for the rate of growth that

$$\begin{cases} \gamma_{1,2} = \dfrac{(\phi_t-\theta)-\theta(\mu+1)}{2} \pm \\[4mm] \pm \dfrac{\left(\left(\theta(\mu+1)-(\phi_t-\theta)\right)^2 - 4\theta\left(\dfrac{\mu\theta}{1-\alpha}-(\phi_t-\theta)\right)\right)^{\frac{1}{2}}}{2} \,, \end{cases} \tag{7.28}$$

$$\text{where } \phi_t = \frac{\beta}{L_t^{\varphi}} \,.$$

The system must generate at least one positive rate of growth. However, at the moment the outcome is a function of steady state employment. Moreover, we see that in the case of full-employment the rate of growth is completely identical to that of the notional system (equation 7.3).

To calculate steady state employment we use the same methodology as in chapter six. Hence we only refer to the derivations presented in the preceding chapter and to the presentation in mathematical appendix A25. In spite of the missing external effect, we yield a result identical to the one cited in chapter six. Thus, in this model there also exists steady state full-employment. Note that population was normalized by one, and therefore the steady state rate of growth simply reduces to equation (7.28) with $\phi_t = \beta$.

We do not analyze the comparative statics of the rate of growth within respect to the respective parameters because we may only refer to the results of chapter six. With similar argumentation, we can show that less willingness to substitute intertemporally decreases the rate of growth whereas it is positively influenced by the "learning efficiency" parameter. Furthermore, we can show that this model also qualitatively generates the same outcome as the original model by Lucas (1988).

7.3 CONCLUSIONS

The economic intuition behind the Lucas-type model presented in this chapter differs greatly from the one presented in chapter six. The economy does not exhibit external effects in production and we introduce a reaction of employed households to the existence of unemployment following the ideas that were presented in chapter five. Hence we assume that employed households that act in an economy where involuntary unemployment exists think that more education and increased skills generation reduces the probability of dismissals. Despite these changes we achieve steady state full-employment and an identical rate of growth in both systems, as we do in the model in chapter six.

Similar to chapter six, we repeat the skills accumulation equation and combine it with the aggregated time constraint to see that

$$\gamma = \frac{\dot{S}_t^e}{S_t^e} = \frac{\beta}{L_t^{-\varphi}}\left(1 - \frac{H_t^e}{L_t} - \frac{F_t^e}{L_t}\right).$$

In contrast to chapter six no external effect in production exits. In a simple comparative static view, we would expect two different effects of an increase in unemployment (hence of lower employment). First, it should increase the rate of growth due to the effect on aggregated educational time (the term in brackets) and, second, it should decrease the rate of growth because of the postulated existence of a fear of becoming unemployed. However, these arguments ignore possible changes in the optimal working and leisure time decisions of still-employed households.

In chapter six we argued that the minimum wage induces a "skills effect" for the still-employed households, leading to an increase in educational time and therefore an increase in skills accumulation. This induces an increase in the growth rate for all points in time outside of the steady state. We described this effect in chapter six in detail and will therefore not repeat the specific argumentation. The economic intuition of the outcome of this chapter is in many points similar to that of chapter six. Here the "skills effect" is supported by fear of unemployment. However, both effects have to reduce unemployment leading to steady state full-employment. In the steady state full-employment is achieved and no fear of becoming unemployed exists. Hence, in both models unemployment outside the steady state does not influence the steady state outcome in terms of the rate of growth and of employment.

8
Conclusions

8.1 MINIMUM WAGES?

This book focuses on the effects of minimum wages on employment and on steady state economic growth. For our point of view it is not significant whether the minimum wage has been introduced by law or is the result of wage negotiations between firms and unions that follow a "right to manage" behavior. In "right to manage" models, the union and the firm only negotiate the wage. Once the wage is fixed, firms unilaterally determine employment. Possible bargaining results are therefore restricted to combinations of wage and employment levels that conform to the standard labor demand function of the firm (i.e. points on its labor demand curve). This situation seems to describe the behavior of unions in the majority of bargaining procedures in advanced countries. The interpretation of results of "right to manage" negotiations as a minimum wage gives rise to the possibility of a generally stronger economic impact of the minimum wage, as only legal minimum wages would do.

A short overview of the stylized facts of minimum wages for select countries (chapter one) shows that we find significant differences in the minimum wage systems of OECD countries. We see that the existence of national minimum wages and wage bargaining is not contradictory, but find the tendency that legal minimum wages can more often be found in countries with a lower union density rate. The US and UK especially seem to exhibit a different wage setting system compared to the group of compared European countries. In the US and the UK, wage bargains predominantly take place at the firm level and are accompanied by legal minimum wages. By contrast, we find many European countries with no legal minimum wage at all; instead they display much-differentiated wage setting systems and an enormous impact of labor unions in terms of union power. In general, the economic impact of minimum wages should by no means be neglected. For instance, in the US the coverage rate is very low (15 percent), but in most of the other countries examined it is higher than 80 percent. In extreme cases (98 percent in Austria) we find almost total coverage leading to influences of the unions in almost all the various working conditions.

8.2 ON THEORY AND METHODOLOGY

A critical review of literature on the employment effects of minimum wages (chapter two) yields two main observations:

- First, in recent literature the predictions of the "textbook theory" have been criticized, both from an empirical and theoretical perspective. In empirical literature, the standard "textbook version" of the theory of minimum wages is contradicted by empirical studies that find no or even positive effects of minimum wages on employment. This leads to a broad discussion on the econometric methods used and – to our point of view much more importantly – on the underlying theoretical foundation. The importance of alternative theoretical models has therefore been pointed out in recent literature. Despite the fact that these models are essentially neoclassically oriented, many of them provide a theoretical foundation for "unexpected," hence positive, employment results of minimum wages. These more recent alternative approaches focus on market failures in different ways, for instance by examining market power, efficiency wages, monopsonistic competition, or search behavior. The possible "unexpected" results, thus no or even positive employment effects, crucially depend on the existence of these market failures.
- Second, we find several drawbacks in the focus and methodology of "mainstream" theoretical analysis of the effects of minimum wages. In particular, most studies are comparative static in nature and are conducted only within a partial equilibrium context. In spite of this, in political discussion it is still common practice to draw analogies for the whole economy from only partial equilibrium standard results.

In this book we focus on these criticisms. First, we think it appropriate to explicitly analyze the change of economic agents' behavior induced by the introduction of a minimum wage in a general equilibrium model. This should help to capture the possible effects on markets other than the labor market. However, the treatment of minimum wages in Walrasian general equilibrium models is analytically problematic because Walras' law must be properly considered. Second, some minimum wage effects are dynamic, so they cannot be analyzed in the static context. A dynamic analysis gives rise to the possibility of "unexpected" and up to now neglected economic effects of minimum wages. Third, we extends the focus of the analysis by additionally taking into account the effects of minimum wages on human capital as a central element of advanced economies.

Chapter three presented the methodological foundation that is necessary for the theoretical analysis performed later. We point out that it is impossible to analyze the effects of minimum wages in a simple Walrasian economy and argue that the work of Malinvaud (1985) can help to generate an appropriate micro-based framework for solving this problem. Hence, our analysis is based on "non-market-clearing general equilibrium models," although our interest lies solely in adapting the models' formal basic structure.

The central argument of the "non-market-clearing equilibrium theory" is that transactions are not always identical to supply, respectively demand. Based on short-term price rigidities, a distinction between notional (corresponding to Walrasian economics) and effective supply, respectively demand, is done. Given disequilibria on the individual markets, price adjustment mechanisms that would allow the model to adjust into Walrasian equilibrium no longer exist. As a result, economic agents make quantity adjustments, and not price adjustments. As a result of the minimum wage, households are unexpectedly and involuntarily confronted with labor market rationing. The remaining analysis continues to move in a Walrasian-oriented economy without real money effects.

With these modifications, the effect of the introduction of a minimum wage on the maximization problems of the households and the possible effects on other markets can be analyzed in the static and dynamic context. Households in particular experience differing budget constraints when employed or unemployed. Individuals who notice the rationing find out that they are on the short side of the market but have no information about how large the excess supply is in aggregate. It is now essential – and here lies the main difference to the pure Walrasian model - that these individuals subsequently attempt to adjust their utility-maximizing behavior to the given situation. This also affects their activities in other markets.

8.3 MINIMUM WAGES AND COMPARATIVE STATICS

The above considerations allow us to develop four different theoretical models for the analysis of the effects of minimum wages. We must mention that, due to formal complexity, some of the results could not be derived analytically and have only been supported with simulation results, which are based on a plausible calibration of the respective parameters. The comparative static results are as follows:

In chapter four a simple general Walrasian model with only three markets has been presented and was modified into a static "non-market-clearing" equilibrium model through the introduction of a minimum wage in order to mainly analyze output and employment effects. We obtain involuntary unemployment, lower equilibrium output, and higher prices for goods. All of these results correspond to economic intuition from partial equilibrium models, but now they have been derived endogenously and are consistently determined by the specific mechanics of the model. We see that in "the best of all worlds" – that is, in a model without market failures other than the minimum wage – we qualitatively yield the same result as with the partial equilibrium approach, even in the framework of a "non-market-clearing" equilibrium model.

Drawing on the work of Lucas (1988), chapter five expands this basic model by the existence of human capital, by endogenously educational decisions of the households and by the assumption that the average level of human capital creates a positive external effect for the production of the individual firm. Furthermore, we assume that the household's process of generating skills is positively influenced by the level of unemployment. The intuition behind this is that the fear of becoming unemployed influences the educational decisions of households. Households tend to think that a higher educational level decreases the probability of becoming unemployed. The outcome of this model seems to contrast many of the standard minimum wage arguments. Aside from the fact that the minimum wage induces unemployment, we yield quite unorthodox results. We think it is of special interest that the output increases and the price of goods declines. These results are based on the changing supply of human capital, which is forced by the implementation of the minimum wage and the implementation of market failures into our model. However, in spite of the unexpected results for output and prices, involuntary unemployment is still present in this context.

8.4   MINIMUM WAGES AND ECONOMIC GROWTH

Chapter six dynamizes the model described in chapter four in order to analyze minimum wage effects on steady state economic growth and steady state employment. Based on a Lucas (1988) model of endogenous growth with micro-based decisions on the optimal use of labor, leisure and educational time, as well as the assumption of external effects in production, we yield results that contrast with those of the partial equilibrium analysis. The steady state rate of growth is not affected by the implementation of the minimum wage and, surprisingly, in steady state the system comes back to full employment. These effects are founded on the dynamic view, which allows for intertemporal adjustment in order to react properly to the minimum wage. Reasons for this can be found in the skills accumulation equation, the changed economic behavior of the still-employed households which create more skills in relative terms, and the production technology. This long-term result stands in contrast to the partial equilibrium predictions of the traditional textbook analysis, as well as to the recent theoretical approaches that yield positive employment effects.

Chapter seven removes the assumption of external effects in production and centers the analysis on the basic idea of chapter five. Hence we develop a Lucas-type model of endogenous growth, where households think that a higher level of education decreases the probability of becoming unemployed. This model repeats the unexpected results of the model presented in chapter six. Qualitatively, the results are identical to those of chapter five. The system achieves steady state full employment, and the steady state rate of growth remains unchanged. Without unemployment, no fear of becoming unemployed exists. The reasons for these effects are similar to those of the preceding chapter, as they can be found in the reaction of still employed households to the additional income due to the minimum wage. This fosters human capital accumulation and induces higher economic growth and full employment.

8.5   DISCUSSION OF THE RESULTS

As we have shown, in recent literature the predictions of the "textbook theory" have been criticized from both an empirical and a theoretical stance. The results of this book are not univocal. They partially confirm the newer theoretical approaches, and partially confirm the qualitative results of the "traditional" textbook-model:

- The effects on unemployment are not clear. We yield a univocal reduction in employment in the two comparative static models. By contrast, in the two dynamic cases steady state employment remains unchanged at the full-employment level.
- In no case do we yield an increase of employment due to the implementation of the minimum wage. This possibility was ruled out by the existence of full-employment in every undisturbed model. Further research could implement minimum wages in the framework of "non-market-clearing equilibrium theory" in an economy with endogenously created unemployment, as for instance induced by search behavior. This would create a possibility for positive employment effects.
- The effects on equilibrium output in the two comparative static models are contradictory. In one of the comparative static models the implementation of the minimum wage decreases it, whereas in the other, which focused on the creation of skills, it increases. Given increases in output and decreases in employment, productivity must also increase. This gives rise to the possibility that effects on output are relatively strong in countries with a very strong human capital-oriented production structure. This could be a possible reason for the situation in many countries in Europe, where high productivity (measured on the basis of working hours) is accompanied by a highly capital-intensive production, and high unemployment rates. Future empirical work could additionally focus on this aspect.
- In the two dynamic cases the steady state rate of growth is not changed by the implementation of the minimum wage. Hence, in contrast to recent literature on the dynamic effects of minimum wages, which is also based on human capital accumulation and the existence of external effects, minimum wages do not internalize parts of the external effects.
- Looking at the employment effects, the results of the two comparative static and two dynamic models show the importance of different time horizons for the analysis of the effects of minimum wages. They essentially change the qualitative results.
- Finally, the results of the implementation of the minimum wage could simply be interpreted as results of the existence of any exogenous wage which is higher than the equilibrium one. Therefore the results could be reinterpreted as the results stemming from any form of classical unemployment. Reasons for this could not only be found in the legal implementation of a minimum wage or in the ex-

istence of labor unions, but also in the existence of sticky wages which are not based on the first two reasons. Other reasons for nominal wage rigidities could for instance be found in social norms, notions of fairness, or the explicit or implicit individual agreements between workers and firms.

Of course, our results strongly depend on the underlying basic assumptions and the methodology of the theoretical models used. This can easily be seen in the assumption that the labor market has to yield full-employment in the notional systems. An increase of employment due to the minimum wage is therefore impossible.

The technical properties of the Cobb-Douglas Production function and log-linear Cobb-Douglas utility function have also influenced the results. There are several reasons for using them. First, of course, they simplify analytical treatment. Second, we wanted to implement minimum wages in a Lucas-type framework. We therefore simply used a qualitatively identical production function as did Lucas (1988). Finally, one of the reasons to develop the Cobb-Douglas production function was to find a production function in accordance with the stylized fact that, in the long run, the labor's share of an economy stays constant. It is easy to show that the labor's share derived from the Cobb-Douglas function is independent of the wage and constant. The wage bill, however, is a function of the output produced. Implementing a minimum wage decreases the income of the now unemployed households, but increases the income of the still-employed. Hence, taking into account that the general effect of minimum wages on the labor's share is at first sight indetermined, we think that the assumption of a constant labor's share is a good compromise for our analytical treatment.

Using the framework of "non-market-clearing equilibrium models" also influences our results. It helps to analyze the effect of minimum wages on markets other than the labor market. It especially helps to analyze the results of the changed behavior of households that are on the one hand confronted with higher income, and on the other hand with unemployment. Moreover, it helps to model a situation where households are involuntarily and unexpectedly confronted with labor market rationing. We think that the unexpected aspect of becoming unemployed better characterizes the situation of households than does the statement of an underlying rational estimation and evaluation of the probability of becoming unemployed.

Of course, the analysis presented in this book could be deepened as well as enlarged in different directions. The transitional dynamics of the two growth models could, for example, be analyzed in detail. Another possibility could be the analysis of the effects of training on the job, instead of just analyzing educational effects. More generally, the analysis of minimum wages in other models of economic growth within the framework of "non-market-clearing equilibrium models" seems to offer productive possibilities. The effects of endogenous growth in R&D-type models seem especially interesting. Finally, at the moment the models all lack empirical verification.

Combining the results found in literature and the contributions of this book, in spite of the very different methodological and theoretical settings we were able to draw two common conclusions:

- First, from the theoretical point of view we see that, in comparison to traditional textbook theory, "unexpected" results such as a decrease in employment or no employment effect depend on the existence of market failures. These could for instance be founded in bargaining power which leads to efficient bargains, market power which leads to monopsony or monopsony-like behavior, market rigidities which lead to monopsony-like behavior, or external effects, such as the external effects in human capital accumulation. Thus, "unexpected results" are achieved if a market with existing market failures is confronted with an additional exogenous restriction by the minimum wage. Therefore, in all of these cases, positive economic effects of the minimum wage present only a second best solution, and not a first best solution.[1] However, the probability of finding undisturbed labor markets seems close to zero.

- Second, from the empirical point of view, we have to rethink the unclear and contradictory empirical results of the recent studies. Aside from methodological problems in the estimation of the employment effects of minimum wages, causes for these contradictory results could also be found in the various underlying forms of market structures, and in the different time horizons of the empirical analysis. Different forms of market structures may involve the existence of different specific forms of market failures, which would lead to completely different effects of the minimum wage. Additionally, different forms of market failures could exhibit employment effects in different directions, leading to very small over-all effects. Moreover, different time horizons could also lead to different economic effects of minimum wages. Finally, as can be seen in the overview of wage setting systems, particularly in Europe, the economic impact of minimum wages could simply be overrated in spite of very high union coverage rates. In these countries, the enormous grade of labor management in different forms often grade of labor management in different forms often makes it impossible to differentiate between the minimum wage and the equilibrium wage. Hence, the minimum wage could simply be so small that the economic impact – independently of its direction – can not be measured.

In summary, the thesis that the minimum wage always creates unemployment should be treated with caution. Contrarily, we think the specific economic situation of the relevant economic sector should be analyzed first. Specific market structures and market failures could lead to completely different causalities of the minimum wage, as could also the different time horizons of the analysis.

Mathematical Appendix

APPENDIX TO CHAPTER 4

A1 Notional Case, Calculation of the Individual's Supply Function of Hours and Demand Function of Goods (Equations 4.7 and 4.8)

The analysis is based on the normalization of the time constraint, $F_i + H_i = 1$, equation (4.5') from the main text, and the FOCs of the household's problem (4.6), which are given by

$$\frac{1}{C_i} = \lambda_i\, p\,, \quad \mu\frac{1}{F_i} = \lambda_i\, w\,, \text{ and } w - wF_i + rK_i = pC_i\,.$$

We express C_i by division of the second by the first FOC and reformulate to yield that $C_i = w\mu^{-1}p^{-1}F_i$. Then we substitute for C_i and for capital, given by equation (4.5'), into the budget constraint to calculate F_i:

$$w - wF_i + \xi\,\overline{K}_i - p\frac{1}{\mu}\frac{w}{p}F_i = 0\,, \quad \Rightarrow wF_i + \frac{1}{\mu}wF_i = w + \xi\,\overline{K}_i\,,$$

$$\Rightarrow F_i = \frac{\mu}{1+\mu}\left(1 + \frac{\xi\,\overline{K}_i}{w}\right).$$

Substitute by the time constraint to obtain the individual's notional supply function of working hours as

$$H_i^{S,n} = 1 - \frac{\mu}{1+\mu}\left(1 + \frac{\xi\,\overline{K}_i}{w}\right). \tag{4.7}$$

From the main text, we know that it has to be valid that

$$\mu(1+\mu)^{-1}(1+\xi\,\overline{K}_i/w) \le 1\,, \quad \Rightarrow \mu + \mu\frac{\xi\,\overline{K}}{w} \le 1 + \mu\,, \quad \Rightarrow \xi\,\overline{K} \le w/\mu\,.$$

We calculate F_i from the first two FOCs, which yields that $F_i = C_i\mu(p/w)$, and substitute for F_i and capital, given by equation (4.5'), into the budget constraint to obtain the notional individual's demand function for goods, $C_i^{D,n}$, as

$$w - w\frac{C_i\mu}{wp^{-1}} + \xi\,\overline{K}_i - pC_i = 0\,, \quad \Rightarrow pC_i\mu_i + pC_i = \xi\,\overline{K}_i + w\,,$$

$$\Rightarrow C_i^{D,n} = \frac{1}{1+\mu} \frac{\xi \overline{K}_i + w}{p} . \tag{4.8}$$

A2   Notional Case, Calculation of the "Conditional" Factor Demand Functions (Equations 4.9 and 4.10)

The analysis is based on equations (4.1) and (4.2) from the main text. The cost minimization problem is given by

$$\begin{cases} \min_{L_j, h_j, K_j} TC_j = \min_{L_j, h_j, K_j} (rK_j + wh_j L_j), \\[2mm] \text{s.t.}: Y_j = K_j^\alpha h_j^{1-\alpha} L_j^{1-\alpha}. \end{cases} \tag{4.3}$$

Reformulate the production function to obtain that

$$K_j = Y_j^{\frac{1}{\alpha}} (h_j L_j)^{-\frac{1-\alpha}{\alpha}}, \quad \text{and} \quad h_j L_j = Y_j^{\frac{1}{1-\alpha}} K_j^{-\frac{\alpha}{1-\alpha}} .$$

Substitution of K_i and $h_j L_j$, respectively, into the cost minimization problem reduces the problem to

$$\min_{h_j L_j} \left(rY_j^{\frac{1}{\alpha}} (h_j L_j)^{-\frac{1-\alpha}{\alpha}} + wh_j L_j \right), \quad \text{and} \quad \min_{K_j} \left(rK_j + wY_j^{\frac{1}{1-\alpha}} K_j^{-\frac{\alpha}{1-\alpha}} \right).$$

We yield that:

$$\frac{\partial(.)}{\partial L_j} = -\frac{1-\alpha}{\alpha} rY_j^{\frac{1}{\alpha}} h_j^{-\frac{1-\alpha}{\alpha}} L_j^{-\frac{1}{\alpha}} + wh_t = 0 ,$$

$$\Rightarrow \frac{\partial(.)}{\partial L_j} = \frac{1-\alpha}{\alpha} rY_j^{\frac{1}{\alpha}} (h_j L_t)^{-\frac{1}{\alpha}} = w ,$$

$$\frac{\partial(.)}{\partial h_j} = -\frac{1-\alpha}{\alpha} rY_j^{\frac{1}{\alpha}} h_j^{-\frac{1}{\alpha}} L_j^{-\frac{1-\alpha}{\alpha}} + wL_j = 0 ,$$

$$\Rightarrow \frac{\partial(.)}{\partial h_j} = \frac{1-\alpha}{\alpha} rY_j^{\frac{1}{\alpha}} (h_j L_t)^{-\frac{1}{\alpha}} = w ,$$

$$\frac{\partial(.)}{\partial K_j} = r - \frac{\alpha}{1-\alpha} wY_j^{\frac{1}{1-\alpha}} K_j^{-\frac{1}{1-\alpha}} = 0 .$$

Hence the FOC for labor and working hours are identical. Reformulate for $h_i L_i$ and K_i, and use the rental price for capital as the numéraire to calculate the "conditional" demand functions for labor and capital:

$$\frac{1-\alpha}{\alpha} Y_j^{\frac{1}{\alpha}} (h_j L_t)^{-\frac{1}{\alpha}} = w, \quad \Rightarrow (h_j L_t)^{S,n} = \left(\frac{\alpha}{1-\alpha} w\right)^{-\alpha} Y_j, \tag{4.9}$$

$$\frac{\alpha}{1-\alpha} w Y_j^{\frac{1}{1-\alpha}} K_j^{-\frac{1}{1-\alpha}} = 1, \quad \Rightarrow K_j^{S,n} = \left(\frac{\alpha}{1-\alpha} w\right)^{1-\alpha} Y_j. \tag{4.10}$$

A3 Notional Case, Calculation of the Cost Function of the Firm (Equation 4.11)

The analysis is based on equations (4.9) and (4.10), derived above, the cost-constraint from the main text (equation 4.2) and the use of the rental price of capital as the numéraire. We substitute equations (4.9) and (4.10) into equation (4.2) to obtain that:

$$TC_j = \left(\frac{\alpha}{1-\alpha} w\right)^{1-\alpha} Y_j + w\left(\frac{\alpha}{1-\alpha} w\right)^{-\alpha} Y_j,$$

$$\Rightarrow TC_j = w^{1-\alpha} Y_j (\alpha^{1-\alpha}(1-\alpha)^{\alpha-1} + \alpha^{-\alpha}(1-\alpha)^{\alpha}),$$

$$\Rightarrow TC_j = w^{1-\alpha} Y_j (1-\alpha)^{\alpha-1} \alpha^{-\alpha}(\alpha+1-\alpha),$$

$$\Rightarrow TC_j = (1-\alpha)^{\alpha-1} \alpha^{-\alpha} w^{1-\alpha} Y_j. \tag{4.11}$$

A4 Notional Case, Calculation of Equilibrium Output (Equation 4.13)

The analysis is based on equations (4.8'), (4.12'), (4.10') and (4.5'') from the main text. Equilibrium on the goods markets directly yields that

$$C^{*,n} = \frac{1}{1+\mu} \frac{\xi \overline{K} + w}{\alpha^{-\alpha}(1-\alpha)^{\alpha-1} w^{1-\alpha}}.$$

Equilibrium on the capital market leads to

$$w = \left(\frac{\xi \overline{K}}{C^{*,n}}\right)^{\frac{1}{1-\alpha}} \frac{1-\alpha}{\alpha}.$$

We substitute for w into equilibrium on the goods market and reformulate:

$$C^{*,n} = \frac{1}{1+\mu} \frac{\xi\,\overline{K} + \left(\dfrac{\xi\,\overline{K}}{C^{*,n}}\right)^{\frac{1}{1-\alpha}} \dfrac{1-\alpha}{\alpha}}{\alpha^{-\alpha}(1-\alpha)^{\alpha-1}\left(\left(\dfrac{\xi\,\overline{K}}{C^{*,n}}\right)^{\frac{1}{1-\alpha}} \dfrac{1-\alpha}{\alpha}\right)^{1-\alpha}},$$

$$\Rightarrow (1+\mu)\alpha^{-\alpha}(1-\alpha)^{\alpha-1}\left(\frac{1-\alpha}{\alpha}\right)^{1-\alpha} \xi\,\overline{K} = \xi\,\overline{K} + \left(\frac{\xi\,\overline{K}}{C^{*,n}}\right)^{\frac{1}{1-\alpha}}\left(\frac{1-\alpha}{\alpha}\right),$$

$$\Rightarrow \xi\,\overline{K}\,\frac{(1+\mu)\alpha^{-\alpha}(1-\alpha)^{\alpha-1}\left(\frac{1-\alpha}{\alpha}\right)^{1-\alpha} - 1}{\frac{1-\alpha}{\alpha}} = \frac{(\xi\,\overline{K})^{\frac{1}{1-\alpha}}}{C^{*,n\frac{1}{1-\alpha}}},$$

$$\Rightarrow C^{*,n} = (\xi\,\overline{K})^{\alpha}\,\frac{\left(\frac{1-\alpha}{\alpha}\right)^{1-\alpha}}{\left((1+\mu)\alpha^{-\alpha}(1-\alpha)^{\alpha-1}\left(\frac{1-\alpha}{\alpha}\right)^{1-\alpha} - 1\right)^{1-\alpha}},$$

$$\Rightarrow C^{*,n} = (\xi\,\overline{K})^{\alpha}\left(\frac{1-\alpha}{(1+\mu)\alpha^{-\alpha}(1-\alpha)^{\alpha-1}\alpha(1-\alpha)^{1-\alpha}\alpha^{\alpha-1} - \alpha}\right)^{1-\alpha},$$

$$\Rightarrow C^{*,n} = \varsigma\,(\xi\,\overline{K})^{\alpha}, \text{ where } \varsigma = \left(\frac{1-\alpha}{1-\alpha+\mu}\right)^{1-\alpha}, \tag{4.13}$$

A5   Notional Case, Calculation of the Equilibrium Wage (Equation 4.14)

Use equilibrium output on the goods market, derived above, and the equilibrium condition on the capital market, which is given by

$$w = \left(\frac{\xi\,\overline{K}}{C^{*,n}}\right)^{\frac{1}{1-\alpha}}\frac{1-\alpha}{\alpha}.$$

Substitution of this equation into equilibrium output yields that

$$w^{*,n} = \left(\frac{\xi \overline{K}}{\left(\frac{1-\alpha}{1-\alpha+\mu} \right)^{1-\alpha} (\xi \overline{K})^{\alpha}} \right)^{\frac{1}{1-\alpha}} \frac{1-\alpha}{\alpha},$$

$$\Rightarrow w^{*,n} = \left(\left(\frac{1-\alpha+\mu}{1-\alpha} \right)^{1-\alpha} (\xi \overline{K})^{1-\alpha} \right)^{\frac{1}{1-\alpha}} \frac{1-\alpha}{\alpha},$$

$$\Rightarrow w^{*,n} = \frac{1-\alpha+\mu}{\alpha} \xi \overline{K} . \tag{4.14}$$

A6 Notional Case, Calculation of Equilibrium Working Hours (Equation 4.14)

Use the equilibrium wage, calculated above, and equilibrium output (equation 4.11). Substitute equilibrium wage and equilibrium output into the demand function for working hours (equation 4.8') to obtain that

$$H^{*,n} = \left(\frac{\alpha}{1-\alpha} \frac{1-\alpha+\mu}{\alpha} \xi \overline{K} \right)^{-\alpha} \left(\frac{1-\alpha}{1-\alpha+\mu} \right)^{1-\alpha} (\xi \overline{K})^{\alpha} ,$$

$$\Rightarrow H^{*,n} = \frac{1-\alpha}{1-\alpha+\mu} . \tag{4.16}$$

A7 Effective Case, Calculation of Equilibrium Employment (Equation 4.23)

We use equilibrium working hours (equation 4.22) and the supply function of hours (equation 4.7'') from the main text. Substitute equilibrium working hours into the supply function of hours and reformulate to yield that

$$\Rightarrow L^{*,e} = \frac{1-\alpha}{\alpha} \frac{\xi \overline{K}}{\overline{w}} \left\{ 1 - \frac{\mu}{1+\mu} \left(\frac{\xi \overline{K}}{\overline{w}} + 1 \right) \right\}^{-1} ,$$

$$\Rightarrow L^{*,e} = \frac{1-\alpha}{\alpha} \frac{\xi \overline{K}}{\overline{w}} \frac{(1+\mu)\overline{w}}{(1+\mu)\overline{w} - \mu\xi \overline{K} - \mu\overline{w}} ,$$

$$\Rightarrow L^{*,e} = (1+\mu) \frac{1-\alpha}{\alpha} \frac{\xi \overline{K}}{\overline{w} - \mu\xi \overline{K}} . \tag{4.23}$$

APPENDIX TO CHAPTER 5

A8   Notional Case, Calculation of the Factor Demand Functions (Equations 5.9 and 5.10)

The firm's problem and the according FOCs are given by:

$$\pi_{\max} = pK_j^{\alpha}(s_j L_j)^{1-\alpha} s^{\psi} - rK_j - ws_j L_j.$$

$$\frac{\partial \pi}{\partial L_j} = p(1-\alpha)L_j^{-\alpha}K_j^{\alpha}s_j^{1-\alpha}s^{\psi} - ws_j = 0,$$

$$\frac{\partial \pi}{\partial K_j} = p\alpha K_j^{\alpha-1}s_j^{1-\alpha}L_j^{1-\alpha}s^{\psi} - r = 0,$$

$$\frac{\partial \pi}{\partial s_j} = p(1-\alpha)K_j^{\alpha}s_j^{-\alpha}L_j^{1-\alpha}s^{\psi} - wL_j = 0.$$

Division of the first by the second FOC yields the tangent condition which turns out as

$$\frac{(1-\alpha)L_j^{-\alpha}K_j^{\alpha}}{\alpha K_j^{\alpha-1}L_j^{1-\alpha}} = \frac{ws_j}{r}, \quad \Rightarrow L_j = \frac{1-\alpha}{\alpha}\frac{rK_j}{ws_j}.$$

Use the rental price for capital as the numéraire. Substitution of L_j back into the production function leads to

$$Y_j = K_j^{\alpha}\left(\frac{1-\alpha}{\alpha}\frac{K_j}{w}\right)^{1-\alpha}s^{\psi}, \quad \Rightarrow Y_j = K_j^{\alpha}\left(\frac{1-\alpha}{\alpha}\right)^{1-\alpha}\frac{K_j^{1-\alpha}s^{\psi}}{w^{1-\alpha}},$$

$$\Rightarrow K_j = w^{1-\alpha}\left(\frac{1-\alpha}{\alpha}\right)^{\alpha-1}Y_j s^{-\psi}.$$

With the exception of aggregated human capital this is equivalent to the result of the basic model, or

$$K_j^{D,n} = \left(\frac{\alpha}{1-\alpha}w\right)^{1-\alpha}Y_j s^{-\psi}. \tag{5.9}$$

Substitution of K_j back into the tangency condition yields that

$$L_j = \frac{1-\alpha}{\alpha}\frac{Y_j w^{1-\alpha}\left(\frac{1-\alpha}{\alpha}\right)^{\alpha-1}s^{-\psi}}{ws_j},$$

$$\Rightarrow (s_j L_j)^{D.n} = \left(\frac{\alpha}{1-\alpha} w\right)^{-\alpha} Y_j s^{-\psi}.$$

(5.10)

Note that division of the first by the third FOC yields a symmetric solution for s_j. Because of the production technology the demand for s_j and L_j cannot be calculated independently.

A9 Notional Case, Calculation of the Individual's "Leisure Supply Function" and the Supply Function of Skills (Equations 5.13 and 5.14)

Division of the second by the first FOC of the household's problem described in the main text (equation 5.12) shows that $(\mu / F_i)/(1/C_i) = w\beta p^{-1}$. It follows that $C_i = (1/\mu)(w\beta / p)F_i$. Substitution into the third FOC yields that

$$w\beta - wF_i\beta + K_i - \frac{1}{\mu}w\beta F_i = 0, \; \Rightarrow F_i = \frac{\mu}{1+\mu}\left(1 + \frac{K_i}{\beta w}\right).$$

Note that $E_i = 1 - F_i$. Hence it has to be fulfilled that

$$F_i = \frac{\mu}{1+\mu}\left(1 + \frac{K_i}{\beta w}\right) \leq 1.$$

Substitute by equation (4.3') to yield the "leisure supply function," $F_i^{S,n}$, or

$$F_i^{S,n} = \frac{\mu}{1+\mu}\left(1 + \frac{\xi \overline{K}_i}{\beta w}\right),$$

(5.13)

It is valid if, $1 + \dfrac{\xi \overline{K}_i}{\beta w} \leq \dfrac{1+\mu}{\mu}, \; \Rightarrow \xi \overline{K}_i \leq \dfrac{\beta}{\mu} w.$

Additionally note that $E_i = 1 - F_i$. Calculate educational time from the expression above and substitute into the production function for skills to obtain that

$$S_i = \beta\left(1 - \frac{\mu}{1+\mu}\left(1 + \frac{\xi \overline{K}_i}{\beta w}\right)\right), \; \Rightarrow S_i = \left(\frac{\beta(1+\mu) - \mu\beta}{1+\mu} - \frac{\mu}{1+\mu}\frac{\xi \overline{K}_i}{w}\right),$$

$$\Rightarrow S_i^{S,n} = \frac{1}{1+\mu}\left(\beta - \mu\frac{\xi \overline{K}_i}{w}\right).$$

(5.14)

In order to guarantee positive supply of skills it is required that

$$\beta - \mu\frac{\xi \overline{K}_i}{w} > 0, \; \Rightarrow \xi \overline{K}_i < \frac{\beta}{\mu} w,$$

which is identical to the restriction because of $E_i + F_i = 1$, mentioned above.

A10 Notional Case, Calculation of the Demand Function for Goods (Equation 5.15)

Division of the second by the first FOC of the household's problem of the main text (equation 5.12) shows that $\mu/F_i)/(1/C_i) = w\beta\, p^{-1}$. It follows that, $F_i = \mu C_i p w^{-1}\beta^{-1}$. Substitution into the third FOC yields:

$$w\beta - \frac{\mu C_i p}{w\beta} w\beta + K_i - pC_i = 0 \,, \;\Rightarrow\; pC_i = w\beta - \mu C_i p + K_i \,,$$

$$\Rightarrow C_i = \frac{1}{1+\mu}\frac{w\beta + K_i}{p}\,.$$

Additionally substitute from equation (4.8') to obtain that

$$C_t^{D,n} = \frac{1}{1+\mu}\frac{w\beta + \xi\,\overline{K}_i}{p}\,. \tag{5.15}$$

A11 Calculation of the Aggregated Demand Function for Human Capital in the Notional and Effective Case (Equations 5.16 and 5.27)

The firm's demand function for human capital is given by

$$L_j s_j = \left(\frac{\alpha}{1-\alpha}w\right)^{-\alpha} Y_j s^{-\psi}\,.$$

Note that normalization of the number of firms leads to $s = S/L$. Therefore in the notional case ($L = 1$) it follows that

$$S = \left(\frac{\alpha}{1-\alpha}w\right)^{-\alpha} Y^n S^{-\psi}\,, \;\Rightarrow\; S^{D,n} = \left(\frac{\alpha}{1-\alpha}w\right)^{-\frac{\alpha}{1+\psi}} Y^{n\frac{1}{1+\psi}}\,. \tag{5.16}$$

In the effective case it is given by

$$S^{D,e} = \left(\frac{\alpha}{1-\alpha}\overline{w}\right)^{-\alpha} Y^e \left(\frac{S^e}{L^{*,e}}\right)^{-\psi}\,. \tag{5.27}$$

We do not rearrange this function to simplify the calculations later on.

A12 Notional Case, Calculation of the Equilibrium Values (Equations 5.17, 5.18, 5.19, and 5.20)

From the main text we know that:

Demand for goods:
$$C^{D,n} = \frac{1}{1+\mu}\frac{w^n\beta + \xi\,\overline{K}}{p^n},$$

Supply of goods:
$$p^n = \alpha^{-\alpha}(1-\alpha)^{\alpha-1}w^{n^{1-\alpha}}S^{n^{-\psi}},$$

Demand for human capital:
$$S^{D,n} = \left(\frac{\alpha}{1-\alpha}w^n\right)^{-\frac{\alpha}{1+\psi}}Y^{n\frac{1}{1+\psi}},$$

Supply of human capital:
$$S^{S,n} = \frac{1}{1+\mu}\left(\beta - \mu\frac{\xi\,K}{w^n}\right),$$

Demand for "physical capital":
$$K^{D,n} = \left(\frac{\alpha}{1-\alpha}w^n\right)^{1-\alpha}Y^nS^{n^{-\psi}},$$

Supply of capital:
$$K^{S,n} = \xi\,\overline{K}.$$

We have to calculate $S^{*,n}$, $w^{*,n}$, $p^{*,n}$, and $C^{*,n}$. We omit all superscripts to simplify the presentation. From equilibrium on the capital market follows that

$$\frac{\xi\overline{K}S^{\psi}}{Y}\left(\frac{1-\alpha}{\alpha}\right)^{1-\alpha} = w^{1-\alpha}, \;\Rightarrow\; w = \frac{1-\alpha}{\alpha}\left(\frac{\xi\,\overline{K}S^{\psi}}{Y}\right)^{\frac{1}{1-\alpha}}.$$

Denote $\beta - \mu\xi\,\overline{K}/w$ by $\mathfrak{S}$. Then we substitute for S from the demand function for human capital to yield that

$$w = \frac{1-\alpha}{\alpha}\left[\xi\overline{K}\left(\frac{1}{1+\mu}\mathfrak{S}\right)^{\psi}\right]^{\frac{1}{1-\alpha}}C^{-\frac{1}{1-\alpha}}.$$

Equilibrium on the market for human capital leads to

$$\left(\frac{\alpha}{1-\alpha}w\right)^{-\frac{\alpha}{1+\psi}}C^{\frac{1}{1+\psi}} = \frac{1}{1+\mu}\mathfrak{S}.$$

Substitution for w from the equilibrium on the capital market obtains that

$$\left(\left(\xi\overline{K}\left(\frac{1}{1+\mu}\mathfrak{S}\right)^{\psi}C^{-1}\right)^{\frac{1}{1-\alpha}}\right)^{-\frac{\alpha}{1+\psi}}C^{\frac{1}{1+\psi}} = \frac{1}{1+\mu}\mathfrak{S},$$

$$\Rightarrow\left(\xi\,\overline{K}\left(\frac{1}{1+\mu}\mathfrak{S}\right)^{\psi}C^{-1}\right)^{-\frac{\alpha}{1-\alpha}}C = \left(\frac{1}{1+\mu}\mathfrak{S}\right)^{1+\psi},$$

$$\Rightarrow (\xi\,\overline{K})^{-\frac{\alpha}{1-\alpha}}\left(\frac{1}{1+\mu}\Im\right)^{-\frac{\alpha\psi}{1-\alpha}}C^{\frac{1}{1-\alpha}} = \left(\frac{1}{1+\mu}\Im\right)^{1+\psi},$$

$$\Rightarrow (\xi\overline{K})^{-\alpha}\left(\frac{1}{1+\mu}\Im\right)^{-\alpha\psi}C = \left(\frac{1}{1+\mu}\Im\right)^{(1+\psi)(1-\alpha)},$$

$$\Rightarrow C = (\xi\,\overline{K})^{\alpha}\left(\frac{1}{1+\mu}\Im\right)^{(1+\psi)(1-\alpha)+\alpha\psi},$$

$$\Rightarrow C = (\xi\,\overline{K})^{\alpha}\left(\frac{1}{1+\mu}\Im\right)^{1-\alpha+\psi}.$$

Substitution of C back into the expression for w helps to calculate $w^{*,n}$ as

$$w = \frac{1-\alpha}{\alpha}\left(\frac{\xi\,\overline{K}\left(\frac{1}{1+\mu}\Im\right)^{\psi}}{(\xi\,\overline{K})^{\alpha}\left(\frac{1}{1+\mu}\Im\right)^{1-\alpha+\psi}}\right)^{\frac{1}{1-\alpha}},$$

$$\Rightarrow w = \frac{1-\alpha}{\alpha}\left((\xi\,\overline{K})^{1-\alpha}\left(\frac{1}{1+\mu}\Im\xi\right)^{\alpha-1}\right)^{\frac{1}{1-\alpha}},$$

$$\Rightarrow w = \frac{1-\alpha}{\alpha}\left(\frac{1}{1+\mu}\right)^{\frac{1}{1-\alpha}}\xi\,\overline{K}\Im^{-1}.$$

Substitute for $\Im$,

$$w\left(\beta - \mu\frac{\xi\,\overline{K}}{w}\right) = \frac{1-\alpha}{\alpha}\left(\frac{1}{1+\mu}\right)^{\frac{1}{1-\alpha}}\xi\,\overline{K},$$

$$\Rightarrow w\beta = \frac{1-\alpha}{\alpha}\left(\frac{1}{1+\mu}\right)^{\frac{1}{1-\alpha}}\xi\,\overline{K} + \mu\xi\,\overline{K},$$

$$\Rightarrow w^{*,n} = \frac{\xi\,\overline{K}}{\beta}\left(\frac{1-\alpha}{\alpha}\left(\frac{1}{1+\mu}\right)^{\frac{1}{1-\alpha}} + \mu\right).$$

We define that: $\omega \equiv \dfrac{1-\alpha}{\alpha}\left(\dfrac{1}{1+\mu}\right)^{\frac{1}{1-\alpha}} + \mu$,

$$\Rightarrow w^{*,n} = \frac{\xi \overline{K}}{\beta}\omega .$$

(5.17)

Note: from the household's problem, it must be fulfilled that, $\xi \overline{K} \le \beta \mu^{-1} w$. Using the term for the equilibrium wage, this condition is equivalent to

$$1 \le \frac{1}{\mu}\omega , \Rightarrow \mu \le \frac{1-\alpha}{\alpha}\left(\frac{1}{1+\mu}\right)^{\frac{1}{1-\alpha}} + \mu , \Rightarrow 0 \le \frac{1-\alpha}{\alpha}\left(\frac{1}{1+\mu}\right)^{\frac{1}{1-\alpha}} .$$

Hence in equilibrium the condition is fulfilled. Substitution of $w^{*,n}$ into the supply function of human capital helps to calculate the equilibrium value for skills which turns out as

$$S^{*,n} = \frac{1}{1+\mu}\left(\beta - \mu\xi \overline{K}\left(\frac{\xi \overline{K}}{\beta}\omega\right)^{-1}\right),$$

$$\Rightarrow S^{*,n} = \frac{\beta}{1+\mu}\left(1-\frac{\mu}{\omega}\right).$$

(5.18)

Note that the derivative of equilibrium skills in respect to β is given by

$$\frac{\partial S^{*,n}}{\partial \beta} = \frac{1}{1+\mu} - \frac{\mu}{(1+\mu)\omega} .$$

Substituting for ω into this expression, it is positive, if

$$\frac{1}{1+\mu} > \frac{\mu}{1+\mu}\left[\frac{1-\alpha}{\alpha}\left(\frac{1}{1+\mu}\right)^{\frac{1}{1-\alpha}} + \mu\right]^{-1} , \Rightarrow \frac{1-\alpha}{\alpha}\left(\frac{1}{1+\mu}\right)^{\frac{1}{1-\alpha}} > 0 ,$$

which is fulfilled by assumption. Additionally, substitution for $w^{*,n}$ into the expression for C yields the equilibrium value for the notional output as

$$C = (\xi \overline{K})^\alpha \left(\frac{1}{1+\mu}\left(\beta - \frac{\mu\xi \overline{K}}{\frac{\xi \overline{K}}{\beta}\omega}\right)\right)^{1-\alpha+\psi} ,$$

$$\Rightarrow C^{*,n} = (\xi \overline{K})^\alpha \left(\frac{\beta}{1+\mu}\left(1-\frac{\mu}{\omega}\right)\right)^{1-\alpha+\psi} .$$

(5.19)

Finally, substitution of $w^{*,n}$ and $S^{*,n}$ into the goods supply helps to calculate $p^{*,n}$. We obtain that

$$p = \alpha^{-\alpha}(1-\alpha)^{\alpha-1}\left(\omega\frac{\xi\,\overline{K}}{\beta}\right)^{1-\alpha}\left(\frac{\beta}{1+\mu}\left(1-\frac{\mu}{\omega}\right)\right)^{-\psi},$$

$$\Rightarrow p^{*,n} = \alpha^{-\alpha}(1-\alpha)^{\alpha-1}\,\beta^{\,\alpha-1-\psi}(1+\mu)^{\psi}(\xi\,\overline{K}\omega)^{1-\alpha}\left(1-\frac{\mu}{\omega}\right)^{-\psi}. \qquad (5.20)$$

A13 Effective Case, Calculation of the Equilibrium Values (Equations 5.28, 5.29, 5.30 and 5.31)

We use all simplifications, neglect superscripts and subscripts and remembering that $s=S/L$. From the main text we know:

Effective demand for goods:
$$C = L\frac{1}{1+\mu}\frac{\overline{w}\frac{\beta}{L}+\xi\,\overline{K}}{p}+(1-L)\frac{\xi\,\overline{K}}{p},$$

Effective supply of goods
$$p = \alpha^{-\alpha}(1-\alpha)^{\alpha-1}\,\overline{w}^{1-\alpha}\left(\frac{S}{L}\right)^{-\psi},$$

Supply of human capital:
$$S = L\frac{1}{1+\mu}\left(\frac{\beta}{L}-\mu\frac{\xi\,\overline{K}}{\overline{w}}\right),$$

Demand for human capital:
$$S = \left(\frac{\alpha}{1-\alpha}\overline{w}\right)^{-\alpha}Y\left(\frac{S}{L}\right)^{-\psi}.$$

First, note that in order for human capital to be positive, it has to be fulfilled that

$$\frac{\beta}{L}-\mu\frac{\xi\,\overline{K}}{\overline{w}}>0,\ \Rightarrow \mu\frac{\xi\,\overline{K}}{\overline{w}}>\frac{\beta}{L}.$$

In equilibrium skills are given by

$$\frac{S}{L}=\frac{1}{1+\mu}\left(\frac{\beta}{L}-\mu\frac{\xi\,\overline{K}}{\overline{w}}\right).$$

Hence the equilibrium price turns out as

$$p = \alpha^{-\alpha}(1-\alpha)^{\alpha-1}\,\overline{w}^{1-\alpha}(1+\mu)^{\psi}\left(\frac{\beta}{L}-\mu\frac{\xi\,\overline{K}}{\overline{w}}\right)^{-\psi}.$$

Use the equilibrium condition in the goods market. From demand for skills it then follows that

$$C = \left(\frac{\alpha}{1-\alpha}\overline{w}\right)^{\alpha}\left(\frac{S}{L}\right)^{\psi}.$$

Substitution for L^e and S yields that

$$C = \left(\frac{\alpha}{1-\alpha}\overline{w}\right)^{\alpha}(1+\mu)^{-\psi}\left(\frac{\beta}{L} - \mu\frac{\xi\,\overline{K}}{\overline{w}}\right)^{\psi}.$$

Using the above functions for C and p and denoting $\chi = \beta L^{-1} - \mu\xi\,\overline{K}\overline{w}^{-1}$, we know that

$$Cp = \left(\frac{\alpha}{1-\alpha}\overline{w}\right)^{\alpha}(1+\mu)^{-\psi}\chi^{\psi}\alpha^{-1}\left(\frac{\alpha}{1-\alpha}\overline{w}\right)^{1-\alpha}(1+\mu)^{\psi}\chi^{-\psi},$$

$$\Rightarrow Cp = \frac{\overline{w}}{1-\alpha}.$$

From demand for goods it follows that

$$Cp = L\frac{1}{1+\mu}\left(\overline{w}\frac{\beta}{L} + \xi\,\overline{K}\right) + (1-L)\xi\,\overline{K}.$$

Substitution for Cp helps to calculate equilibrium employment, $L^{*,n}$, as

$$\frac{\overline{w}}{1-\alpha} = L\frac{1}{1+\mu}\left(\overline{w}\frac{\beta}{L} + \xi\,\overline{K}\right) + (1-L)\xi\,\overline{K},$$

$$\Rightarrow \frac{w}{1-\alpha} = \frac{w\beta}{1+\mu} + \frac{L\xi\,\overline{K}}{1+\mu} + \xi\,\overline{K} - L\xi\,\overline{K},$$

$$\Rightarrow \overline{w}\left(\frac{1}{1-\alpha} - \frac{\beta}{1+\mu}\right) - \xi\,\overline{K} = -L\frac{\xi\,\overline{K}\mu}{1+\mu},$$

$$\Rightarrow L^{*,e} = \frac{1+\mu}{\mu\xi\,\overline{K}}\varphi, \text{ where } \varphi \equiv \overline{w}\left(\frac{\beta}{1+\mu} - \frac{1}{1-\alpha}\right) + \xi\,\overline{K}. \tag{5.28}$$

Finally, substitution for L into the expressions of C, p and S, described above, helps to calculate the equilibrium values (denoted with superscripts). For equilibrium consumption we yield that:

$$C = \left(\frac{\alpha}{1-\alpha}\overline{w}\right)^{\alpha}\left(\frac{(1+\mu)^2\varphi}{\mu\xi\,\overline{K}}\right)^{-\psi}\left(\frac{\beta}{\frac{(1+\mu)\varphi}{\mu\xi\,\overline{K}}} - \mu\frac{\xi\,\overline{K}}{\overline{w}}\right)^{\psi},$$

$$\Rightarrow C = \left(\frac{\alpha}{1-\alpha}\overline{w}\right)^{\alpha}\left(\frac{\mu\xi\,\overline{K}}{(1+\mu)^2\varphi}\right)^{\psi}\left(\frac{\mu\xi\,\overline{K}\beta}{(1+\mu)\varphi} - \mu\frac{\xi\,\overline{K}}{\overline{w}}\right)^{\psi},$$

$$\Rightarrow C^{*,e} = \left(\frac{\alpha}{1-\alpha}\overline{w}\right)^{\alpha}\left(\frac{(\mu\xi\,\overline{K})^2}{(1+\mu)^2\varphi}\left(\frac{\beta}{(1+\mu)\varphi} - \frac{1}{\overline{w}}\right)\right)^{\psi}. \tag{5.29}$$

The equilibrium price is calculated as follows:

$$p = \alpha^{-\alpha}(1-\alpha)^{\alpha-1}\,\overline{w}^{1-\alpha}(1+\mu)^{\psi}\left(\frac{1+\mu}{\mu\xi\,\overline{\overline{K}}}\varphi\right)^{\psi}\left(\frac{\beta}{\frac{1+\mu}{\mu\xi\,\overline{K}}\varphi}-\mu\frac{\xi\,\overline{K}}{\overline{w}}\right)^{-\psi},$$

$$\Rightarrow p = \alpha^{-\alpha}\left(\frac{\overline{w}}{1-\alpha}\right)^{1-\alpha}\left(\frac{\frac{\beta}{\frac{(1+\mu)\varphi}{\mu\xi\,\overline{K}}}-\frac{\mu\xi\,\overline{K}}{w}}{\frac{(1+\mu)^2\varphi}{\mu\xi\,\overline{K}}}\right)^{-\psi},$$

$$\Rightarrow p = \alpha^{-\alpha}\left(\frac{\overline{w}}{1-\alpha}\right)^{1-\alpha}\left(\frac{\frac{\beta\mu\xi\,\overline{K}}{(1+\mu)\varphi}-\frac{\mu\xi\,\overline{K}}{w}}{\frac{(1+\mu)^2\varphi}{\mu\xi\,\overline{K}}}\right)^{-\psi},$$

$$\Rightarrow p = \alpha^{-\alpha}\left(\frac{\overline{w}}{1-\alpha}\right)^{1-\alpha}\left(\frac{\mu\xi\,\overline{K}\left(\frac{\beta\overline{w}}{(1+\mu)\varphi}-\frac{1}{\overline{w}}\right)}{\frac{(1+\mu)^2\varphi}{\mu\xi\,\overline{K}}}\right)^{-\psi},$$

$$\Rightarrow p^{*,e} = \alpha^{-\alpha}\left(\frac{\overline{w}}{1-\alpha}\right)^{1-\alpha}\left(\frac{(\mu\xi\,\overline{K})^2}{(1+\mu)^2\varphi}\left(\frac{\beta\overline{w}}{(1+\mu)\varphi}-\frac{1}{\overline{w}}\right)\right)^{-\psi}. \tag{5.30}$$

Finally, we calculate equilibrium skills.

$$\frac{S}{\frac{(1+\mu)\varphi}{\mu\xi\,\overline{K}}} = \frac{1}{1+\mu}\left(\frac{\beta}{\frac{(1+\mu)\varphi}{\mu\xi\,\overline{K}}}-\mu\frac{\xi\,\overline{K}}{\overline{w}}\right),\ \Rightarrow S = \frac{\frac{(1+\mu)\varphi}{\mu\xi\,\overline{K}}}{1+\mu}\left(\frac{\beta}{\frac{(1+\mu)\varphi}{\mu\xi\,\overline{K}}}-\mu\frac{\xi\,\overline{K}}{\overline{w}}\right),$$

$$\Rightarrow S = \frac{1}{1+\mu}\left(\beta-\frac{(1+\mu)\varphi}{\overline{w}}\right),\ \Rightarrow S^* = \frac{\beta}{1+\mu}-\frac{\varphi}{\overline{w}}.$$

We substitute for φ,

$$\Rightarrow S^* = \frac{\beta}{1+\mu}-\frac{\overline{w}\left(\frac{\beta}{1+\mu}-\frac{1}{1-\alpha}\right)+\xi\,\overline{K}}{\overline{w}},$$

$$\Rightarrow S^* = \frac{1}{1-\alpha}-\frac{\xi\,\overline{K}}{\overline{w}}. \tag{5.31}$$

Equilibrium output and equilibrium price are positive if

$$\frac{\beta}{1+\mu} > \frac{\varphi}{\overline{w}}, \quad \text{where} \quad \varphi \equiv \overline{w}\left(\frac{\beta}{1+\mu} - \frac{1}{1-\alpha}\right) + \xi\,\overline{K}.$$

Reformulation reduces this condition to $\overline{w} > (1-\alpha)\xi\,\overline{K}$, which also guarantees that equilibrium skills are positive.

A14 Proof of Proposition 5.3, "The Effective Demand Function is positioned to the Right of the Notional one."

At an identical price level, the effective demand function is positioned to the right of the notional one, if

$$L^{,e}\frac{1}{1+\mu}\frac{\overline{w}\dfrac{\beta}{L^{*,e}}+\xi\,\overline{K}}{p^{*,e}} + (1-L^{*,e})\frac{\xi\,\overline{K}}{p^{*,e}} - \frac{1}{1+\mu}\frac{\overline{w}\beta+\xi\,\overline{K}}{p^{*,e}} > 0,$$

$$\frac{1}{1+\mu}(\overline{w}\beta + L^{*,e}\xi\,\overline{K}) + (1-L^{*,e})\xi\,\overline{K} - \frac{1}{1+\mu}(\overline{w}\beta + \xi\,\overline{K}) > 0,$$

$$\Rightarrow \overline{w}\beta + L^{*,e}\xi\,\overline{K} + (1+\mu)(1-L^{*,e})\xi\,\overline{K} - \overline{w}\beta - \xi\,\overline{K} > 0,$$

$$\Rightarrow L^{*,e}\xi\,\overline{K} + (1+\mu)(1-L^{*,e})\xi\,\overline{K} - \xi\,\overline{K} > 0,$$

$$\Rightarrow \xi\,\overline{K}(L^{*,e} + (1+\mu)(1-L^{*,e}) - 1) > 0, \;\rightarrow\; L^{*,e} + (1+\mu)(1-L^{*,e}) > 1,$$

$$\Rightarrow L^{*,e} + (1+\mu) - (1+\mu)L^{*,e} > 1, \;\Rightarrow\; L^{*,e}(1-(1+\mu)) + 1 + \mu > 1,$$

$$\Rightarrow -\mu L^{*,e} + 1 + \mu > 1, \;\Rightarrow\; 1 > L^{*,e}.$$

We know that employment is smaller than one. Hence the inequality is fulfilled.

APPENDIX TO CHAPTER 6

A15 Identical Maximization Results for Different Starting Points of Maximization

We do not present a formal proof, but an exemplary comparison of the outcomes of the maximization problems for two different points in time, which has to hold for all other points in time, too. The analysis is based on the first five FOCs which were derived from equation (6.10) in the main text at starting point τ. Next imagine a derivation of the FOCs at starting point $\tau+1$. Independently of the maximization time, all endogenous variables except the shadow prices have to be formally identical, because the shadow prices are the only variables which are changed by different starting point terminations. Therefore, in the following we only indicate the shadow prices according to the different starting points of the maximization problem. From the chapter "technical notes" of the main text we know that the general definition of the shadow prices and the transversality conditions are given by

$$\tilde{\upsilon}_{i,t} \equiv \upsilon_{i,t}e^{\theta(t-\tau)}, \quad \tilde{\lambda}_{i,t} \equiv \lambda_{i,t}e^{\theta(t-\tau)}, \quad \text{and}$$

$$\lim_{t\to\infty}(e^{-\theta(t-\tau)}\lambda_{i,t}K_{i,t}) = 0, \quad \lim_{t\to\infty}(e^{-\theta(t-\tau)}\upsilon_{i,t}S_{i,t}) = 0.$$

We compare the situation for $\tau = 0$ with the situation for $\tau + 1 = 1$. Denote all according results of time τ by the superscript zero and the results of time $\tau + 1$ by the superscript one. Then we yield for the starting point τ that

$$\tilde{\upsilon}_{i,t}^{0} \equiv \upsilon_{i,t}^{0}e^{\theta t}, \quad \tilde{\lambda}_{i,t}^{0} \equiv \lambda_{i,t}^{0}e^{\theta t}, \quad \text{and}$$

$$\lim_{t\to\infty}(e^{-\theta t}\lambda_{i,t}^{0}K_{i,t}) = 0, \quad \lim_{t\to\infty}(e^{-\theta t}\upsilon_{i,t}^{0}S_{i,t}) = 0.$$

Additionally, for point $\tau + 1$ it is valid that

$$\tilde{\upsilon}_{i,t}^{1} \equiv \upsilon_{i,t}^{1}e^{\theta(t-1)}, \quad \tilde{\lambda}_{i,t}^{1} \equiv \lambda_{i,t}^{1}e^{\theta(t-1)}, \quad \text{and}$$

$$\lim_{t\to\infty}(e^{-\theta(t-1)}\lambda_{i,t}^{1}K_{i,t}) = 0, \quad \lim_{t\to\infty}(e^{-\theta(t-1)}\upsilon_{i,t}^{1}S_{i,t}) = 0.$$

Hence the FOCs for time τ may be written as:

$$\frac{1}{C_{i,t}} - \tilde{\upsilon}_{i,t}^{0} = 0, \tag{A15.1}$$

$$\frac{\mu}{F_{i,t}} - \lambda_{i,t}^{0}\beta\, S_{i,t} = 0, \tag{A15.2}$$

$$\tilde{\upsilon}_{i,t}^{0}w_{t}S_{i,t} - \tilde{\lambda}_{i,t}^{0}\beta\, S_{i,t} = 0, \tag{A15.3}$$

$$\dot{\tilde{\upsilon}}_{i,t}^{0} = -\frac{\partial h(.)}{\partial K_{i,t}} + \theta\,\tilde{\upsilon}_{i,t}^{0}, \quad \Rightarrow \frac{\partial h(.)}{\partial K_{i,t}} = \theta\,\tilde{\upsilon}_{i,t}^{0} - \dot{\tilde{\upsilon}}_{i,t}^{0}, \tag{A15.4}$$

$$\dot{\tilde{\lambda}}_{i,t}^{0} = -\frac{\partial h(.)}{\partial S_{i,t}} + \theta\,\tilde{\lambda}_{i,t}^{0}, \quad \Rightarrow \frac{\partial h(.)}{\partial S_{i,t}} = \theta\,\tilde{\lambda}_{i,t}^{0} - \dot{\tilde{\lambda}}_{i,t}^{0}, \tag{A15.5}$$

and the maximization results for time $\tau + 1$ are given by:

$$\frac{1}{C_{i,t}} - \tilde{\upsilon}_{i,t}^{1} = 0, \tag{A15.6}$$

$$\frac{\mu}{F_{i,t}} - \tilde{\lambda}_{i,t}^{1}\beta\, S_{i,t} = 0, \tag{A15.7}$$

$$\tilde{\upsilon}_{i,t}^{1}w_{t}S_{i,t} - \tilde{\lambda}_{i,t}^{1}\beta\, S_{i,t} = 0, \tag{A15.8}$$

$$\dot{\tilde{\upsilon}}_{i,t}^{1} = -\frac{\partial h(.)}{\partial K_{i,t}} + \theta\,\tilde{\upsilon}_{i,t}^{1}, \quad \Rightarrow \frac{\partial h(.)}{\partial K_{i,t}} = \theta\,\tilde{\upsilon}_{i,t}^{1} - \dot{\tilde{\upsilon}}_{i,t}^{1}, \tag{A15.9}$$

$$\dot{\lambda}_{i,t}^{1} = -\frac{\partial \hbar(.)}{\partial S_{i,t}} + \theta \, \tilde{\lambda}_{i,t}^{1}, \quad \Rightarrow \frac{\partial \hbar(.)}{\partial S_{i,t}} = \theta \, \tilde{\lambda}_{i,t}^{1} - \dot{\lambda}_{i,t}^{1}. \tag{A15.10}$$

From (A15.1) and (A15.6) follows that $v_{i,t}^{0} = v_{i,t}^{1}$. Equate (A15.4) and (A15.9) and use the information that $v_{i,t}^{0} = v_{i,t}^{1}$ to yield that $\dot{\tilde{v}}_{i,t}^{1} = \dot{\tilde{v}}_{i,t}^{0}$. Next, equate (A15.2) and (A15.7) to obtain that $\lambda_{i,t}^{1} = \lambda_{i,t}^{0}$. With use of this relationship, we equate equations (A15.5) and (A15.10) to yield that $\tilde{\lambda}_{i,t}^{0} = \tilde{\lambda}_{i,t}^{1}$. Therefore, the maximization results are completely identical. An analogous argumentation holds for the effective case too.

A16 Notional Case, Derivation of Equation (6.24)

From the main text we know that

$$\frac{\dot{\tilde{v}}_{t}}{\tilde{v}_{t}} - \frac{\dot{\tilde{\lambda}}_{t}}{\tilde{\lambda}_{t}} = (\alpha - \psi)\frac{\dot{S}_{t}}{S_{t}} - \alpha \frac{\dot{K}_{t}}{K_{t}}.$$

Substitute for the growth rate for skills from equation (6.23) and for the growth rate of capital by equation (6.22), which are both derived in the main text, to yield that

$$\frac{\dot{\tilde{v}}_{t}}{\tilde{v}_{t}} - \frac{\dot{\tilde{\lambda}}_{t}}{\tilde{\lambda}_{t}} - \frac{(\alpha - \psi)(1 - \alpha)}{1 - \alpha + \psi}\gamma \quad \alpha\gamma,$$

$$\Rightarrow \frac{\dot{\tilde{v}}_{t}}{\tilde{v}_{t}} - \frac{\dot{\tilde{\lambda}}_{t}}{\tilde{\lambda}_{t}} = \gamma \frac{(\alpha - \psi)(1 - \alpha) - \alpha(1 - \alpha + \psi)}{1 - \alpha + \psi},$$

$$\Rightarrow \gamma = \left(\frac{\dot{\tilde{\lambda}}_{t}}{\tilde{\lambda}_{t}} - \frac{\dot{\tilde{v}}_{t}}{\tilde{v}_{t}}\right)\frac{1 - \alpha + \psi}{\psi}. \tag{6.24}$$

A17 Notional Case, Derivation of the Steady State Rate of Growth (Equation 6.28)

The analysis is based on equations (6.24), (6.25), (6.26) and (6.27) from the main text. Substitute equations (6.25) and (6.26) into equation (6.24) to obtain that

$$\gamma = \left(-\gamma \frac{1 - \alpha}{1 - \alpha + \psi} - \beta H_{t} + \theta + \gamma\right)\frac{1 - \alpha + \psi}{\psi},$$

$$\Rightarrow \gamma \left(\frac{\psi}{1 - \alpha + \psi} + \frac{1 - \alpha}{1 - \alpha + \psi} - \frac{1 - \alpha + \psi}{1 - \alpha + \psi}\right) = -\beta H_{t} + \theta,$$

$$\Rightarrow H_{t} = \frac{\theta}{\beta}.$$

Substitute in equation (6.27), and remember that $(1-\alpha) \equiv \Phi$:

$$\frac{\theta}{\beta} = 1 - \frac{\mu \dfrac{\theta}{\beta}(\gamma + \theta - \alpha\gamma)}{(1-\alpha)(\gamma + \theta)} - \gamma \frac{\Phi}{\beta\,\Omega},$$

$$\Rightarrow (\theta - \beta) = -\mu\,\theta \frac{\gamma(1-\alpha) + \theta}{(1-\alpha)(\gamma + \theta)} - \gamma \frac{\Phi}{\Omega},$$

$$\Rightarrow (\theta - \beta) = -\frac{\mu\,\theta\gamma}{(\gamma + \theta)} - \frac{\mu\,\theta^2}{(1-\alpha)(\gamma + \theta)} - \gamma \frac{\Phi}{\Omega},$$

$$\Rightarrow (\theta - \beta)(\gamma + \theta) = -\mu\,\theta\gamma - \frac{\mu\,\theta^2}{1-\alpha} - \gamma \frac{\Phi}{\Omega}(\gamma + \theta),$$

$$\Rightarrow (\theta - \beta)\gamma + (\theta - \beta)\theta = -\mu\,\theta\gamma - \frac{\mu\,\theta^2}{1-\alpha} - \gamma^2 \frac{\Phi}{\Omega} - \theta\gamma \frac{\Phi}{\Omega},$$

$$\Rightarrow (\theta - \beta)\gamma + \mu\,\theta\gamma + \gamma^2 \frac{\Phi}{\Omega} + \theta\gamma \frac{\Phi}{\Omega} = -\frac{\mu\,\theta^2}{1-\alpha} - (\theta - \beta)\theta,$$

$$\Rightarrow \gamma^2 + \gamma \frac{\Omega}{\Phi}\left(\theta - \beta + \mu\,\theta + \theta \frac{\Phi}{\Omega}\right) = -\frac{\Omega}{\Phi}\theta\left(\frac{\mu\,\theta}{\dfrac{\mu\,\theta^2}{1-\alpha}} + \theta - \beta\right),$$

$$\Rightarrow \gamma^2 + \gamma\left((\theta - \beta)\frac{\Omega}{\Phi} + \frac{\Omega}{\Phi}\mu\,\theta + \theta\right) = \theta \frac{\Omega}{\Phi}\left(\beta - \theta - \frac{\mu\,\theta}{1-\alpha}\right),$$

$$\Rightarrow \gamma^2 \frac{\Phi}{\Omega} + \gamma\left(\theta\left(\mu + \frac{\Phi}{\Omega}\right) - (\theta - \beta)\right) + \theta\left(\frac{\mu\,\theta}{\Phi} - (\theta - \beta)\right) = 0.$$

The Discriminant (to be seen in the main text) in any case is positive if

$$4 \frac{\Phi}{\Omega}\theta\left(\frac{\mu\,\theta}{\Phi} - (\theta - \beta)\right) < 0, \ \Rightarrow \beta - \theta > \frac{\mu\,\theta}{\Phi}?, \ \Rightarrow \frac{\beta}{\theta} > 1 + \frac{\mu}{\Phi}?$$

We assume that $\beta/\theta > 1 + \mu/\Phi$. Hence equation (6.28) in the main text, which will not be repeated here, directly follows from the equation above.

A18 Effective Case, Derivation of Equation (6.44)

Equate equation (6.43) with the Euler Equation (6.38), which both are derived in the main text to obtain that

$$\tilde{v}_t^u \alpha K_t^{\alpha-1} H_t^{e^{1-\alpha}} S_t^{e^{1-\alpha+\psi}} L_t^{\alpha-\psi-1} = \frac{\dot{L}_t C_t^u + \dot{C}_t^u(1 - L_t)}{C_t^{u^2}} + \theta \tilde{v}_t^u.$$

Substitute for the Lagrange multiplier from equation (6.31) of the main text to yield that

$$\frac{1-L_t}{C_t^u}\alpha K_t^{\alpha-1}H_t^{e^{1-\alpha}}S_t^{e^{1-\alpha+\psi}}L_t^{\alpha-\psi-1}=\frac{\dot{L}_t C_t^u+\dot{C}_t^u(1-L_t)}{C_t^{u^2}}+\theta\frac{1-L_t}{C_t^u}\,,$$

$$\Rightarrow(1-L_t)\alpha K_t^{\alpha-1}H_t^{e^{1-\alpha}}S_t^{e^{1-\alpha+\psi}}L_t^{\alpha-\psi-1}=\dot{L}_t+\frac{\dot{C}_t^u}{C_t^u}(1-L_t)+\theta(1-L_t)\,,$$

$$\Rightarrow\alpha K_t^{\alpha-1}H_t^{e^{1-\alpha}}S_t^{e^{1-\alpha+\psi}}L_t^{\alpha-\psi-1}=\frac{\dot{L}_t}{1-L_t}+\frac{\dot{C}_t^u}{C_t^u}+\theta\,,$$

$$\Rightarrow\alpha K_t^{\alpha-1}H_t^{e^{1-\alpha}}S_t^{e^{1-\alpha+\psi}}L_t^{\alpha-\psi-1}=-\frac{(1-\dot{L}_t)}{1-L_t}+\frac{\dot{C}_t^u}{C_t^u}+\theta\,.$$

Note that the first term of the right side in steady state is zero, and denote the rate of growth of the consumption of unemployed households by γ^u to get that

$$\gamma^u=\alpha K_t^{\alpha-1}H_t^{e^{1-\alpha}}S_t^{e^{1-\alpha+\psi}}L_t^{\alpha-\psi-1}-\theta\,. \tag{6.44}$$

A19 Effective Case, Derivation of Equation (6.56)

Reformulate equation (6.51) from the main text to obtain that

$$K_t=\frac{\mu H_t^e}{F_t^e}C_t^e\left(\frac{1-\alpha}{\alpha}(\gamma+\theta)\right)^{-1}\,.$$

Additionally, from the main text we know that

$$\frac{1-\alpha}{\alpha}(\gamma+\theta)K_t+\theta\,K_t^e=C_t^e\,.$$

Substitute for the aggregate capital stock from the first equation to calculate equation (6.56):

$$\frac{1-\alpha}{\alpha}(\gamma+\theta)\frac{\mu H_t^e}{F_t^e}C_t^e\left(\frac{1-\alpha}{\alpha}(\gamma+\theta)\right)^{-1}+\theta K_t^e=C_t^e\,,$$

$$\Rightarrow\frac{\mu\,H_t^e}{F_t^e}C_t^e+\theta K_t^e=C_t^e\,,\quad\Rightarrow C_t^e\left(\frac{\mu H_t^e}{F_t^e}C_t^e-1\right)=-\theta K_t^e\,,$$

$$\Rightarrow\frac{C_t^e}{K_t^e}=\theta\left(1-\frac{\mu H_t^e}{F_t^e}\right)^{-1}\,. \tag{6.56}$$

A20 Effective Case, Derivation of Equation (6.57)

Equate equations (6.51) and (6.56) from the main text to yield that

$$\frac{1-\alpha}{\alpha\mu}(\gamma+\theta)\frac{F_t^e}{H_t^e}=\theta\left(1-\frac{\mu H_t^e}{F_t^e}\right)^{-1},$$

$$\Rightarrow \frac{1-\alpha}{\alpha\mu}(\gamma+\theta)=\frac{\theta H_t^e}{F_t^e-\mu H_t^e}\ ,\ \Rightarrow \frac{1-\alpha}{\alpha\mu}(\gamma+\theta)(F_t^e-\mu\,H_t^e)=\theta H_t^e\ ,$$

$$\Rightarrow F_t^e\frac{1-\alpha}{\alpha\mu}(\gamma+\theta)=H_t^e\left(\theta+\mu\frac{1-\alpha}{\alpha\mu}(\gamma+\theta)\right),$$

$$\Rightarrow \frac{F_t^e}{H_t^e}=\frac{\theta+\dfrac{1-\alpha}{\alpha}(\gamma+\theta)}{\dfrac{1-\alpha}{\alpha\mu}(\gamma+\theta)}\ ,$$

$$\Rightarrow \frac{F_t^e}{H_t^e}=\frac{\alpha\mu}{1-\alpha}\frac{\theta}{\gamma+\theta}+\mu\ . \tag{6.57}$$

A21 Effective Case, Derivation of the Steady State Rate of Growth (Equation 6.60)

The analysis is based on equations (6.57), (6.58) and (6.59) from the main text. Substitute for working and leisure time from equations (6.58) and (6.59) into equation (6.57) and define that $\Phi\equiv(1-\alpha)$, and $\Omega\equiv(1-\alpha+\psi)$ to obtain that:

$$\frac{L_t}{\beta}\left(\beta-\theta-\gamma\frac{\Phi}{1-\alpha+\psi}\right)\left(\frac{L_t\theta}{\beta}\right)^{-1}=\frac{\alpha\mu}{\Phi}\frac{\theta}{\gamma+\theta}+\mu\ .$$

$$\Rightarrow \beta-\theta-\gamma\frac{\Phi}{\Omega}=\frac{\alpha\mu}{\Phi}\frac{\theta^2}{\gamma+\theta}+\theta\mu\ ,$$

$$\Rightarrow (\beta-\theta)(\gamma+\theta)-\gamma\frac{\Phi}{\Omega}(\gamma+\theta)=\frac{\alpha\mu\theta^2}{\Phi}+\theta\mu(\gamma+\theta)\ ,$$

$$\Rightarrow \begin{cases}-(\beta-\theta)\gamma-(\beta-\theta)\theta+\gamma^2\dfrac{\Phi}{\Omega}+\gamma\dfrac{\Phi\theta}{\Omega}=\\[2ex] =-\dfrac{\alpha\mu\theta^2}{\Phi}-\gamma\theta\mu-\theta^2\mu,\end{cases}$$

$$\Rightarrow \gamma^2\frac{\Phi}{\Omega}+\gamma\theta\mu+\gamma\frac{\Phi\theta}{\Omega}-(\beta-\theta)\gamma=\theta\left((\beta-\theta)-\frac{\theta\mu}{\Phi}\right),$$

$$\Rightarrow \gamma^2 + \gamma \frac{\Omega}{\Phi}\left(\theta\mu + \frac{\Phi\theta}{\Omega} - (\beta - \theta)\right) = \theta \frac{\Omega}{\Phi}\left((\beta - \theta) - \frac{\theta\mu}{\Phi}\right),$$

$$\Rightarrow \gamma^2 \frac{\Phi}{\Omega} + \gamma\left(\theta\left(\mu + \frac{\Phi}{\Omega}\right) - (\beta - \theta)\right) = \theta\left((\beta - \theta) - \frac{\theta\mu}{\Phi}\right).$$

Equation (6.60) directly follows from this expression.

A22 Effective Case, Calculation of $\dot{K}^e_t / K^e_t$

From the main text we know that $\gamma^e = \dot{K}_t / K_t = \gamma = \dot{K}^u_t / K^u_t$. Remember that the rates of growth of all three elements of consumption are identical and that this rate of growth is equal to the rate of growth of the aggregated capital stock. We know that

$$\dot{K}_t = \dot{K}^e_t + \dot{K}^u_t ,$$

$$\Rightarrow \dot{K}_t / K_t * K_t = \dot{K}^e_t / K^e_t * K^e_t + \dot{K}^u_t / K^u_t * K^u_t ,$$

$$\Rightarrow \gamma (K_t - K^u_t) = \dot{K}^e_t / K^e_t K^e_t .$$

Furthermore we know that $K_t - K^u_t = K^e_t$, hence $\dot{K}^e_t / K^e_t = \gamma$.

A23 Effective Case, The Firm's Problem, Derivation of the FOCs and the Factor Demand Function for Human Capital (Equations 6.8', 6.9' and 6.62)

The analysis is based on the firm's problem (6.2) from the main text. Additionally note that skills and working hours are only provided by employed households which is denoted by the index "e." We obtain that:

$$\max_{} \pi = K^{\alpha}_{j,t}(s^e_{j,t}h^e_{j,t}L_{j,t})^{1-\alpha} s^{e\psi}_t - r_t K_{j,t} - \overline{w}^e_t\, _{j,t} s^e_{j,t} h^e_{j,t} L_{j,t} ,$$

$$\frac{\partial \pi_{j,t}}{\partial s^e_{j,t}} = (1-\alpha)K^{\alpha}_{j,t}s^{e-\alpha}_{j,t} h^{e1-\alpha}_t L^{1-\alpha}_{j,t} s^{e\psi}_t = \overline{w}_t h^e_{j,t} L_{j,t} ,$$

$$\frac{\partial \pi_{j,t}}{\partial h^e_{j,t}} = (1-\alpha)K^{\alpha}_{j,t}s^{e1-\alpha}_{j,t} h^{e-\alpha}_{j,t} L^{1-\alpha}_{j,t} s^{e\psi}_t = \overline{w}_t s^e_{j,t} L_{j,t} ,$$

$$\frac{\partial \pi_{j,t}}{\partial L_{j,t}} = (1-\alpha)K^{\alpha}_{j,t}s^{e1-\alpha}_{j,t} h^{e1-\alpha}_{j,t} L^{-\alpha}_{j,t} s^{e\psi}_t = \overline{w}_t s^e_{j,t} h^e_{j,t} .$$

Reformulation leads to:

$$\frac{\partial \pi_{j,t}}{\partial L_{j,t}} = \frac{\partial \pi_{j,t}}{\partial s^e_{j,t}} = \frac{\partial \pi_{j,t}}{\partial h^e_{j,t}} = (1-\alpha)K^{\alpha}_{j,t}s^{e-\alpha}_{j,t} h^{e-\alpha}_{j,t} L^{-\alpha}_{j,t} s^{e\psi}_t = \overline{w}_t ,$$

$$\frac{\partial \pi_{j,t}}{\partial K_{j,t}} = \alpha K_{j,t}^{\alpha-1} s_{j,t}^{e\,1-\alpha} h_{j,t}^{e\,1-\alpha} L_{j,t}^{1-\alpha} s_j^{e\psi} = r_t .$$

Division of the FOC for human capital by the FOC for capital obtains the tangent condition, which is given by

$$\frac{1-\alpha}{\alpha} \frac{K_{j,t}^{\alpha} s_{j,t}^{e-\alpha} h_{j,t}^{e-\alpha} L_{j,t}^{-\alpha} s_t^{e\psi}}{K_{j,t}^{\alpha-1} s_{j,t}^{e\,1-\alpha} h_{j,t}^{e\,1-\alpha} L_t^{1-\alpha} s_t^{e\psi}} = \frac{\overline{w}_t}{r_t} , \quad \Rightarrow s_{j,t}^e h_{j,t}^e L_{j,t} = \frac{1-\alpha}{\alpha} \frac{r_t}{\overline{w}_t} K_{j,t} .$$

Substitute human capital back into the production function,

$$Y_{j,t} = K_{j,t}^{\alpha} \left(\frac{1-\alpha}{\alpha} \frac{r_t}{\overline{w}_t} K_{j,t} \right)^{1-\alpha} s_t^{e\psi} , \quad \Rightarrow K_{j,t} = Y_{j,t} \left(\frac{1-\alpha}{\alpha} \frac{r_t}{\overline{w}_t} \right)^{\alpha-1} s_t^{e-\psi} ,$$

and substitute K_j back into the tangency condition to calculate the demand function for human capital as

$$s_{j,t}^e h_{j,t}^e L_{j,t} = \frac{r_t}{\overline{w}_t} Y_{j,t} \left(\frac{1-\alpha}{\alpha} \frac{r_t}{\overline{w}_t} \right)^{\alpha-1} s_t^{e-\psi} ,$$

$$\Rightarrow s_{j,t}^e h_{j,t}^e L_{j,t} = \left(\frac{1-\alpha}{\alpha} \frac{r_t}{\overline{w}_t} \right)^{\alpha} Y_{j,t} s_t^{e-\psi} . \tag{6.62}$$

Substitute for the wage and the interest rate from the FOCs to yield an expression for labor which is given by

$$\Rightarrow s_{j,t}^e h_{j,t}^e L_{j,t} = \left(\frac{1-\alpha}{\alpha} \frac{\alpha K_{j,t}^{\alpha-1} s_{j,t}^{e\,1-\alpha} h_{j,t}^{e\,1-\alpha} L_{j,t}^{1-\alpha} s_j^{e\psi}}{(1-\alpha) K_{j,t}^{\alpha} s_{j,t}^{e-\alpha} h_{j,t}^{e-\alpha} L_{j,t}^{-\alpha} s_t^{e\psi}} \right)^{\alpha} Y_{j,t} s_t^{e-\psi} ,$$

$$\Rightarrow s_{j,t}^e h_{j,t}^e L_{j,t} = K_{j,t}^{-\alpha} s_{j,t}^{e\alpha} h_{j,t}^{e\alpha} L_{j,t}^{\alpha} Y_{j,t} s_t^{e-\psi} ,$$

$$\Rightarrow L_t^{1-\alpha} = K_{j,t}^{-\alpha} s_{j,t}^{e\alpha-1} h_{j,t}^{e\alpha-1} Y_{j,t} s_t^{e-\psi} ,$$

For consistency it has to be valid that

$$L_t^{1-\alpha} = K_{j,t}^{-\alpha} h_{j,t}^{e\alpha-1} Y_{j,t} s_t^{e-\psi+\alpha-1} .$$

Express this equation in aggregated values in order to expression output, which turns out as

$$L_t^{1-\alpha} = K_t^{-\alpha} \frac{H_t^{\alpha-1} S_t^{e^{-\psi+\alpha-1}}}{L_t^{\alpha-1} L_t^{-\psi+\alpha-1}} Y_t, \quad \Rightarrow Y_t = K_t^{\alpha} H_t^{1-\alpha} S_t^{e^{1-\alpha+\psi}} L_t^{\alpha-\psi-1}.$$

Finally, express the FOCs for human capital and capital in aggregated variables:

$$(1-\alpha) K_t^{\alpha} S_t^{e^{\psi-\alpha}} H_t^{e^{-\alpha}} L_t^{\alpha-\psi} = \overline{w}_t, \tag{6.8'}$$

$$\alpha K_t^{\alpha-1} S_t^{e^{1-\alpha+\psi}} H_t^{e^{1-\alpha}} L_t^{\alpha-\psi-1} = r_t. \tag{6.9'}$$

A24 Effective Case, Derivation of Equations (6.65) and (6.67)

Reformulate equation (6.63) from the main text in per capita terms,

$$\tilde{v}_t^u \alpha C_t + K_t \tilde{v}_t^u \alpha \gamma = K_t (-\dot{\tilde{v}}_t^u + \theta \tilde{v}_t^u),$$

$$\Rightarrow \tilde{v}_t^u \alpha c_t + k_t \tilde{v}_t^u \alpha \gamma = k_t (-\dot{\tilde{v}}_t^u + \theta \tilde{v}_t^u),$$

$$\Rightarrow \tilde{v}_t^u \alpha \frac{c_t}{k_t} + \tilde{v}_t^u \alpha \gamma = -\dot{\tilde{v}}_t^u + \theta \tilde{v}_t^u,$$

$$\Rightarrow \tilde{v}_t^u \frac{c_t}{k_t} \alpha = -\dot{\tilde{v}}_t^u + \theta \tilde{v}_t^u - \tilde{v}_t^u \alpha \gamma, \tag{6.65}$$

and equate equation (6.66) from the main text and equation (6.65) to obtain that

$$\tilde{v}_t^u \frac{c_t}{k_t} \alpha = \frac{\gamma}{c_t^u} \frac{1-L_t}{L_t} + \theta \tilde{v}_t^u - \tilde{v}_t^u \alpha \gamma,$$

$$\Rightarrow \tilde{v}_t^u \frac{c_t}{k_t} \alpha - \theta \tilde{v}_t^u + \tilde{v}_t^u \alpha \gamma = \frac{\gamma}{c_t^u} \frac{1-L_t}{L_t},$$

$$\Rightarrow \tilde{v}_t^u \left(\frac{c_t}{k_t} \alpha - \theta + \alpha \gamma \right) = \frac{\gamma}{c_t^u} \frac{1-L_t}{L_t},$$

$$\Rightarrow \tilde{v}_t^u c_t^u = \gamma \frac{1-L_t}{L_t} \left(\frac{c_t}{k_t} \alpha - \theta + \alpha \gamma \right)^{-1}. \tag{6.67}$$

A25 Effective Case, Proof that Steady State Employment is Identical to Population

Substitute equation (6.67) into equation (6.64), both presented in the main text,

$$L_t = \left(\gamma \frac{1-L_t}{L_t} \left(\frac{c_t}{k_t} \alpha - \theta + \alpha\gamma \right)^{-1} + 1 \right)^{-1},$$

$$\Rightarrow L_t = \left(\frac{\gamma(1-L_t) + L_t \left(\frac{c_t^u}{k_t} \alpha - \theta + \alpha\gamma \right)}{L_t \left(\frac{c_t}{k_t} \alpha - \theta + \alpha\gamma \right)} \right)^{-1},$$

define that $\dfrac{c_t}{k_t}\alpha - \theta + \alpha\gamma \equiv \xi$ to obtain that

$$\Rightarrow L_t = \frac{L_t \xi}{\gamma(1-L_t) + L_t \xi}, \Rightarrow 1 = \frac{\xi}{\gamma(1-L_t) + L_t \xi}, \Rightarrow \gamma(1-L_t) + L_t \xi = \xi,$$

$$\Rightarrow \gamma - \gamma L_t + L_t \xi = \xi, \Rightarrow \gamma + L_t(\xi - \gamma) = \xi, \Rightarrow L_t(\xi - \gamma) = \xi - \gamma,$$

$$\Rightarrow L_t = 1.$$

APPENDIX TO CHAPTER 7

A26 Effective Case, Derivation of Equation (7.24)

The analysis is based on equations (7.10), (7.23) and the Euler-Equation from the unemployed's system (7.23). Equal equation (7.23) with the Euler Equation to yield that

$$\tilde{v}_t^e \alpha K_t^{\alpha-1} S_t^{e^{1-\alpha}} H_t^{e^{1-\alpha}} L_t^{\alpha-1} = -\frac{\dot{L}_t C_t^e - \dot{C}_t^e L_t}{C_t^{e^2}} + \theta \tilde{v}_t^e.$$

Substitute for the Lagrange multiplier from equation (7.10),

$$\frac{L_t}{C_t^e} \alpha K_t^{\alpha-1} S_t^{e^{1-\alpha}} H_t^{e^{1-\alpha}} L_t^{\alpha-1} = -\frac{\dot{L}_t C_t^e - \dot{C}_t^e L_t}{C_t^{e^2}} + \theta \frac{L_t}{C_t^e},$$

$$\Rightarrow \alpha K_t^{\alpha-1} S_t^{e^{1-\alpha}} H_t^{e^{1-\alpha}} L_t^{\alpha-1} = -\frac{\dot{L}_t}{L_t} + \frac{\dot{C}_t^e}{C_t^e} + \theta,$$

note that in steady state the rate of growth of employment is zero and rearrange to reduce the expression to

$$\frac{\dot{C}_t^e}{C_t^e} \equiv \gamma^e = \alpha K_t^{\alpha-1} S_t^{e^{1-\alpha}} H_t^{e^{1-\alpha}} L_t^{\alpha-1} - \theta. \tag{7.24}$$

A27 Effective Case, Derivation of $\tilde{\lambda}_t^e$ with Respect to Time

We reformulate equation (7.11) from the main text and remember that $\phi_t = \beta L_t^{-\varphi}$ to get that

$$\tilde{\lambda}_t^e = \frac{\mu}{\beta} \frac{L_t^{2+\varphi}}{F_t^e S_t^e} \ .$$

Taking the derivative with respect to time yields,

$$\dot{\tilde{\lambda}}_t^e = \frac{\mu}{\beta} \frac{(2+\varphi)L_t^{\varphi+1}\dot{L}_t F_t^e S_t^e - (L_t^{\varphi+2}\dot{F}_t^e S_t^e + L_t^{\varphi+2}\dot{S}_t^e F_t^e)}{F_t^{e^2} S_t^{e^2}} ,$$

$$\Rightarrow \dot{\tilde{\lambda}}_t^e = \frac{\mu}{\beta}\left((2+\varphi)\frac{L_t^{\varphi+2}}{F_t^e S_t^e}\frac{\dot{L}_t}{L_t} - \frac{L_t^{\varphi+2}}{F_t^e S_t^{e^2}}\frac{\dot{F}_t^e}{F_t^e} - \frac{L_t^{\varphi+2}}{F_t^e S_t^{e^2}}\dot{S}_t^e \right).$$

The rates of growth of the first two elements in brackets in steady state are by definition zero:

$$\Rightarrow \dot{\tilde{\lambda}}_t^e = -\frac{\mu}{\beta} \frac{L_t^{\varphi+2}}{F_t^e S_t^e} \frac{\dot{S}_t^e}{S_t^e} ,$$

We know that $\phi_t = \beta L_t^{-\varphi}$. Hence the expression reduces to

$$\dot{\tilde{\lambda}}_t^e = -\frac{\mu}{\phi_t} \frac{\dot{S}_t^e}{S_t^e} \frac{L_t^2}{F_t^e S_t^e} \ .$$

A28 Effective Case, Derivation of Equation (7.28)

In order to calculate the rate of growth in terms of parameters and employment substitute for C_t^e / K_t from equation (7.27), into equation (7.26), which are both derived in chapter seven:

$$\gamma = \phi_t - \frac{\alpha\mu\theta}{(1-\alpha)(\gamma+\theta)}\left(\frac{1-\alpha}{\alpha}(\gamma+\theta)+\theta \right) - \theta \ .$$

$$\Rightarrow \gamma + \theta = \phi_t - \mu\theta - \frac{\theta^2\alpha\mu}{(1-\alpha)(\gamma+\theta)} ,$$

$$\Rightarrow \gamma + \theta(1+\mu) = \phi_t - \frac{\theta^2\alpha\mu}{(1-\alpha)(\gamma+\theta)} ,$$

$$\Rightarrow \gamma(\gamma+\theta)+\theta(1+\mu)(\gamma+\theta) = \phi_t(\gamma+\theta) - \frac{\theta^2\alpha\mu}{1-\alpha} ,$$

$$\Rightarrow \gamma^2 + \theta\gamma + \gamma\theta(1+\mu) + \theta^2(1+\mu)) = \gamma\phi_t + \theta\phi_t - \frac{\theta^2\alpha\mu}{1-\alpha},$$

$$\Rightarrow \gamma^2 + \gamma\theta\left(2+\mu-\frac{\phi_t}{\theta}\right) + \theta^2\left(1+\mu+\frac{\alpha\mu}{1-\alpha}-\frac{\phi_t}{\theta}\right) = 0,$$

$$\Rightarrow \gamma^2 + \gamma\theta\left(2+\mu-\frac{\phi_t}{\theta}\right) + \theta^2\left(\frac{(1+\mu)(1-\alpha)+\alpha\mu}{1-\alpha}-\frac{\phi_t}{\theta}\right) = 0,$$

$$\Rightarrow \gamma^2 + \gamma\theta\left(2+\mu-\frac{\phi_t}{\theta}\right) + \theta^2\left(1+\frac{\mu}{1-\alpha}-\frac{\phi_t}{\theta}\right) = 0.$$

After some reformulations equation (7.28) follows directly from the expression above.

Notes

1 Introduction

1. Even if claims on specific unemployment benefits are part of the wage negotiations, they depend solely on previous employment.
2. The formal description of the bargaining situations follows Oswald (1985) in a simplified and adapted form.
3. Manning (1987) showed that all three models may be regarded as special cases of a two-stage bargaining problem.
4. This is pointed out precisely by McDonald and Solow (1981). For a very short presentation and discussion see Blanchard and Fischer (1989), 442.
5. See Booth (1995) for a detailed discussion.
6. Compare the argumentation in chapter 2.2.2.
7. A discussion about this possibility has taken place in recent literature, which was mainly based on the publications of Card and Krueger (1994 and 1995).
8. The examples follow Ragacs and Zagler (1998).

2 An Inquiry into the Theory of Minimum Wages

1. A very good presentation of the standard model can for instance be found in Fallon and Verry (1988).
2. For a short overview see Layard, Nickel und Jackman (1991).
3. Because of the existence of monopsony we are able to omit the index for the number of firms.
4. These developments are best summarized by Boal and Ransom (1997).
5. For the description of the model see Zavodny (1998, 24).
6. Paragraphs one and two of this chapter are based on Zagler and Ragacs (1999), paragraph three is based on Zagler and Ragacs (1998).
7. One of the basic ideas for endogenizing economic growth was contributed much earlier by Arrow (1962).
8. Advisable books are: Barro and Sala-I-Martin (1995), Aghion and Howitt (1998), Zagler (1999b), Solow (2000), Lucas (2002) Romer (2001 chapters 1–3); and on an introductory level: Jones (1997), and Gylfason (1999).
9. For an overview see Temple (1999).
10. The first to propose a correlation between unemployment and growth was Arthur Okun (1970), but he described only an empirical correlation that was not theoretically founded.
11. For an overview of newer studies see Brown (1999).
12. See e.g. Card und Krueger (1995).
13. Meyer and Wise (1983). For the presentation see OECD (1998), 46.
14. For the discussion of elasticities see Ghellap (1998), 44–46 and 64 f., and OECD (1998).

3   Minimum Wages and "General Equilibrium": Methodological Problems

1. A simple and recommendable introduction to Walrasian economics is provided by Katzner (1988).
2. A quick view of these theories can be found in Snowdown, Vane and Wynarczyk (1994), 109–23. Benassy (1982), Cuddington, Johansson and Löfgren (1984), and Dréze (1991) are also recommended.
3. Malinvaud first published his work in 1977. The second edition of his work (Malinvaud 1985, 16 ff.) serves as a basis for the illustration and the notation in this chapter. It has, however, been partly adapted. The assumptions that deviate from Malinvaud have been marked. The state sector was left out of the analysis completely.
4. The argumentation in this paragraph follows Rothschild (1981, 77 f.).
5. A7–A10 and A12 follow directly from Malinvaud (1985), 21 ff.
6. Endowment e.g. could be the maximum quantity of possible labor hours, initial financial wealth or initial amount of goods.

4   Supporting the Partial Equilibrium Results

1. As will be shown later, the minimum wage has a positive effect on the price level of goods. It is, however, in such a small amount that in equilibrium the real minimum wage is also higher than the original real market wage, as will be explained later.
2. We have to use this unusual notation because in later models we will denote educational time by E and we will also introduce investment, then denoted by I.
3. The process introduced here corresponds with the standard solution for the problem described in several textbooks. Compare for instance Varian (1992, 54 f.), where the corresponding functions are generally derived for the Cobb-Douglas production function with unspecified scales of return and for the special case of constant returns.
4. Rearrange the utility function,

$$\ln C_i = U_i(.) - \mu \ln F_i \,,$$

and differentiate to yield,

$$\left. \frac{d \ln C_i}{d \ln F_i} \right|_{U_i(.) = \overline{U}_i(.)} = -\mu \, .$$

5. For a Lagrange representation of the Kuhn-Tucker Problem see for instance Chiang (1984), 724 ff.
6. See mathematical appendix, A1.
7. See mathematical appendix, A1.
8. See mathematical appendix, A1.
9. See mathematical appendix, A2.
10. See mathematical appendix, A3.
11. See mathematical appendix, A4.

12. See mathematical appendix, A5.
13. See mathematical appendix, A6.
14. See mathematical appendix, A7.
15. In the growth models presented later, investments are meaningful. Higher total wages can lead to an increase in savings and hence in investment.

5 Minimum Wages, Unemployment and the Creation of Human Capital

1. Given the technical properties of the Cobb-Douglas production function, it is impossible for $L^{*,e}$ to become zero.
2. The technical properties of the consumption function are described in chapter four.
3. A similar assumption has to be implicitly set in any partial equilibrium micro model with labor-leisure choice.
4. See mathematical appendix, A8.
5. The calculation of the cost function follows the same methodology as the calculation of the cost function in chapter four. See mathematical appendix, A3.
6. See mathematical appendix, A9.
7. See mathematical appendix, A9. The parameter restriction necessary to guarantee a positive function is identical to the restriction necessary for the time constraint (see mathematical appendix). Note that for any deviation from the assumption of $L=1$, we would yield the formulation β/L instead of β.
8. See mathematical appendix, A10.
9. See mathematical appendix, A11.
10. See mathematical appendix, A12.
11. See mathematical appendix, A12.
12. Of course, this expression could be easily reformulated as a function of "physical labor" alone, but the used representation helps to simplify the analytical treatment. Note that

$$s^e L^{*,e} = S^e / L^{*,e} * L^{*,e} = S^e.$$

13. See mathematical appendix, A13.
14. At first sight, there exist some other necessary restrictions, but they can all be reduced to the two restrictions given above.

6 Minimum Wages, Human Capital and Growth

1. A good and short technical description of the basic Lucas model may be found in Sala-I-Martin (1990) or Barro and Sala-I-Martin (1995).
2. Remember that we use this unusual notation because we will denote educational time by E_t.
3. Here we must anticipate the analysis presented later, where the behavior of the households is described precisely.
4. Due to the production technology presented later and the existence of perfect competition, economic profits must be zero.

5. Compare Barro and Sala-I-Martin (1995, 172) for the case without endogenous working time.
6. The felicity function fulfills the Inada conditions:

   $u'(.) \to \infty$ as $(.) \to 0$, and $u'(.) \to 0$ as $(.) \to \infty$.

7. The formal proof of the properties of a more broadly defined utility function, where the one used represents a subcase, was given by Barro and Sala-I-Martin (1995, 326 ff.).
8. Compare Barro and Sala-I-Martin (1995, 172).
9. Of course, households do not care about average levels of skills and working time, as firms do.
10. The argumentation of A15 is based on the derivation of the FOCs from equation (6.10), which will be presented in the beginning of the next chapter. Hence we recommend reading this part of the text first.
11. A very good representation of Hamiltonian maximization can for example be found in Chiang (1992, 210 ff.).
12. The derivation of the FOCs in the notional case follows the same methodology as the derivation in the effective case with the additional assumption that employment is normalized to one. See mathematical appendix, A23.
13. Substitute back into equation (6.21) to prove that this is one of the possible solutions.
14. See mathematical appendix, A16.
15. All remaining necessary mathematical derivations for the calculation of the steady state rate of growth of the economy are presented in the mathematical appendix, A17.
16. Compare the presentations in Barro and Sala-I-Martin (1995, 65, and 182 ff.).
17. The equilibrium wage w_i^* at point zero is identical to the equilibrium wage of the notional system.
18. See mathematical appendix, A23.
19. Given the information about the maximization problems of employed and unemployed households the equations presented in the chapter „macroeconomic relations“ could be adapted easily for this model.
20. To see that this assumption is fulfilled, substitute by the rate of growth that will be derived later.
21. See mathematical appendix, A18.
22. To see that this assumption is fulfilled, substitute by the rate of growth that will be derived later.
23. See mathematical appendix, A18.
24. See mathematical appendix, A22.
25. See mathematical appendix, A19.
26. Note, for the proof that shows that in steady state we will achieve full-employment, this assumption and all results derived from it, are not necessary. We present the proof later to provide a structure of the model's presentation, which is mostly identical to that of the notional case.
27. See mathematical appendix, A20.
28. See mathematical appendix, A23.
29. See mathematical appendix, A23.
30. We do not have to change the shadow prices.

31. See mathematical appendix, A24.
32. See mathematical appendix, A24.
33. See mathematical appendix, A25.
34. Remember the standard properties of the utility function.

7   Minimum Wages, Unemployment and Growth

1. This formulation of the production function of skills is only used to simplify the presentation as much as possible. However, it induces an over-proportional reaction on unemployment. A linear reaction could for instance be expressed by,

$$\phi_t = \beta(1+\varphi(1-L_t)), \quad \varphi > 0.$$

2. We do not simplify the rate of growth in order to show the connection to the result of chapter six, equation (6.28).
3. The solution of the firm's problem and the aggregation is obtained by using the same methodology as is presented in the mathematical appendix A23, with the exception that there exists no external effect in production.
4. Compare the derivation of equations (6.42) – (6.48) in chapter six.
5. See mathematical appendix, A26.
6. See mathematical appendix, A27.
7. Note, for the proof that shows that in steady state we will achieve full-employment, this assumption and all results derived from this assumption are not necessary.
8. See mathematical appendix, A28.

8   Conclusions

1. The theory of the "Second Best" states that violating one Pareto-criterion also induces the violation of all other criteria, which is problematic for decision-finding.

Bibliography

1. In light of the importance of some specific publications on minimum wages which have not been available to the author, we must in some cases refer to the literature in which they have been cited.

Bibliography

Abowd, J. M., Kramarz, F., Lemieux, T. and Margolis, D. N. (1997) "Minimum Wages and Youth Employment in France and the United States," *National Bureau of Economic Research, Working Paper*, 6111.

Acemoglu, D. and Pischke, J. S. (1999) "Minimum Wages and On-The-Job Training," *National Bureau of Economic Research, Working Paper*, 7184.

Acemoglu, D., Pischke, J. S. (2002) "Minimum Wages and On-the-Job Training," *Centre for Economic Performance, Discussion Papers*, CEPDP0527 (http://cep.lse.ac.uk/pubs/download/DP0527.pdf).

Aghion, P. and Howitt, P. (1998) *Endogenous Growth Theory* (Cambridge: MIT Press).

Aghion, P., Caroli, E. and Garcia-Penalosa, C. (1999) "Inequality and Economic Growth: The Perspective of the New Growth Theories," *Journal of Economic Literature*, 37(4), December, 1615–60.

Albrecht, J. W. and Axell, B. (1984) "An Equilibrium Model of Search Unemployment," *Journal of Political Economy*, 92(5), 824–40.

Arrow, K. J. (1962) "The Economic Impact of Learning by Doing," *Review of Economic Studies*, 29, 155–73.

Arulampalam, W., Booth, A. L. and Bryan, M. L. (2002) "Work-related Training and the New National Minimum Wage in Britain," *Institute for the Study of Labor (IZA), Discussion Paper*, 595 (ftp://repec.iza.org/ RePEc/Discussionpaper/dp595.pdf).

Ashenfelter, O., Card, D., eds (1999) *Handbook of Labor Economics*, Volume 3B (Princeton: Princeton University Press).

Baker, M., Dwayne, B. and Stanger, S. (1997) "The Highs and Lows of the Minimum Wage Effect: A Time Series-Cross Section Study of the Canadian Law," Toronto University, mimeo; cited according to OECD (1998), *Employment Outlook*, 77 (Paris: OECD Publications).[1]

Baker, M., Benjamin, D. and Stanger, S. (1999) "The Highs and Lows of the Minimum Wage Effect: A Time-Series Cross-Section Study of the Canadian Law," *Journal of Labor Economics*, 17(2), 318–50.

Ball, L. and Mankiw, G. N. (1995) "What do Deficits do?," *National Bureau of Economic Research, Working Paper*, 5263.

Barro, R. J. and Sala-I-Martin, X. (1995) *Economic Growth* (New York: McGraw Hill).

Bazen, S. and Martin, J. P. (1991) "The Impact of the Minimum Wage on Earnings and Employment in France," *OECD Economic Studies*, 16, 199–221.

Bazen, S. and Marimoutou, V. (1997) "Looking for a Needle in a Haystack? A Re-examination of the Time Series Relationship Between Teenage Employment and Minimum Wages in the United States, " Université Montesquieu Bordeaux IV, France, mimeo; cited according to OECD (1998), *Employment Outlook*, 77 (Paris: OECD Publications).

Bazen, S. and Skourias, N. (1997) "Is there a Negative Effect of Minimum Wages in France?," *European Economic Review*, 41, 723–32.

Bazen, S. and Marimoutou, V. (2002) "Looking for a Needle in a Haystack? A Re-examination of the Time Series Relationship between Teenage Employment and Minimum Wages in the United States," *Oxford Bulletin of Economics and Statistics*, 64/ Supplement, 699–725.

Bean, C. and Pissarides, C. (1993) "Unemployment, Consumption and Growth," *European Economic Review*, 37, 837–59.

Bell, L. A. (1995) "The Impact of Minimum Wages in Mexico and Columbia," *The World Bank Policy Research, Working Paper*, No. 1514; cited according to OECD (1998), *Employment Outlook*, 77 (Paris: OECD Publications).

Benassy, J. P. (1982) *The Economics of Market Disequilibrium* (New York: Academic Press).

Ben-David, D. (1996) "Trade and Convergence Among Countries," *Journal of International Economics*, 40(3/4), 279–98.

Benhabib, J. and Spiegel, M. (1994) "The Role of Human Capital in Economic Development: Evidence from Aggregate Cross-Country Data," *Journal of Monetary Economics*, 34, 143–74.

Benhayoun, G. (1994) "The Impact of Minimum Wages on Youth Employment in France Revisited: A Note on The Robustness of the Relationship," *International Journal of Manpower*, 15, 82–5.

Bhaskar, V. and To, T. (1998) "Minimum Wages for Ronald McDonald Monopsonies: A Theory of Monopsonistic Competition," Universities of Essex and Warwick, mimeo (http://econwpa.wustl.edu:8089/eps/lab/papers/ 9603/9603001.pdf).

Bhaskar, V. and To, T. (1999) "Minimum wages for Ronald McDonald monopsonies: a theory of monopsonistic competition, " *Economic Journal*, 109, p190-203.

Black, D. A. and Loewenstein, M. A. (1991) "Self-enforcing Labor Contracts with Costly Mobility," in: Ehrenberg, R. G. (ed.), *Research in Labor Economics. A Research Annual*, 12, 3–83 (Greenwich: JAI Press).

Blanchard, O. J. and Fischer, S. (1989) *Lectures on Macroeconomics* (Cambridge and London: MIT-Press).

Boal, W. M. and Ransom, M. R. (1997) "Monopsony in the Labor Market," *Journal of Economic Literature*, 35(1), 86–112.

Booth, A. L. (1995) *The Economics of the Trade Union* (Cambridge: Cambridge University Press).

Brander, J. and Dowrick, S. (1994) "The Role of Fertility and Population in Economic Growth: Empirical Results from Aggregate Cross-national Data," *Journal of Population Economics*, 7(1), 1–25.

Brown C., Gilroy C. and Kohen, A. (1982) "The Effects of the Minimum Wage on Employment and Unemployment," *Journal of Economic Literature*, 20(2), 487–528.

Brown C., Gilroy C. and Kohen, A. (1983) "Time Series Evidence of the Effects of the Minimum Wage on Youth Employment and Unemployment," *Journal of Human Resources*, 18(1), 3–31.

Brown, C. (1988) "Minimum Wage Laws, Are They Overrated?," *The Journal of Economic Perspectives*, 2(3), 133–45.

Brown, C. (1999) "Minimum Wages, Employment and the Distribution of Income," in: Ashenfelter, O., Card, D., eds *Handbook of Labor Economics*, Volume 3B (Princeton: Princeton University Press).

Bruno, M. and Easterly, W. (1998) "Inflation Crises and Long-run Growth," *Journal of Monetary Economics*, 41(1), 3–26.

Burdett, K. and Mortenson, D. T. (1989) "Equilibrium Wage Differentials and Employer Size," *Northwestern University, Working Paper*, 860; cited according to Zavodny, M. (1998) "Why Minimum Wage Hikes May not Reduce Employment," *Federal Reserve Bank of Atlanta Economic Review*, Second Quarter, 18–28.

Burkhauser, R. V., Couch, K. A. and Wittenburg, D. (1977) "Who Minimum Wage Increases Bite: An Analysis Using Monthly Data from the SIPP and the CPS," Centre for Policy Research, Syracuse University, New York, mimeo; cited according to OECD (1998), *Employment Outlook*, 77 (Paris: OECD Publications).

Burkhauser, R. V., Couch, K. A and Wittenburg, D. C. (2000) "A Reassessment of the New Economics of the Minimum Wage Literature with Monthly Data from the Current Population Survey," *Journal of Labor Economics*, 18(4), 653–80.

Cahuc, P. and Michel, P. (1996) "Minimum Wage, Unemployment and Growth," *European Economic Review*, 40(7), 1463–82.

Calmfors, L. and Driffill, J. (1988) Bargaining Structure, Corporatism and Macroeconomic Performance, *Economic Policy*, 6, 13–61.

Calvo, G. A. and Wellisz, S. (1979) "Hierarchy, Ability, and Income Distribution," *Journal of Political Economy*, 87(5), Part 1, 991–1010.

Card, D. (1992) "Using Regional Variation in Wages to Measure the Effects of the Federal Minimum Wage," *Industrial and Labor Relations Review*, October, 38–54.

Card, D. and Krueger, A. B. (1994) "Minimum Wages and Employment: A Case Study of the Fast Food Industry in New York and Pennsylvania," *American Economic Review*, 84, 772–93.

Card, D. and Krueger, A. B. (1995) *Myth und Measurement, The New Economics of the Minimum Wage* (Princeton: Princeton University Press).

Card, D. and Krueger, A. B. (1998) "A Reanalysis of the Effect of the New Jersey Minimum Wage Increase on the Fast-Food Industry with Representative Payroll Data," *Industrial Relations Section, Princeton University, Working Paper*, 293, (http://netec.mimas.ac.uk/WoPEc/data/Papers/nbrnberwo6386.html).

Card, D. and Krueger, A., B. (2000) "Minimum Wages and Employment: A Case Study of the Fastfood Industry in New Jersey and Pennsylvania – Reply," *American Economic Review*, 90(5), 1397–420.

Carley, M. (2002) "Industrial Relations in the EU, Japan and USA, 2000," *European Industrial Relations Observatory* (http://www.eiro.eurofound.ie/2001/11/feature/tn0111148f.html, 1.4.2003, 2002).

Carley, M. (2003) "Industrial Relations in the EU, Japan and USA, 2001," *European Industrial Relations Observatory* (http://www.eiro.euro-found.ie/2002/12/feature/TN0212101F.html, 1.4.2003, 2003).

Carter, T. J. (1998) "Minimum Wage Laws: What does an Employment Increase imply about Output and Welfare?," *Journal of Economic Behaviour & Organization*, 36, 473–85.

Cass, D. (1965) "Optimum Growth in an Aggregative Model of Capital Accumulation," *Review of Economic Studies*, 32, 233–40.

Chapple, S. (1997) "Do Minimum Wages Have an Adverse Impact on Employment? Evidence from New Zealand," *Labour Market Bulletin*, 2; cited according to OECD (1998), *Employment Outlook*, 77 (Paris: OECD Publications).

Chiang, A. C. (1984) *Fundamental Methods of Mathematical Economics*, 3rd edn (Auckland: McGraw-Hill).

Chiang, A. C. (1992) *Elements of Dynamic Optimization* (New York et al.: McGraw-Hill).

Cooley, T. F., ed. (1995) *Frontiers of Business Cycle Research* (Princeton: Princeton University Press).

Cooley, T. F. and Prescott, E. C. (1995) "Economic Growth and Business Cycles," in: Cooley. T. F., ed. *Frontiers of Business Cycle Research* (Princeton: Princeton University Press), 1–38.

Crouch, C. and Traxler, F. (1995) *Organized Industrial Relations in Europe: What Future?* (Aldershot: Avebury).

Cuddington, J. T., Johansson, P. O. and Löfgren, K. G. (1984) *Disequilibrium in Open Economies* (Oxford: Basil Blackwell).

Currie, R. P. and Fallick, B. C. (1996) "The Minimum Wage and the Employment of Youth: Evidence from the NLSY," *Journal of Human Resources*, Spring, 404–28.

Davidson, P. (1994) *Post Keynesian Macroeconomic Theory* (Brookfield: Edward Elgar).

Deere, D., Murphy, K. M. and Welch, F. (1995) "Reexamining Methods of Estimating Minimum Wage Effects: Employment and the 1990–91 Minimum Wage Hike," *American Economic Review, Papers und Proceedings*, May, 232–37.

Deininger, K. and Squire, L. (1997) "Economic Growth and Income Inequality: Reexamining the Links," *Finance and Development*, March, 38–41.

Dickens, R., Machin, S. and Manning, R. (1994) "Estimating the Effect of Minimum Wages on Employment from the Distribution of Wages: A Critical Review," *Centre for Economic Performance, Discussion Paper*, 203, (http:// netec.mimas.ac.uk/WoPEc/data/Papers/cepcepdps0203.html).

Dickens, R. and Machin, S. (1999) "The Effects of Minimum Wages on Employment: Theory and Evidence from Britain," *Journal of Labor Economics* 17(1), 1–22.

Dolado, J., Kramarz, F., Machin, S., Manning, A., Margolis, D. and Teulings, C. (1996) "The Economic Impact of Minimum Wages in Europe," *Economic Policy*, October, 319–70.

Domar, E. D. (1946) "Capital Expansion, Rate of Growth, and Employment," *Econometrica*, 14, 137–47.

Dreze, J. H. (1991) *Underemployment Equilibria. Essays in Theory, Econometrics and Policy* (Cambridge: Cambridge University Press).

Ehrlich, I. and Lui, F. (1997) "The Problem of Population and Growth: A Review of the Literature from Malthus to Contemporary Models of Endogenous Population and Endogenous Growth," *Journal of Economic Dynamics and Control*, 21, 205–42.

Evans, G. W., Honkapohja, S. and Romer, P. M. (1998) "Growth Cycles," *American Economic Review*, 88(3), 495–515.

Fallon, P. and Verry, D. (1988) *The Economics of Labour Markets* (Oxford and New Jersey: Phillip Allan Publishers).

Ghellap, Y. (1998) "Minimum Wages and Youth Unemployment," *International Labour Office, Employment and Training Department, Employment and Training Papers*, 26.

Gramlich, E. (1976) "The Impact of Minimum Wages on Other Wages, Employment and Family Incomes," *Brookings Papers of Economic Activity*, 2, 409–51.

Gregory, M. and Swaffield, J. K. (2002) "Preface: Evaluating the Impact of the UK National Minimum Wage," *Oxford Bulletin of Economics and Statistics*, 64/ Supplement, 565–66.

Grossman, J. B. (1983) "The Impact of the Minimum Wage on other Wages," *Journal of Human Resources*, 90, 359–78.

Grossman, G. M. and Helpman, E. (1991) *Innovation and Growth in the Global Economy* (Cambridge and London: The MIT Press).

Grossman, G. M. and Helpman, E. (1994) "Endogenous Innovations and the Theory of Growth," *Journal of Economic Perspectives*, 8, 23–44.

Gylfason, T. (1999) *Principles of Economic Growth* (Oxford: Oxford University Press).

Harrod, R. F. (1939) "An Essay in Dynamic Theory," *The Economic Journal*, 49, 14–39.

Huemer, G., Mesch, M., and Traxler, F., eds (1999) *The Role of Employer Associations and Labour Unions in the EMU. Institutional Requirements for Europe and Economic Policies* (Aldershot: Avebury).

Jones, C. I. (1997) *An Introduction to Economic Growth* (New York and London: W.W. Norton and Company)

Jones, S. R. G. (1987) "Minimum Wage Legislation in a Dual Labor Market," *European Economic Review*, 31, 1229–46.

Katzner, D. W. (1988) *Walrasian Microeconomics. An Introduction to the Economic Theory of Market Behavior* (New York: Addison-Wesley).

Koopmans, T. C. (1965) "On the Concept of Optimal Economic Growth," in: *The Econometric Approach to Development Planning*, (Amsterdam: North Holland).

Kosters, M. and Welch, F. (1972) "The Effects of Minimum Wage by Race, Sex, and Age," in: Pascall, A., ed. *Racial Discrimination in Economic Life* (Lexington: Heath) 103–18.

Koutsogeorgopoulou, V. (1994) "The Impact of Minimum Wages on Industrial Wages and Employment in Greece," *International Journal of Manpower*, 2/3, 86–99.

Lang, K. and Kahn, S. (1998) "The Effect of Minimum Wage Laws on the Distribution of Employment: Theory and Evidence," *Journal of Public Economics*, 69, 67–82.

Larçon, J. P., ed. (1998) *Entrepreneurship and Economic Transition in Central Europe* (Boston, Dortrecht and London: Kluwer Academic Publishers)

Layard, N., Nickel, S. and Jackman, R. (1991) *Unemployment, Macroeconomic Performance and the Labour Market* (Oxford: Oxford University Press).

Lindahl, M. and Krueger, A. B. (1998) "Education in Sweden and the World," Harvard University, mimeo (http://www.nuff.ox.ac.uk/Economics/Growth/ refs/humanc.htm).

Lucas R. E., Jr. (1988) "On the Mechanics of Economic Development," *Journal of Monetary Economy,* 22(1), July, 3–42.

Lucas, R. E., Jr. (2002) *Lectures on Economic Growth* (Cambridge and London: Harvard University Press).

Machin, S. and Manning, A. (1994) "The Effects of Minimum Wages on Wage Dispersion and Employment: Evidence from the UK Wage Councils," *Industrial and Labor Relations Review,* January, 319–329.

Machin, S. and Manning, A. (1997) "Minimum Wages and Economic Outcomes in Europe," *European Economic Review,*" 41, 733–742.

Malinvaud, E. (1985) *The Theory of Unemployment Reconsidered,* 2nd edn (Oxford and New York: Basil Blackwell).

Maloney, T. (1995) "Does the Adult Minimum Wage Affect Employment and Unemployment in New Zealand?," *New Zealand Economic Papers,* 1, 1–19; cited according to OECD (1998), *Employment Outlook,* 77 (Paris: OECD Publications).

Mankiw, G., N., Romer, D. and Weil, D. N. (1992) "A Contribution to the Empirics of Economic Growth," *Quarterly Journal of Economics,* 107 (2), 407–37.

Manning, A. (1987) An Integration of Trade Union Models in a Sequential Bargaining Framework, *The Economic Journal,* 97, 121–39.

Mare, D. (1995) "Comments on Maloney, T., Does the Adult Minimum Wage Affect Employment and Unemployment in New Zealand?," New Zealand Department of Labour, mimeo; cited according to OECD (1998), *Employment Outlook,* 77 (Paris: OECD Publications).

Marshall, A. (1890) *Principles of Economics* (London: Macmillan).

McDonald, I. M. and Solow, R. M. (1981) "Wage Bargaining and Employment," *American Economic Review,* 71(5), 896–908.

Meyer, R. H. and Wise, D. A. (1983) "Discontiniuous Distributions and Missing Persons: The Minimum Wage and Unemployment Youth," *Econometrica,* 51/6, 1677–98.

Mincer, J. (1976) "Unemployment Effects of Minimum Wages," *Journal of Political Economy,* 84, 87–104.

Murat, M. and Pigliaru, F. (1998) "International Trade and Uneven Growth: A Model with Intersectoral Spillovers of Knowledge," *Journal of International Trade and Economic Development,* 7, 221–36.

Neumark, D. and Wascher, W. (1992) "Employment Effects of Minimum and Sub-minimum Wages: Panel Data in State Minimum Wage Laws, *Industrial and Labor Relations Review,* October, 55–8.

Neumark, D. and Wascher, W. (1995) "Minimum Wage Effects on Employment and Enrolment: Evidence from Matched CPS Surveys," *National Bureau of Economic Research, Working Paper,* 5092.

Neumark, D. and Wascher, W. (2000) "Minimum Wages and Employment: A Case Study of the Fastfood Industry in New Jersey and Pennsylvania – Comment," *American Economic Review*, 90(5), 1397–420.

Neumark, D. and Wascher, W. (2003) "Minimum Wages, Labor market Institutions and Youth Employment: A Cross-National Analysis," *Board of Governors of the Federal Reserve System, Finance and Economics Discussion Series*, 2003–23 (http://www.federalreserve.gov/pubs/feds/2003/200323/ 200323pap.pdf).

Nickel S. J., and Andrews, M. (1983) "Unions, Real Wages and Employment in Britain 1951–79: The Minimum Wage and Unemployment Youth," *Oxford Economic Papers*, 35(0), Supplement 1983, 183–206.

OECD (1998) *Employment Outlook, 77* (Paris: OECD Publications).

Okun A. (1970) "Potential GDP: Its Measurement and Significance," reprinted in Okun, A., ed., *The Political Economy of Prosperity* (Washington, D.C: Brookings Institution).

Okun, A., ed. (1970), *The Political Economy of Prosperity* (Washington, D.C: Brookings Institution).

Orazem, P. F. and Mattila, P. J. (1998) "Minimum Wage Effects on Hours, Employment and Number of Firms: The Iowa Case," Iowa State University, mimeo (http://www.econ.iastate.edu/research/webpapers/ NDN0020.pdf).

Oswald, A. J. (1985) "The Economic Theory of Trade Unions: An Introductory Survey," *Scandinavian Journal of Economics*, 87(2), 160–93.

Pascall, A., ed., *Racial Discrimination in Economic Life* (Lexington: Heath).

Penrod, J. H. (1995) "A Test for Monopsony in the Academic Labor Market," *University of Michigan, Working Paper*, Sept.; cited according to Boal, W. M. and Ransom, M. R. (1997) "Monopsony in the Labor Market," *Journal of Economic Literature*, 35(1), 86–112.

Ragacs, C. (1993a) "Minimum Wages in Austria: Estimation of Employment Functions," *Vienna University of Economics and Business Administration, Department of Economics Working Paper Series*, 20.

Ragacs, C. (1993b) "Employment, Productivity, Output and Minimum Wages in Austria: A Time Series Analysis," *Vienna University of Economics and Business Administration, Department of Economics, Working Paper Series*, 21.

Ragacs, C. and Zagler, M. (1998) "Wachstumsstrategien für Österreich in einem veränderten Mitteleuropa," in: *Kompetenzzentrum Wien* (Vienna: Service Verlag), 261–69.

Ramsey, F. (1928) "A Mathematical Theory of Saving," *Economic Journal*, 38 (December), 543–59.

Raven, M. O. and Sorenson, J. R. (1995) "Minimum Wages: Curse or Blessing," *Centre for Economic Policy Research, Discussion Paper*, 1212.

Raven, M. O. and Sorenson, J. R. (1999) "Schooling, Training, Growth and Minimum Wages," *Scandinavian Journal of Economics*, 101(3), 441–57.

Rebitzer, J. B. and Taylor, L. J. (1991) "The Consequences of Minimum Wage Laws, Some New Theoretical Ideas," *National Bureau of Economic Research, Working Paper*, 3877.

Rebitzer, J. B. and Taylor, L. J. (1995) "The Consequences of Minimum Wage Laws, Some New Theoretical Ideas," *Journal of Public Economics*, February, 245–55.

Romer, D. (2001) *Advanced Macroeconomics*, 2nd edn (Boston, Mass.: McGraw-Hill).

Romer, P. M. (1990) "Endogenous Technological Change," *Journal of Political Economy*, 98, 71–102.

Romer, P. M. (1986) "Increasing Returns and Long-Run Growth," *Journal of Political Economy*, 94, 1002–35.

Rosen, S. (1972) "Learning and Experience in the Labor Market," *Journal of Human Resources*, 7, 326–442.

Rothschild, K. W. (1981) *Einführung in die Ungleichgewichtstheorie* (Berlin: Springer).

Sala-I-Martin, X. (1990) "Lecture Notes on Economic Growth (II), Five Prototype Models of Endogenous Growth," *National Bureau of Economic Research, Working Paper*, 3564.

Schumpeter, J. A. (1912) *Theorie der wirtschaftlichen Entwicklung* (Leipzig: Duncker & Humblot).

Shapiro, C. and Stiglitz, J. E. (1984) "Equilibrium Unemployment as a Workers Discipline Device," *The American Economic Review*, 74(3), 433–44.

Skinner, C., Stuttard, N., Beissel-Durrant, G., and Jenkins, J. (2002) "The Measurement of Low Pay in the UK Labour Force Survey," *Oxford Bulletin of Economics and Statistics*, 64/Supplement, 653–76.

Snowdown, B., Vane, H. and Wynarczyk, P. (1994) *A Modern Guide to Macroeconomics. An Introduction to Competing Schools of Thought* (Brookfield: Edward Elgar).

Solow, R. M. (1956) "A Contribution to the Theory of Economic Growth," *Quarterly Journal of Economics*, 71, 65–94.

Solow, R. M. (2000) *Growth Theory: An Exposition*, 2nd edn (Oxford: Oxford University Press).

Soskice, D. (1990), "Wage Determination: The Changing Role of Institutions in Advanced Industrialized Countries," *Oxford Review of Economic Policy*, 6/4, 36–61.

Stewart, M. B. (2002) "Estimating the Impact of the Minimum Wage Using Geographical Wage Variation," *Oxford Bulletin of Economics and Statistics*, 64/Supplement, 583–605.

Stigler, G. (1946) "The Economics of Minimum Wage Legislation," *American Economic Review*, 36, 358–365.

Swinnerton, K. A. (1996) "Minimum Wages in an Equilibrium Search Model with Diminishing Returns to Labor in Production," *Journal of Labor Economics*, 2, 340–355.

Temple, J. R. W. (1999) "A Positive Effect of Human Capital on Growth," *Economic Letters*, 65(1), 131–34.

Temple, J. R. W. (1999) "The New Growth Evidence," *Journal of Economic Literature*, 18(1), 112–56.

Teulings, C. N. (1998) "Aggregation Bias in Elasticities of Substitution and the Minimum Wage Paradox," *Tinbergen Institute, Discussion Papers*, 98–118/3 (http://www.tinbergen.nl/discussionpapers/98118.pdf)

Topel, R. (1998) "Labor Markets and Economic Growth," University of Chicago, mimeo (http://gsbmxn.uchicago.edu/sole/topel.pdf).

Traxler, F. (1999) "Wage-Setting Institutions and European Monetary Union," in: Huemer, G., Mesch, M. and Traxler, F., eds, *The Role of Employer Associations and Labour Unions in the EMU. Institutional Requirements for European Economic Policies* (Aldershot: Avebury), 115–36.

Traxler, F. and Kittel, B. (2000) "The Bargaining System and Performance. A Comparison of 18 OECD Countries," *Comparative Political Studies*, 33/9, 1154–90.

Traxler, F., Blaschke, S. and Kittel, B. (2001) *National Labour Relations in Internationalized Markets: A Comparative Study of Institutions, Change, and Performance* (Oxford: Oxford University Press).

Traxler (2002) "Funktion und Wandel der Institutionen der Lohnregulierung," *Wirtschaft und Gesellschaft*," 28/4, 471–88.

Varian, H. G. (1992) *Microeconomic Analysis*, 3rd edn (New York: W. W. Norton and Company)

Walsh, F. (2003) "Comment on 'Minimum Wages for Ronald McDonald Monopsonies: A Theory of Monopsonistic Competition'," *The Economic Journal*, 113, 718–22.

Welch, F. (1974) "Minimum Wage Legislation in the United States," *Economic Inquiry*, 12(3), 285–318.

WIFO (1999) *Database of the "Austrian Institute of Economic Research* (Österreichisches Institut für Wirtschaftsforschung), restricted access.

Zagler, M. (1999a) "Endogenous Growth, Efficiency Wages, and Persistent Unemployment," *Vienna University of Economics and Business Administration, Department of Economics, Working Paper Series*, 66, (http://www.wu-wien.ac.at/inst/vw2/papers/wu-wp66.pdf).

Zagler, M. (1999b) *Endogenous Growth, Market Failures, and Economic Policy* (Basingstoke: Macmillan).

Zagler, M. and Ragacs, C. (1998) "Company Co-operations between Eastern and Western Europe: A Key Role in the Development of Eastern Europe," in: Larçon, J. P., ed., *Entrepreneurship and Economic Transition in Central Europe* (Boston, Dortrecht and London: Kluwer Academic Publishers), 163–75.

Zagler, M. and Ragacs, C. (1999) "Endogenous Growth, Division of Labour, and Fiscal Policy," in: Zagler, M., *Endogenous Growth, Market Failures, and Economic Policy* (Basingstoke: Macmillan), 27–45.

Zagler, M. (2004) *Growth and Employment in Europe* (Basingstoke: Palgrave/Macmillan).

Zavodny, M. (1998) "Why Minimum Wage Hikes may not Reduce Employment," *Federal Reserve Bank of Atlanta Economic Review*, Second Quarter, 18–28.

Index of Names

Index of Subjects